C000163325

Otto Pfleiderer

Paulinism

a contribution to the history of primitive Christian theology - Vol. 1

Otto Pfleiderer

Paulinism

a contribution to the history of primitive Christian theology - Vol. 1

ISBN/EAN: 9783348023245

Printed in Europe, USA, Canada, Australia, Japan

Cover: Foto ©Lupo / pixelio.de

More available books at **www.hansebooks.com**

PAULINISM

A Contribution to the

HISTORY OF PRIMITIVE CHRISTIAN THEOLOGY.

BY

OTTO PFLEIDERER,

DOCTOR AND PROFESSOR OF THEOLOGY AT JENA, ETC.

TRANSLATED BY EDWARD PETERS,

LATE OF THE MADRAS CIVIL SERVICE.

VOL. I.

EXPOSITION OF PAUL'S DOCTRINE.

WILLIAMS AND NORGATE,

14, HENRIETTA STREET, COVENT GARDEN, LONDON;
AND 20, SOUTH FREDERICK STREET, EDINBURGH.

1877.

LONDON :
PRINTED BY C. GREEN AND SON,
178, STRAND.

PREFACE.

THIS work is intended as a contribution to the history of the primitive Christian theology, a portion of the history of early Christian dogma, not a biography of Paul, nor a critical introduction to Pauline literature, which forms the principal subject-matter of Baur's " Paul." The criticism of the Epistles is throughout presupposed, and is only treated of here where it is affected by questions of dogma. And the critical consideration of the Acts of the Apostles cannot, on this plan, be made the starting-point, but must be introduced at the conclusion ; since this document can in nowise serve as the source of the Pauline theology, but rather as a test of the correctness of the view taken of the development of Pauline doctrine after the time of Paul.

Much has been done in late years to elucidate Pauline theology, especially by the able investigations of Dr. Holsten, which have been of the greatest assistance to me in this work, and indeed first set me upon it. It was his brilliant idea of starting from Paul's conversion and the psychological presuppositions and inferences connected with it, in order to grasp the kernel of his gospel in its peculiarity, that suggested to me the task of endeavouring to understand how, from this nucleus of Paul's faith in Christ, on the one hand, and the presuppositions of his Jewish theology, on the other, the Pauline doctrine as a whole came into existence; and what is the particular significance of each portion. The solution of this problem has been attempted in the first Part of the present work. The second Part then traces, by the same genetic method, the gradual transformation of the original Pauline doctrine through the changing influence of new theoretical and practical factors, until it was resolved into the common consciousness of the Roman Catholic Church. In this way I have attempted to write a portion of the history of early Christian dogma, as I think the history of dogma should always be treated—not as a herbarium of dead forms, but as the history of the development of living religious ideas, in their birth, growth and change, as the creations of real religious life, acted upon by the surrounding world and acting on it in its turn.

It is evident that this is not so easy a task as the simple disinterment of the several doctrines of an Apostle or of an early Christian literature. It has seldom been attempted, still less has it been anywhere satisfactorily accomplished. Nay, it almost appears to me that the main direction of the scientific exegesis of the day (and that without distinction of the lines taken by different parties) rather tends from than towards this goal. If an attempt was made some time ago to transfer the representations of the Bible into too imme- diate proximity to modern thought, by which means they were changed in a rationalistic sense and stripped of their histori- cal significance, there is now great danger of falling into the other extreme, by confining these representations, taken just as they stand, to their literal historical sense, and never inquiring how it comes to pass, if there is nothing more in them than thus meets the eye, that the writers of the Bible so often lighted on ideas strangely attractive to us, and whether the religious impulse that prompted them may not, perhaps, be a religious idea natural to the religious spirit, and therefore still living in our own time. This external mode of treatment may, no doubt, be advantageously used as a help to ascertain the exact meaning of single passages, and has been so used in many instances of late ; but by such means the understanding of the religious world of thought as a whole cannot be promoted, nor can the object of all Biblical theology be thus attained ; for this, after all, can only be to unlock the treasures of the Bible, and make them fruitful for the religious life of the present. Whither we should ultimately be led by this one-sided formalism in Biblical theology, has just been strikingly shown by the astonishing announcement of a hypercritical theologian, who roundly declares that Scientific Theology and the Christian Church are irreconcilable opponents, for whom the only possible *modus vivendi* is for each to ignore the other ! As if Christianity, that power which has been so eminently a maker of history, had to shun the light of history ! As if Theology, the self-consciousness of the Christian Church, could ever tear itself away from its own soul ! No ; it can be no sound theology which leads to such a fatal end, but rather its morbid ossification in a scholasticism (no matter whether it be orthodox or critical) which forgets the spirit in the letter, the matter in the form, and the reality and permanence of the spiritual idea in the contingency and transitoriness of the historical clothing. To such a poor and narrow view, whose admitted unfruitfulness betrays its abortive nature, the words of Mephistopheles are still applicable :

> " He who'd know and describe some living thing,
> First drives out the soul that dwells therein :
> With the severed parts before him spread,
> He lacks but the spirit-bond that's fled."

In opposing to this scholastic direction of the study of the Bible at the present day, the genetic development of doctrine from the religious impulse as the fundamental requisite for a really scientific Biblical Theology, I am aware that I am likely enough to be assailed with the old reproach of " constructing;" but I must here candidly confess that this always moves me with a slight sense of the ridiculous, for it too forcibly reminds me of the fable of the fox and the sour grapes. It cannot be denied that one is more liable to make mistakes in what the literalists call " constructing " (which is in fact nothing but the genetic method of synthesis common to every true scientific production), than in the common empirical description of something that is given; but does it follow from the difficulty of solving a problem, that one can or ought to evade it ? It may be pleasant to do so, but whether it is particularly reasonable is another question. With regard, then, to this particular work, I am quite aware that many parts of it will be found to contain error, and require correction; nevertheless, I entertain the firm conviction, and will venture boldly to express it, that the method here pursued is the right one, and the only way in which the science of Biblical Theology can be advanced to a satisfactory position.

CONTENTS.

INTRODUCTION.

How are we to conceive the *genesis of the Pauline doctrine?* From what root did it spring? It is more necessary that such questions should be answered with regard to this than to any other doctrine contained in the New Testament. For not only was Paul no immediate disciple of Jesus, but he did not even derive his peculiar teaching from the Apostles who were disciples. The Apostle himself has a most lively consciousness of this peculiarity and independence of his gospel; he repeatedly brings it strongly forward, especially against his Judaizing adversaries.[1] And the truth of this assertion of his is plainly enough attested by the actual facts. For in reality we find but few traces of acquaintance with the particulars of the life or teaching of Jesus in Paul's enunciation of his doctrine; only the most prominent events of the institution of the Lord's Supper, the death of Christ, and his appearance after the resurrection,[2] were received by him from without as historical data; his death, no doubt, together with the dogmatic justification of it, that it was a death for our sins, according to the Scriptures; this was a

---

[1] Cf. Gal. i. 11 f. with i. 6, ἕτερον εὐαγγ.: ii. 2, 7, τὸ εὐαγγ. τῆς ἀκροβυστίας: Rom. ii. 16, τὸ εὐαγγέλιόν μου: Rom. xvi. 25; 2 Cor. iv. 3, τὸ εὐαγγ. ἡμῶν: 2 Cor. xi. 4, εὐαγγ. ἕτερον, ἄλλον Ἰησοῦν ὃν οὐκ ἐκηρύξαμεν.

[2] The Lord's Supper, 1 Cor. xi. 23. Christ's death and appearance, 1 Cor. xv. 3 f. Again, 1 Cor. ix. 14 is most likely an allusion to Luke x. 7, and 1 Cor. vii. 10 probably refers to Matt. v. 32. Whether, and to what extent, the eschatological description in 1 Thess. iv. is to be directly referred to the words of Jesus (cf. Matt. xxiv.) it is difficult to determine, because the genuineness of that speech of Jesus' is as doubtful on the one hand, as it is certain on the other that those eschatological views were common to the whole community of early Christians.

matter of course, because the disciples could never speak of the
death of Jesus the Messiah without at once giving to this awk-
ward-looking fact the aspect of an expiation, by showing that the
Scripture itself declared (e.g. Is. liii.) that the Messiah was to
die for the sins of mankind. But then how thoroughly original
was the system of doctrine that grew up under the hands of Paul
from those few elements of historical tradition! How widely
did it deviate, in the view of Christ which was its basis, and the
scheme of Christian doctrine and life raised thereon, from all
that had hitherto been the established faith and practice of the
Jewish Christian community! Well might the Apostle speak of
"*his* gospel" in contradistinction to the "*other*" gospel which the
Judaizers sought to introduce in Corinth and Galatia; and so
great appeared to him the antagonism of the two systems, that
he saw in the latter quite another Christ than the one whom he
preached, a fleshly Christ whom he knew not; while his Christ
was in like manner concealed from them, because they had not
that light shining in the heart to manifest the glory of Christ as
the image of God which had been imparted to him through the
revelation of Christ himself.[1]

Now whence came this doctrinal system of the Apostle Paul,
with its deviation from that of the more ancient type? He himself gives us this short and plain answer: "I was taught it by
the revelation of Jesus Christ" (Gal. i. 12); which he then proceeds to explain more fully, and to corroborate by the *historical
narrative of his conversion* and the events that followed it, laying
special emphasis on his intentional retirement from Jerusalem
for the first three years, and further on the fact that on his first
visit he met none of the Apostles except Peter and James. This
last circumstantial and solemnly asseverated narrative serves to
corroborate the negative assertion, "I neither received nor was
taught of man the gospel which I preached." And in the same
connection with the historical narrative of his conversion, the

---

[1] Cf. 2 Cor. xi. 4 with v. 16 and iv. 3—6.

positive assertion, "I have received it through revelation of Jesus Christ," is also taken up again and illustrated in the sentence, "As it pleased God to reveal his Son in me, that I might preach him among the heathen." It is to be noted here how his calling to be an Apostle of the heathen is placed in such close and marked connection with the revelation of the Son of God at his conversion, that an intimate relation between them is necessarily suggested to our minds. The peculiar character of the revelation of Christ made to him must, one would think, have consisted precisely in this, that the right and duty of the mission to the heathen followed with logical necessity from it. But the right and duty of the mission to the heathen, as Paul first, and for a long time alone, understood and practised it, was nothing but the clear and simple practical consequence of the fundamental idea that in the Christian community the law peculiar to the Jews was abrogated. From this conviction followed immediately the consequence that the heathen had an equal right with the Jews to Christian salvation, and therefore that the gospel was to be imparted to them, not merely incidentally, but by express appointment; as, on the contrary, the opposite conviction of the permanent validity of the Jewish law involved the practical consequence of confining the mission of the gospel to Israel, as is clearly proved by the example of the original Apostles. If, then, the revelation of Christ made to Paul at his conversion contained within itself, as its immediate consequence, the task of converting the heathen, we may thence plainly see that Paul's faith in Christ, as regards its distinguishing characteristics, namely, its antinomianism and universality, really dated from his conversion, and had the same root with it.

And here the science of history has to face the problem of seeking for such a psychological explanation of the conversion of Paul as may contain at the same time the germ of his peculiar doctrine. As we have here to deal with inward processes of the religious spirit, of which we have no immediate knowledge, it is self-evident that scientific investigation can never arrive at exact demonstrative knowledge, but only at *hypotheses.* In fact, hypotheses have constantly been set up about the psychological conditions which preceded Paul's conversion; only these were of little value so long as there was no canon by means of which their probability could be tested. But we have now found one, in that we require the psychological antecedents of the conversion to exhibit at the same time the root of his peculiar gospel. For by this means we obviously obtain this canon, that the hypothetical attempts to explain the conversion of Paul acquire probability (which is all that science can here aspire to) in proportion as they are capable of explaining at the same time the genesis of the Pauline gospel with reference to its distinguishing characteristics.

Tested by this canon, the assumption which used to be generally accepted, and is to this day the most popular one regarding the psychological antecedents of the conversion of Paul, is decidedly unsatisfactory. Even before his conversion, it is said,[1] Paul had deeply felt the inadequacy of the righteousness of the law, the impossibility of man's attaining to the complete fulfilment of the law: herein was contained not only the negative preparation for his conversion, but also the germ of his later antithesis of the righteousness of faith and the righteousness of the law. But let us reflect for a moment on the vast difference between the subjective feeling of one's own imperfect righteousness according to the law, and the objective conviction that such righteousness is altogether impossible. A Jew might be penetrated with the most lively feeling that he fell far short of the requirements of the holy will of God revealed in the law; but he could by no possibility from this premise arrive at the conclusion that the law, this undoubted revelation of God, was absolutely incapable of placing a man in a state of righteousness before God, and was not intended for that purpose, consequently that it was not the right way of salvation. He would undoubtedly

---

[1] See, for instance, Beyschlag, Theol. St. and Kr., 1864, p. 249 f.

be much more inclined to seek the cause of the subjective want of righteousness in himself, in the insufficiency of his past efforts to attain to higher morality, than in the imperfection of what was fixed in his mind *a priori* as the absolute truth of God. And even if, from his own and other men's experience, he had arrived at the conviction that man, as we find him, could never remain quite free from guilt before the law, which guilt would require an expiation, and that a full and perfect one, like the expiatory sacrifices of the Old Testament, he might certainly be led by this conviction to regard the expiatory death of Christ as a necessary *completion* of the law, but never as an *abrogation* of it, and a *substitution* in its place of an entirely new scheme of salvation.

This and no other must have been the view taken of the matter by the *Jewish Christians;* they also believed that the law alone was not sufficient for the Messianic salvation, otherwise there could have been no inducement for them to become believers in Christ instead of remaining Jews; they saw also in the death of the Messiah on the cross the means of expiation ordained by God, which was to cancel the guilt of sin in God's people more powerfully than the expiatory sacrifices of the Old Testament, and so fill up what was defective in their righteousness before the law. But so far from concluding hence that this new expiatory institution was opposed to the old institution of the law and abrogated it, and that faith in Christ was now to *take the place* of works of the law, the Jewish Christians saw rather, in this consequence deduced by Paul, a downright falsification of the word of God, by which Christ was changed into a promoter of sin rather than of righteousness (Gal. ii. 17: for details see ch. viii.). The cancelling of guilt through the expiatory death of the Messiah was to them rather the "restitutio in integrum" whereby the law for the first time properly attained to its rights, whereby consequently its authority was not only not to be abrogated, but was for the first time to be properly established; according to them, therefore, the true believer in Christ could not only not become an ἄνομος and ἁμαρτωλός, as the heathen were, but he must, on the contrary, even more than before, and more than the unbelieving Jews, be a ζηλωτὴς νόμου (Acts xxi. 20, μυρίαδες εἰσὶν Ἰουδαίων τῶν πεπιστευκότων, καὶ πάντες ζηλωταὶ τοῦ νόμου ὑπάρχουσιν. Cf. James "the Just").

Now to this illogical combination of the works of the law and faith in Christ, which contained no principle, Paul opposed his sharply defined and logical alternative of either the one or the other (Gal. ii. 21, v. 4; Rom. xi. 6); and this fundamental difference presupposes also a different point of departure for his dogmatic views. This cannot be sought in the feeling of the imperfection of his own righteousness before the law, for *this* was shared more or less by the Jewish Christians, who, however, could only infer from it the half-truth of the *completion* of the law by Christ. And it is important to observe that in the principal dogmatic passages in which Paul treats of the relativity of the efficacy of the law and its abrogation in Christ, he does not ground these doctrines on the inadequacy of the natural works of the law. It would be vain to argue from Gal. iii. and iv., and Rom. iv. and v., that it was on *this* ground that he based his degradation of the law. One would certainly have thought this the simplest and most obvious ground; but in fact he proves his thesis by somewhat far-fetched and not always very forcible exegetical arguments, which, one may very plainly see, are calculated only to give an external support to that which the Apostle has other and internal grounds for believing.

But he himself leaves us in no doubt whatever as to what was the conclusive ground of his whole doctrine regarding the law. He speaks it out boldly in Gal. ii. 21: εἰ διὰ νόμου δικαιοσύνη, ἄρα Χριστὸς δωρεὰν ἀπέθανεν——the death of Christ would have been barren and aimless, if the law were to remain, after it as before, the way of righteousness. Now, as we cannot conceive the death of the Messiah on the cross to have beem aimless, it must have been designed by God as the essential means of Messianic righteousness and the Messianic salvation connected with it; but if the death of Christ upon the cross is once admitted to be the means of righteousness ordained by God, it follows by reasoning back from this conclusion, that the law is no longer this means; *the death of the Messiah on the cross thus becomes the end of the law.* No doubt the death of Christ was to the Judaizing Christian too an expiatory means of cancelling guilt, but yet it was to him in nowise the essential means of establishing the entire and positive righteousness of the Messianic people; on the contrary, righteousness was in his eyes still an essentially human achievement, the conformity of the actions of man with the will of God contained in the law; and he regarded the cancelling of guilt granted by God through the expiatory death of Christ as a mere completion of this human performance, and of quite secondary importance. In the system of the Jewish Christians, then, this death had by no means a central significance, with consequences affecting the principle of the law. In the eyes of Paul, on the contrary, the crucifixion of Christ occupied from the first the central place; he called his gospel the "preaching of the cross," 1 Cor. i. 18; he preached "Christ crucified, unto the Jews a stumbling-block, and to the Greeks foolishness," i, 23; he knows and glories in nothing save Jesus Christ the crucified, ii. 2, Gal. vi. 14. But the crucifixion of Christ, thus placed in the centre of his religious contemplation, had necessarily quite other consequences for him than for the Jewish Christians —it became the lever with which he lifted the law out of its difficulties. As an institution of divine grace, the expiatory death was the means of creating *a completely new righteousness*, which is no longer in any respect a human achievement, but solely and entirely a gift of God, which is not obtained by works of the law, but by faith in the new divine scheme of salvation by the death and resurrection of Christ. Thus the peculiar gospel of Paul was the development of the central idea of the expiatory death of Christ.

The problem which presented itself to us, as stated above, was to find a common source in which an explanation might be

8   *INTRODUCTION.*

found, both of the psychological process of the conversion of
Paul, and of the genesis of his peculiar gospel. The question,
therefore, now is, whether we can conceive the idea of the crucified Messiah to be also the starting-point of the psychological
process which prepared the conversion. Let us consider the
position of Paul the Pharisee with regard to the announcement
of a crucified Messiah. History confirms Paul's testimony that
the cross of Christ was a chief offence to the Jews. And this is
also exactly what we should expect. For in this idea was contained beyond doubt the negation of all that a Jew regarded as
most sacred in the hopes and aspirations connected with his
national theocracy. Further, as the Pharisees were the most
vehement representatives of this side of Judaism, it was very
natural that the offence of the cross of Christ should have been
repugnant to them above all others, and that they should therefore most violently have hated and persecuted the proclaimers
of it.[1] They had here to do, not with some merely theoretical

---

[1] The statement of Beyschlag (ut supra, p. 245 f.), that the chief point of dispute
between the Pharisees and Christians lay in the question of the true righteousness, is
erroneous. Righteousness was never the highest or ultimate end to the Pharisees, but
only the means for the advent of the Messiah's kingdom as they understood it; nor
was it the deeper morality of Jesus that most repelled them; indeed, this had many
points of contact with that of the better Pharisees, such as Hillel. But the real stumbling-block was, that Jesus assumed to be the Messiah, and yet was the opposite of
that which they expected and wished the Messiah to be. This is proved by their questions as to his authority (as Messiah), their requiring a sign (of the Messiah), their
tempting him with a penny (which turned entirely on the popular expectation of a
Messiah in opposition to the Roman sovereignty). That this opposition to the Messiahship of Jesus must have become much more violent after the crucifixion is obvious.
This death itself must have appeared to the Pharisees to be a judgment of God upon
Jesus the false Messiah, and the preaching by his disciples of the Messiahship of him
who had been crucified, must have appeared to them only so much the more criminal.
But their assertion that he who had been crucified was risen, must have seemed a
gross deception, worse than the first, because the truth of this assertion must have
changed the judgment of God against Jesus into a judgment against his murderers.
Everything, therefore, must have turned on the question, Was he who was crucified after
all the Messiah, proved to be such by the resurrection which followed ? This burning
question, in which dogma and fact were in immediate contact, was the turning-point
of the whole attack on the one side, and of the defence on the other—this, and by no
means the purely theoretical question of true righteousness. In addition to this, let
us reflect whether it is psychologically conceivable, and not rather contradictory in
itself, that Paul should so violently have persecuted the Christians on account of their

question of dispute, but with absolute right and absolute wrong, with the divine sanction or rejection of the whole of their inner life and its aspirations. For, according to outward appearances, the crucifixion of Jesus had been a judgment of God against his pretension to be the Messiah, consequently a judgment of God in justification of the Pharisees who had rejected such a Messiah as Jesus had been. According to the assertion of the disciples, on the contrary, that God had raised from the dead that Jesus whom the Jews had crucified, and by this stupendous miracle acknowledged his Messiahship and established him in his Messianic kingdom, the Pharisees, by taking part in the death of Jesus, had incurred the guilt of the greatest sin it was possible to commit against God, and the curse had recoiled from Jesus upon the head of his murderers. Thus the question of the Messiahship of Jesus grew into a question of life or death for the Pharisees; no wonder, then, that so zealous a Pharisee as Paul should not be able to rest, but should see in the persecution of the disciples a sacred duty. But it was this very persecution that brought him into closer contact with the Christians. He would be certain to fight against them, not only with external force, but also with those weapons of argument which he was ever ready to employ. In this way he must of necessity have listened to the proofs brought forward by the Christians in their defence. Foremost among these would be the appeal to the appearance of him who had been crucified, in which the disciples

doctrine of a better righteousness, while he was at the same time (according to Beyschlag's own statement) penetrated with the deepest feeling of the inadequacy of the righteousness of the law. How is this possible? Would not this consciousness of the weakness of his position have restrained him from the first from attacking those who held out the prospect of a better righteousness, and inclined him rather in favour of the Christian doctrine than against it? Thus the violence of his persecuting zeal proves that the turning-point of the contest was a very different question,—one, namely, in which Paul, in consistency with his whole past life as a Pharisee, must have regarded his own side as absolutely and unconditionally in the right, and his adversaries as not only theoretically in the wrong, but as deceivers hateful in God's sight. Precisely such a question was that of the significance of the crucifixion of Jesus. Was it the penal death of a criminal, or the expiatory death of a Messiah? The settlement of this question depended, for Paul, on the truth of the resurrection.

could see nothing but a proof of the miraculous raising to life again of the crucified Jesus by the almighty power of God. But, in the next place, they would try to prove from the Scriptures that suffering and death was in no way inconsistent with the Messiahship; nay, rather, that according to the prediction of the prophets, notably Isaiah, ch. liii., the Messiah *must* have suffered, partly for the purpose of his own glorification, partly as a propitiation for the sins of the people. This last idea was clearly enough contained in the words of the prophet, "The chastisement that gave us peace lay upon him, and with his stripes we are healed;" it was moreover symbolically foreshadowed in the expiatory sacrifices and the Passover of the Jewish worship; and the application of this idea of sacrifice to the blood of Christ as the (paschal) "lamb slain" (Rev. v. 6, 12, xiii. 8, &c.), had become familiar to the Christian community through the institution of the Lord's Supper. They would not, therefore, have omitted to make use of it on this occasion, in their defence of the crucified Messiah. At all events, it is certain that Paul had heard this scriptural proof from the disciples; for among the few things which he had received from external tradition he expressly mentions this, "that Jesus died for our sins according to the Scriptures" (1 Cor. xv. 3).

Now what had Paul the Pharisee to oppose to this two-fold defence grounded on the appearance of him who had been raised from the dead, and on the proofs from Scripture? He could neither deny the possibility of the one nor the cogency of the other, in the abstract: not the former, because the resurrection was one of the dogmas of the Pharisees; nor the latter, because that proof from Scripture agreed so well with the fundamental principles of the typical exegesis of his school, that it could not have failed to impress him. But the less he was able to combat the arguments of the Christians objectively, the more powerfully would the subjective feeling of the Jew and the Pharisee rise against the idea that Jesus the crucified should turn out to be the promised Messiah!—he on whom the curse of the law lighted through his ignominious death (Gal. iii. 13) be the bringer of the Messianic salvation, consequently also of the Messianic righteousness! That could not possibly be a righteousness according to the law, which was brought by one who was accursed by the law; it could only be an entirely new righteousness, without any relation to the law ($\chi\omega\rho\grave{\iota}s$ $\nu\acute{o}\mu\sigma\nu$). Thus just that which was the pride of a Pharisee, to be righteous according to the law, would become wholly worthless on the supposition of a Messiah who had been subject to the curse of the law. All the prejudices and prerogatives of the Jews which depended on the law would come to naught, the whole religious world of the Jews must vanish under such a Messiah and give place to a new one! So the contradiction between a crucified Messiah and the sentiments of the Jewish nation would have been intensified for the subjective consciousness of Paul the Pharisee, in proportion as he was the less able to meet the arguments of the Christians with counter arguments. Whilst the religious interest of the immediate disciples of Jesus, from the moment of their Master's death, lay in extenuating as far as possible the paradoxical nature of this catastrophe and reconciling it to a Jewish consciousness, in order to assist themselves and others as quickly and easily as possible to get over the " offence of the cross," the interest of Paul the Pharisee, on the contrary, lay in thinking out to its extreme limits the contradiction between the crucified Messiah and the presuppositions of the Jews; for the more decided was this contradiction, the more he felt himself justified in the hatred to Christ which he evinced by his acts as well as his convictions. We may thus quite naturally explain how Paul, even before he became a Christian, realized much more distinctly than any of the elder disciples before him the essential incompatibility of faith in the crucified and the old religion of the law; it was simply the old hatred of the Pharisee for the suffering Messiah that enabled him to see so clearly all that was involved in the new faith in the crucified one.

But, it may be asked, will not the conversion itself be all the more inexplicable under the circumstances here supposed ? If we turn our attention to two other points, perhaps we shall see that it is not. The first point is this :—however paradoxical to the consciousness of a Jew and mortifying to the pride of a Pharisee might be the idea of a new righteousness, brought about, without any relation to the law, by the expiatory death of the Messiah, yet in *one* respect it exactly satisfied one of the Pharisaic postulates. The Pharisees believed in the immediate approach of the Messianic salvation ; but it postulated for its actual coming *a righteous people.* Now as the people were not righteous in point of fact, nor was there any prospect of their ever becoming so in the Pharisaic sense, here was evidently an unsolved antinomy. What if perchance the Messianic righteousness, which the Pharisee postulated as a condition of the Messiah's kingdom, were not to be understood in the ordinary sense of the fulfilment of the law by man, but was really a gift of God, which might be procured through this very means, now newly proclaimed, of salvation by the expiatory death of the Messiah ? In this way the antinomy, which was eternally insoluble, according to the judgment of man, in the old way of the law, was solved in the simplest way by an ordinance of God, and henceforth nothing would stand in the way of the reception of the Messianic salvation on the part of sinful man ; he had only, sinful as he was, to believe and to lay hold of this free gift of righteousness, and he would be already in possession of the salvation itself. When once a reflection of this kind had impressed itself on the mind of Paul the Pharisee (and it was certainly not far to seek for such a keen intellect as his), it would be a heavy weight in the scale in favour of the persecuted faith. But to this was added the second point to which we have referred. The alleged objective fact of the resurrection was opposed to the subjective conviction of Paul as a difficulty which to a tender conscience must ever have become more alarming. That nothing was to be said against the possibility of such a miracle in the abstract from the Pharisaic point of view, has been already observed ; but the Pharisee would of course at the commencement have violently protested against its truth in this concrete instance ; it could not be true, for in that case he who had been crucified and was by the law accursed would have been declared to be the Messiah by God himself. Consequently the disciples, who professed to have seen Jesus after he had risen, lied in making this assertion, as he must have been compelled to think from his point of view; for according to the psychology of that time there was no middle term between the objective truth of the resurrection and conscious deception. But was this possible ? Did the Christians who allowed themselves to be put to death for their faith look like liars ? Is it likely that the dying Stephen, who, when in the hands of his murderers, saw the heavens open and him who had risen sitting on the right hand of God, would have conveyed the impression of his being a hypocrite ? On the contrary, it is certain that the truth-loving spirit of Paul could not, on witnessing this and many similar scenes, have resisted the impression that the conviction of the Christians, that the crucified Jesus had risen from the dead, was genuine and unalterable. What had he then to oppose to such a conviction of a decisive objective fact ? Nothing but subjective feeling ; and that is a bad state of things for a truth-loving spirit, doubly fatal when, on the ground of such subjective feeling, one has to act, to persecute, and to put to death ! This we may conclude to have been Paul's state of mind on his way to Damascus, on his way to a renewed persecution of the believers in Christ, all the while uncertain on the fundamental question, whether after all this were not the true faith, and whether the crucified one whom he was persecuting were not the ardently longed-for Messiah. On the one hand, we can hear the passionate "No ! it cannot be that the crucified Jesus was declared by the resurrection to be the Messiah ; for a crucified Messiah would put an end to the law, whose curse would lie on him ;" on the other hand, and this would ever be growing louder, "Yes ! but it can be, for it agrees with the Scripture, and the truthfulness of the

first witnesses of it is being placed beyond a doubt by the joyful
death of the believers."

That is a situation which it was simply impossible for a sensi-
tive spirit to endure long. It would press with irresistible
urgency for a solution; what this solution would be, must
depend in every case on individual character. In the present
instance, that the objective truth of the Christian idea should
prevail over the subjective prejudices and antagonistic feelings
of the Pharisee, is exactly what we should expect in a character
like that of Paul; but that the decision arrived at within his
mind should take the form of a sensuous experience, quite agrees
with what happened on similar occasions in his life, and we
must therefore in all of them alike seek the cause in his peculiar
temperament. We need only here call to mind the numerous
revelations and visions related to us by the Apostle himself, and
in the Acts of the Apostles, to see that the analogy they present
to the incident on the road to Damascus is so complete as to
leave no doubt of the essential similarity of the psychological
phenomenon in every instance. The accompanying external
circumstances agree with the description given by Paul of
another vision (2 Cor. xii.), for instance, the falling down, the
ecstatic seeing and hearing (in which he knows not whether he
is in the body or out of the body, and we therefore see that the
ordinary control of the organs of sense by self-consciousness is
suspended), and the great weakness and paralytic affection that
followed. Nor is this all; but it is especially to be observed in
every instance, that at a momentous crisis the decisive resolu-
tion, after previous strong inward excitement, assumes the form
of external revelation; see Gal. ii. 2; Acts xvi. 9. The fact that
this form is different in the different cases—at one time hearing a
voice, at another seeing and hearing, then being carried into
heaven, and again the appearance of a being from heaven—is so
little to be wondered at, that the truth is, it could not be otherwise from the nature of such visions. The very thing that moves
the feelings presents itself to the ecstatic consciousness as an

object of sensuous perception; that which had previously lain buried in the depths of the consciousness comes forth without a mental effort into the view of the imagination, and connects itself with real affections of the nerves of sense, in consequence of which the appearance of external objectivity and corporeal reality presents itself to him who sees the vision. It can only be asked, therefore, whether the image of Christ, glorified and raised to heaven, could already have been an object of consciousness to Paul before his conversion; and after careful reflection upon the situation, we shall be so far from denying the possibility of it, that we shall be forced to the conclusion that it must have been the case. How could he have heard the persecuted Christians, the dying Stephen for instance, speak of their Master as glorified and raised to heaven, without reproducing on his side this mental image? That he did not of course attribute any truth to it at first, does not affect the question; for the *content* of a representation remains, as is well known, precisely the same, whether I attribute or deny *existence* to it in my judgment. Now that Paul would not merely have taken momentarily into his consciousness the representation of him who had risen from the dead, but that it must again and again have occurred to him as the very point on which the decision depended in the mental struggles which preceded his conversion, follows of necessity from the way in which we have supposed the conversion to have been psychologically brought about. The whole question turned on whether the crucified Jesus was really, as his disciples said, declared by the resurrection to be the Messiah, and his death thus proved to be the expiatory death of the Messiah, and a new means of salvation; or whether he had remained among the dead, and was therefore no Messiah, his death no expiatory sacrifice, but the death of a malefactor. The decision depended on Paul's being able or unable to convince himself of the truth of the alleged resurrection; and are we to believe that this cardinal point did not fill and excite the very depths of his consciousness? How could he have turned over and over in his mind the debateable possibility of the resurrection, without forming an image of the risen one ?   But when he had once formed this image, if it were only mentally to reject it at first, nothing is more natural than that the decisive turn of his convictions should clothe itself in the form of the sudden appearance before him, as an objective reality, and in the overpowering brightness of heavenly majesty, of that image of the risen Jesus, which he had so vehemently struggled against, and each time more vainly endeavoured to reject.   Upon this the struggle was decided, every doubt was vanquished ; and Paul the persecutor had attained to the same certainty founded on experience as the first disciples, that the crucified one was the Messiah.   But then he was the Messiah, not only, as they said, *in spite of the cross*, but precisely *because of the cross ;* his crucifixion was the turning-point of his work as Messiah, the end of the old, the beginning of a new covenant, an offence to the Jews, and to the Greeks foolishness, but the power of God and the wisdom of God to those who are called, both Jews and Gentiles, to believe in him (1 Cor. i. 23 f.).

Looked at in this way, the conversion of Paul was certainly at the commencement an intellectual process, a dialectical struggle of religious thought, as it could not but be where he had to deal with the truth or falsehood of objective ideas, and with convictions relating to dogma bound up with history.   And we cannot fail to see unmistakable traces of this theoretical point of departure in his system of doctrine ; his scheme of faith certainly always has for basis the intellectual element of a judgment as to truth of conviction, and in the structure raised thereon the objective truths of the resurrection and the expiatory death of Christ stand first.   And yet this is but one side.   The question with which he had to deal at the time of his conversion was undoubtedly no merely intellectual one, concerned only with the apprehension of knowledge by the understanding, but it comprehended the highest interests of the religious feelings. The whole religious world in which Paul the Pharisee lived, in which he had taken root with all the fibres of his soul, with his thought, feelings and will, his whole being as it had existed up to that day was at stake if the faith in Christ prevailed. The process of his conversion, therefore, was anything but a cold calculation of thought; it was, on the contrary, the deeply moral act of obedience of a tender conscience to the higher truth which irresistibly forced itself upon him (hence faith is to him a ὑπακοή), an act of splendid self-denial, the giving up of the old man and his whole religious world to death, so that henceforth he should not "glory," nay, he should not live; save in Christ the crucified. This is in truth the key-note of which we may hear the sound in all the Apostle's letters, in which he is constantly depicting his personal relation to the cross of Christ; it is never a mere relation of objective theory, but always, at the same time and essentially, the relation of the subjective union of the inmost feelings with the crucified, a mystic communion with the death on the cross and with the life of Christ risen. With his death upon the cross; for by placing there all that had hitherto been his pride, giving himself to Christ for his own by faith, and seeking in his cross his only "glory," the world is crucified to him, and he to the world (Gal. vi. 14); by letting go all that had hitherto made his religious life, especially the law, he is crucified with Christ (Gal. ii. 19); and that is true not only of him, but of all who are Christ's, for "as one died for all, so are all dead" (2 Cor. v. 14). But as Christ is not only dead, but also risen, to live henceforth unto God (Rom. vi. 10), so faith is likewise not only communion with the death, but also with the new life of Christ. In the passing away of the old, everything has at the same time become new (2 Cor. v. 17); in the crucifixion of the old man with Christ, a new creature has come into being (ibid. and Gal. vi. 15). And that new life consists primarily in this, that those for whom Christ died are to show their gratitude for this by living henceforth for Christ, and devoting their lives to him and his interests, or, as he himself did, to God (2 Cor. v. 15; Gal. ii. 19; Rom. xiv. 8). And further, the life of Christians is not only devoted to Christ, but consists also in communion with him; it is a συζῆν, ζῆν ἅμα σὺν Χριστῷ, a κοινωνία Χριστοῦ (1 Thess. v. 10; Rom. vi. 4—8; 1 Cor. i. 9; 2 Cor. xiii. 4); nay, this communion is in its nature so intimate, that the Apostle loves to describe it as a mutual indwelling, as the being and living of the man ἐν Χριστῷ, and of Christ ἐν ἐμοί (Gal. ii. 20), so that the man's own life is completely absorbed and taken up into the life of Christ in him (ἐμοὶ τὸ ζῆν Χριστός, Phil. i. 21).

But now, out of this idea of the mystical communion of the faithful with Christ, which again was but a consequence of the conversion, of this painful dying and becoming a new creature, there grows a second branch of the doctrinal system of Paul, which became as important for its positive formation and further construction, as the consequence of the expiatory death was decisive in forming the negative part of the Pauline Gospel in opposition to the Jews or the Jewish Christians. The life of the risen Jesus, with which the faithful enter into communion, belongs to that heavenly world on the other side of the grave, whose element is not earthly substance, not the weak, transitory and unclean σάρξ, but the higher substance of the πνεῦμα, to which belong life and strength, incorruptibility and purity, and which shines forth as radiant light (δόξα). As Christ himself, through his resurrection, has entered into the sphere of pure spirit, he has absolutely become spirit (2 Cor. iii. 18); which, however, does not exclude the σῶμα πνευματικὸν or σῶμα τῆς δόξης (Phil. iii. 21), in which we are told he actually appeared to Paul himself. But Christ does not only become a living spirit himself, he is also a life-giving principle, πνεῦμα ζωοποίουν (1 Cor. xv. 45), to those who unite themselves to him in faith. And this primarily in the transcendent-physical or eschatological sense of the "eternal heavenly life," though secondarily in the most comprehensive sense of the word "life." It is in the former sense that, just as we bear, as natural men, the image of the first earthly Adam, so shall we, as Christians, bear the image of the second heavenly Adam (1 Cor. xv. 49); as in Adam all die, so in Christ shall all be made alive (ib. ver. 22); or, as we have grown into oneness with Christ through imitation of his death (in baptism), so shall we also through the imitation of his resurrection; if we have died with Christ, so we believe that we shall live with him (Rom. vi. 5—8). In all these passages, the immediate sense of the word "live" is primarily eschatological. Only it inevitably followed from the way in which this whole view originated, that *the transcendent eschatological idea* became of necessity an *immanent ethical* one. For as our future participation in his resurrection-life depends on our having died with him in baptism, and on our being ἐν Χριστῷ in believing, consequently on our *present* mystical communion with Christ, so our participation in his πνεῦμα-life cannot be only future, but must also be *already present.* Hence at the very moment when we entered into mystical communion with Christ (when we, through ἐνδύσασθαι Χριστὸν, became ἐν Χριστῷ ὄντες), that is to say, *at our baptism, we must have received at the same instant the πνεῦμα of Christ,* as an immediate commencement and earnest of our future complete conformity with his πνεῦμα-life. Thus baptism, as the moment of ἐνδύσασθαι τὸν Χριστόν, is at the same time *the beginning of a καινότης ζωῆς,* namely, of the ζωὴ ἐν πνεύματι (Gal. iii. 27; Rom. vi. 4, vii. 6), which is essentially identical with the ζωὴ αἰώνιος and ἐπουράνιος of the risen Jesus and of our own resurrection—as it were, the present inward anticipation of the future heavenly state, under the veil of the earthly corporeality of the σάρξ.

We have here a turn of Christian thought which has bearings of immeasurable importance. Whilst the direction of the primitive Christian consciousness was predominantly, one may almost say exclusively, eschatological, and the life of a Christian on earth appeared for this reason to be still an expectation, not yet a completion, the old that perishes, not the new that endures (αἰὼν οὗτος, not αἰὼν μέλλων), Paul makes the "newness of life" to begin not with that completion on the other side of the grave,

but with the life of faith on earth of the Messiah's community.
And this change in the time of its commencement immediately
leads to a transformation of the idea itself; the Messianic ζωή,
by commencing at once in the life of faith on earth, is stripped
of its one-sided, supernatural, apocalyptic character, and becomes
the new life of Christians in the truly spiritual, in the *ethical*
sense of the word, the renewal of the νοῦς, the self that thinks,
feels and wills. Not, indeed, that the eschatological sense of
the Christian ζωή is eliminated; on the contrary, in the chief
passages bearing on the point, this forms, as has been already
remarked, so essential an element, that no unbiassed commentator can avoid regarding it as the primitive sense, which under-
lies the whole development. But it is just the development by
Paul of the immanent ethical out of the transcendent eschatological idea that was so original and so fruitful for Christian
dogma;[1] and for this we are ultimately indebted to that deeply
religious mysticism of faith, by which Paul knew himself to be
already one with "the Son of God who loved him and gave himself for him."

As the idea of the Messianic ζωή was changed when regarded
from the standpoint of Pauline mysticism, so likewise was that
of the Messianic πνεῦμα. That man obtained the Messianic
πνεῦμα in baptism, was taught by Paul in accordance with the
universal opinion of primitive Christianity. But by this πνεῦμα
was understood a "donum superadditum" peculiar to the Messianic time, which manifested itself as a purely supernatural

---

[1] If we add to the foregoing consideration, that the other fundamental idea upon
which Paul's system of salvation rested—namely, justification—also originated in the
eschatological representation of the Messianic judgment, and if we remember further
that precisely in the same manner the decisive words in the Gospel message of Jesus
himself, "The kingdom of heaven is among you," sprang from the simple anticipation
of the future and external kingdom of the Messiah, in the present and internal consciousness of the community, we thus come by a purely empirical method on the
traces of one of the deepest *laws of development of the history of religion*—namely,
that the religious spirit loves to conceal its deepest mysteries and its most fruitful
germs in the calyx of richly coloured apocalyptic imagery, in order that they may
grow and gain strength under the protection of that covering, until they are capable of
flourishing alone and defying both storm and cold by their own strength.

force by extraordinary miracles. Now with Paul, this notion, again, of the wonder-working spirit is by no means eliminated (cf. 1 Cor. xii.), but it is stripped of its one-sided supernatural character, and completed on the truly spiritual, ethical side. The Messianic πνεῦμα thus no longer remains as something which transcends humanity, and only works upon men in an extraordinary and abrupt manner, but it enters into the Christian himself, and becomes his own ever-working principle of life, the principle of the καινὸς ἄνθρωπος. This Messianic πνεῦμα is here no other than the share of man in that πνεῦμα which Christ himself has as the essence of his life. Now as the faithful have their life in Christ, and the life of Christ in themselves, so also will the πνεῦμα of Christ fuse itself with the πνεῦμα of the Christian into the essence of *one καινή κτίσις*. In fact, in many passages all distinction between the πνεῦμα of Christ and that of the Christian is done away with, whereas in others these two are again opposed to each other as active and passive principle. It is clear in any case, that by means of this new doctrine of the Christian πνεῦμα which proceeded from the mysticism of Paul, the foundation is laid for the immanent ethical view of Christianity.

Paul himself had already drawn a direct inference from this doctrine of the πνεῦμα, and used it for the *foundation of Christian morality*. This point was all the more important on account of the ease with which the Pauline doctrine of the abrogation of the law by grace could be misunderstood in an immoral and libertine sense, and was in fact so misunderstood both by friends and enemies. Paul refuted this apparent consequence of his doctrine concerning the law, by the true consequence of his doctrine of the πνεῦμα. As the Christian has entered by baptism into community with the crucified and risen Christ, so is the old man, whose principle was the σάρξ, crucified with Christ, and a new man, whose principle of life is the πνεῦμα, has risen. Now since the πνεῦμα is the pure element of the heavenly world, that which proceeds from it in the sphere of morality can only be good, and the Christian has only to give himself up to the natural desire of this spirit which dwells in him, in order to do good; good is therefore the truly natural for him, so far as he has the spirit. If, on the contrary, he does evil, then he follows the lusts of the flesh, the impure nature of which can only bring forth evil fruit in the sphere of morality, as the pure nature of the spirit brings forth only good fruit (Gal. v. 19—23). But as this sinful flesh was only the principle of the old man who died with Christ, it has no further claim on the new man who lives with Christ; it cannot and dare not have the mastery over him; he cannot and dare not any longer be under an obligation to compliance with it (Rom. viii. 12, vi. 14). Thus evil is for the Christian as such that which is contrary to his nature; the power and domination of sin is necessarily abrogated for the Christian, together with the law that was its provocation. The requirement, therefore, to keep from evil and to do good, is for the Christian the self-evident consequence of his new nature; *he has only to exhibit in action that which he already is in fact, a spiritual man.* ("If we live in the spirit, let us also walk in the spirit! Walk in the spirit, and ye shall not fulfil the lusts of the flesh." Gal. v. 25, 15).

Thus the Apostle made his doctrine of πνεῦμα the principle of an entirely new ethical system, which completely overcomes as well the mere constraint of a slavish obedience to law, as the mere license of a lawless freedom (that is to say, the Jewish as well as the heathen morality), and elevates them to a freedom which is a law to itself, and to a law which first makes man truly free. "The law of the spirit of life in Christ hath made me free from the law of sin and death. Where the spirit of the Lord is, there is freedom" (Rom. viii. 2; 2 Cor. iii. 17). This new ethical principle is no less a landmark in the history of morality, than justification by faith is in the history of religion. And how close is the connection between them is shown by the whole course of our exposition, inasmuch as it is precisely the mysticism of Paul's faith in Christ which has led to his doctrine of the πνεῦμα, and hence to the new ethical principle.

But now it is in exact accordance with the Apostle's method of dogmatizing to fix the connection between the ethical consequence and its religious foundation also in an immediate and objective fashion, without reference to the subjective psychological process by which it is brought about. That which completes itself in the belief in the crucified one, by means of an inward moral process, namely, the dying of the old man or of the flesh, as the principle of life which rules the natural man, is connected by the Apostle with the crucifixion of Christ, as if it had actually happened here, once for all, as an objective fact ; Christ himself has through his death died to sin (is placed out of all relation to it) ; sin (thought of as an objective power) has been put to death on the cross (Rom. vi. 10, viii. 3). The death of Christ now obtains, therefore, a new significance ; it is not merely an expiatory death for cancelling guilt and bringing ideal imputed righteousness, but it is also the destruction of the σάρξ, or of the real principle of sin ; it is therefore not only a means of reconciliation, but also of the real moral renovation of humanity—not only of their justification, but also of their sanctification. This is undoubtedly a most important extension of Paul's doctrine of the redeeming death of Christ ; for by this means the moral element of the Christian idea of redemption is brought into the most immediate connection with its religious element (reconciliation), and represented as equally essential. Only we must not understand by this that the moral side of Paul's doctrine of redemption is the chief thing, and the true spiritual essence of his dogma. The proposition that the bodily death of Christ has destroyed the power of sin, is, when expressed in this unqualified manner, just as unspiritual and incomplete as the other, that he has cancelled the guilt of sin by taking the place of the sinner. Both propositions require in equal measure to be qualified by Paul's fundamental idea of the

mystical communion of the believer with Christ, by which his
death is no longer an isolated historical event apprehended by
the senses, but a manifestation and a visible type of the Christian principle of salvation, and is only a cause of salvation just
so far as faith perceives and lays hold, in it, of the true spiritual
principle of salvation. Thus regarded, the death of Christ is
expiatory, because faith perceives in it the reconciling love of
God (2 Cor. v. 19; Rom. v. 8, viii. 32); and it is a conquest of
the power of sin, because faith from that reconciliation draws at
the same time the power of moral renovation. But the reconciliation still remains in the Apostle's mind, from the beginning to
the end, the foundation and the main element of his scheme of
redemption; nor ought this to appear strange to any one who
reflects that Christianity is in the first place and above all things
a religion, and only in the second place a system of morality.
However, there is no need to depend on this train of thought,
grounded on the philosophy of religion, since Paul's writings
themselves speak plainly enough. The doctrine of the expiatory
death of Christ pervades in perfectly equal proportions all the
letters of Paul, and is everywhere the point on which hinge his
doctrines of righteousness before God and of the abrogation of
the law; nay, more, on this turns his dominant religious tone of
trusting, grateful love. The doctrine of the destruction of the
flesh and of sin by the death of Christ, on the contrary, appears
for the first time in Rom. xvi. 8, and precisely stated only in the
two verses, vi. 10 and viii. 3. Its roots, indeed, pervade all the
other letters, and are to be found in all those passages in which
the Apostle describes the entering into the possession of Christ
by faith, and baptism as dying with Christ, as a crucifying of
the world and of self, of the flesh with its lusts; thus especially
in Gal. ii. 19, vi. 14, v. 24; 2 Cor. v. 14 f. But in these passages, this "crucifying of the flesh" still appears as what it
really is, as an ethical process in a subject who feels his coming
to believe as a dying and being born again (just as Paul felt his
conversion). And the "progress" made in Rom. vi.—viii. con-

sists accordingly in nothing else than in a more definite dogmatic fixing, but at the same time also an externalizing of that ruling idea of Paul's system of faith, which is so far from being inconsistent with justifying faith in the atoning death of Christ, that, on the contrary, the latter is precisely that out of which it sprang. And so we find in the last letter of Paul,.Phil. iii. 9 f., justification through faith, and the mystic communion with Christ in faith, woven together in indissoluble unity.

Moreover, the doctrine contained in the Epistle to the Romans, of the mortification of the flesh through the death of Christ, is closely connected with the fact that the *ethical conception of σάρξ* is in this very passage (ch. vi.—viii.) for the first time employed by the Apostle for a dogmatic purpose. He had, indeed, previously introduced it in Gal. v., but there only for the purpose of moral exhortation. That Paul, neither in the Epistle to the Galatians nor in Rom. i.—v., used this conception for the basis of his fundamental doctrine of the impossibility of righteousness according to the law, is an unmistakable proof that it did not at that time form part of the foundation of his system (as is generally stated). But without doubt this moral conception of σάρξ first came into his mind as an analogy and consequence of the corresponding conception of πνεῦμα. We saw above how the original transcendent-physical conception of πνεῦμα acquired an ethical application under the influence of Paul's mystic faith. From this it was no violent transition to give a corresponding ethical application to the physical conception of σάρξ, forming in the Hebraic scheme the standing antithesis to the transcendent-physical conception of πνεῦμα—at least where it is opposed to πνεῦμα in the sphere of ethics: for elsewhere the σάρξ is to Paul simply the weak and transient element of the earthly existence of created beings. In brief, then, the actual (morally intensified) dualism of σάρξ and πνεῦμα is not an element of the philosophical anthropology of Paul, nor a presupposition of his dogmatic teaching, but a secondary product of his Christian speculation; it is *the psychological reflex of his dogmatical anti-*

thesis of sin and favour.[1]   The case is precisely the same with
the so-called "dualism" of John.   This is the reason why in
both cases the application of philosophical categories, or reference to the metaphysical dualism of philosophical systems, is
decidedly inadmissible, and produces nothing but error and
confusion.

The antithesis of sin and favour, which dominates Paul's
thinking, first presented itself to us under the religious categories of law and righteousness by faith; and, secondly, in the
sphere of ethical psychology under the categories of flesh and
spirit.   Finally, it acquires its most pregnant and comprehensive expression in the contrast of the historical types *Adam and
Christ,* or *the first and second Adam.*   Viewed by the Apostle
from the height of his Christian philosophy of history, the
development of humanity divides itself into two periods of
opposite religious and moral character.   The first period, which
dates from and is represented by the first Adam, was under
the dominion of sin, the flesh, death, and the law (as taskmaster
of those under the bondage of sin, and a provocation to the
sinful action of the flesh).   Adam, therefore, represents the
principle of sin, of death, and of bondage.   Christ, on the contrary, was the second Adam, because he was the founder of a new
religious and moral development of humanity, which is no
longer under the law, but under favour; no longer under the
dominion of the flesh, but under that of the spirit; no longer in
a state of bondage, but of sonship to God; no longer subject to
death, but in possession of (eternal) life.   But in both instances
Paul sees in the founder of a race the personification of the
type of the race, or of its ruling principle.   Thus Christ, as the
founder of a humanity in the condition of sonship to God, becomes
in his eyes the personified principle of divine sonship, the absolute ideal of the very Son of God.   But in consequence of this

---

[1] The translator has ventured to substitute for the technical term "grace," in
which the original notion is almost entirely obscured by theological accretions, the
word "favour," by which that notion is always expressed in ordinary English.

identification of the historical person with the absolute principle, the former is snatched from the limit of the finite, his course is transferred to heaven and eternity; Christ becomes the pre-existing heavenly man who is sent hither from heaven in the fulness of time, to take upon him our sinful flesh, by the death of which he is to cancel the guilt and power of sin, but by his resurrection to become a quickening spirit to humanity, that we also through the communion of his spirit may be changed into spiritual men and children of God, after the image of the "first-born among many brethren."

Thus Paul's Christology comprehends the fundamental ideas of his gospel, and reflects it truly in strict accordance with its origin; for his Christology, like his whole doctrinal system, is neither derived from tradition, nor the result of abstract speculation or extraneous philosophic dicta, but is derived from reflection on the blessings of salvation granted in the death and resurrection of Christ, as these presented themselves to the faith of Paul as facts of his inward experience. Paul was conscious of having himself become a new man through faith in him who was crucified and raised from the dead, of having painfully worked his way out of the bondage of the flesh and of the law into the freedom of the spirit of sonship: this consciousness, when he extended it to the whole company of believers, naturally led him to apply to the cause of this change the conception of "the second Adam," of the "life-giving Spirit," of "the first-born Son of God," the "prototype of the spiritual or heavenly man" (1 Cor. xv.; Rom. viii. 29). Thus we have before us *the first dogmatic Christology*, i.e. a doctrine about Christ which is in reality an exposition of the Christian consciousness of the community in the form of declarations respecting the person of its Founder. As a free (speculative) expression of the Christian idea, it has an ideal height and breadth which constitute it the common point of departure for all further Christian speculation; but the uniting of the idea with the historical person of the Founder, and especially with his greatest moral act, the sacrifice

of his death upon the cross, adds to the ideal thought the real
power of religious pathos and of heartfelt sympathy; and in so
doing creates that mysticism of feeling, which we find everywhere in the history of religion to be the most genuine and
fruitful source of religious life and thought. Indeed, this mysticism leads directly to speculation; for while the pious subject
through sympathy feels himself as one with his object, the limits
of individual life and the separation of individual from individual are by this act done away, the particular is elevated to
the universal, and thus that is accomplished in the immediate
form of feeling which speculation does in the mediated form
of thought.* Thus, the deepest speculations of Paul concerning
a second Adam, the spiritual man, &c., do in fact issue only
from the depth of his religious feeling. This should be taken
more into account than has commonly been done in recent
treatises,[1] which, ever looking only on the dialectical side of
Paul's character, are on the point of turning him into a hair-
splitting schoolman, of whom it is impossible to conceive how
he became the great Apostle of the Gentiles, who knew how to
bring into captivity every thought to the obedience of Christ
(2 Cor. x. 5).

It remains, in conclusion, to raise the question, whether Paul's
system of doctrine, as it has here been sketched, can be set forth
at all as a completed whole, or whether it passed through changes
and developments by which our statement must be modified.
Now the answer to this question depends of course essentially
on the critical judgment respecting the genuineness or spurious-
ness of certain letters which have come down to us under the

[1] The only decided exception in this respect is the treatise of *Reuss,* Histoire de
la Théol. Chrèt. au Siècle Apostolique, which indeed requires to be supplemented
again on the other side, as it gives less than its just weight to the Judaizing form of
Paul's dogmatic teaching.

* The reader who is not familiar with the technical terms of German philosophy
will derive much enlightenment as to the meaning of these and some of the other un-
English terms, which it has been impossible altogether to exclude from this translation, by consulting the Vocabulary given in the Prolegomena to Mr. Wallace's Hegel.
(The Logic of Hegel, &c., with Prolegomena, by William Wallace. Oxford, 1874.)

name of Paul. Since the thorough investigation of critical questions does not fall within the plan of this work (for criticism concerns us here only in so far as it is affected by the dogmatic teaching which will occupy us in the course of the book), I can here only briefly express my critical views for the information of the reader.

In addition, then, to the four undisputed Epistles, I hold to be *genuine* the first to the Thessalonians, the Epistle to Philemon, and that to the Philippians ; as *unqualifiedly spurious*, that to the Ephesians and the three pastoral Epistles ; as *spurious with qualifications*, the second to the Thessalonians, and that to the Colossians. In these two, and especially in the last, it appears to me as impossible to conceive that they are genuine in every part as that they are in every part spurious ; and since this is so, scarcely any other conclusion remains for us than the view elaborated by Holtzmann in the most recent work on the Epistle to the Colossians and the Ephesians, *that the Epistle to the Colossians which we have is founded on a genuine letter of Paul retouched by a later hand.* But I cannot agree with Holtzmann in thinking that the hand is that of the author of the Epistle to the Ephesians. I rather hold it to be that of an Alexandrian follower of Paul holding similar views with the writer of the Epistle to the Hebrews. As regards the separation of the genuine from the spurious parts, whilst fully recognizing the ability displayed in Holtzmann's attempt, I am yet on several points unable to agree with him, and have no confidence in my ability to make an exact separation and a complete reconstruction of the original letter. But since in any case the peculiarities of the letter proceed from the later hand, its real use is as a monument *of a development of Paul's doctrine after the time of Paul.* With the Epistle to the Hebrews and that to Barnabas, it marks *the first phase of this development*, determined chiefly by Alexandrian influence. The *second* phase of it is mainly represented by the Epistle to the Ephesians, the tendency of which towards church union has already been foreshadowed in the first Epistle of Clement and

the first of Peter. The *third* phase represented by the pastoral
and pseudo-Ignatian letters, exhibits Paul's doctrine after it had
passed over into the faith of the universal (catholic) Church.
Lastly, we shall have to show from the Acts of the Apostles,
how the original system of Paul and its historical struggles were
reflected in a subdued light in the system as catholicized.

Part II. of this book will be occupied with these phases of
Paul's doctrine after the time of Paul.   But the *original system*
as it is to be extracted from the genuine letters forms the subject
of *Part I.*   In these there occur, it is true, differences of such a
kind as show an advance in the dogmatic thought of the Apostle ;
but this consists here, not in a transformation, but simply in a
more precise development and articulation of the dogma.   Hence
there is no good reason, in my opinion, for arranging the exposition of the whole in phases of development following each other
in order of time ; on the contrary, nothing but an *exposition of
the entire system as one* will correspond to the essential unity of
the fundamental views undeniably presented to us in the original
letters.   Due notice will, however, be taken, in every instance
in which they occur, of shades of difference in the earlier and
later letters.   In considering these we must not fail to observe
that local circumstances had their share in producing these differences.   Thus we find in the first Epistle to the Thessalonians
no mention of the doctrine of justification, and this doctrine is
also thrown very much into the background in the Epistles to
the Corinthians ; in both cases doubtless for the same obvious
reason, that there was no need to explain the doctrine of justification to a purely Gentile community in that precise form into
which it was thrown by the categories of Jewish thought ;
though the nucleus of this doctrine, namely, the idea of the
favour of God through Christ, is by no means absent from these
letters.   It is more reasonable to suppose that the absence
of the notion of σάρξ in 1 Thessalonians is an indication that
this conception in its precise dualistic significance was not
worked out by Paul till a later period, since the opportunity of

applying it was not wanting in the Epistle to the Thessalonians. But as regards the Epistle to the Philippians, my conviction is that it is no further removed from that to the Romans, with reference both to questions of dogma and relations of party, than this latter is from the Epistle to the Galatians; whereas we find in it no trace of any of the peculiar characteristics of the Epistles to the Colossians and Ephesians. I therefore consider the grouping together of these three Epistles under a common title, which has now become the fashion in both the opposing camps[1] of New Testament theology, to be a decided error, and I believe that they will soon be again separated. If we examine each of these letters attentively by itself, we find, in the first place, that no one of them has the same general purpose as either of the others, so that they ought at all events to be expounded separately and not together; and, secondly, that the Epistles to the Colosssians and the Ephesians are closely related, and that both of them deviate widely from the original doctrine of Paul, but that the Epistle to the Philippians, on the contrary, has as *little* in common with these two as it has *much* in common with the older and undoubtedly original letters; and that its peculiar character exactly corresponds with the personality of Paul in general, and in particular with his personal relations to

---

[1] The defenders of the genuineness of these three letters (*Weiss, R. Schmidt, Sabatier*), who nevertheless separate them from the older letters and present them all three together, under the heading "Letters of the Imprisonment," are in the awkward position of being bound to explain how it happened that the Apostle during his imprisonment suddenly entered on a new method of teaching. Could the short interval that elapsed between the composition of the letter to the Romans and his imprisonment, have sufficed to account for so radical a difference between that letter and those to the Colossians and Ephesians? And even on this most improbable supposition, how can it, in the next place, be explained that the supposed last of the three "Letters of the Imprisonment," the Epistle to the Philippians, is precisely the one which exhibits the least of these radical changes in the Apostle's dogma, or rather does not show them at all, but again closely resembles the Epistle to the Romans? Are we here again to suppose a retrogression in the dogmatic thought of Paul? Surely we cannot imagine the Apostle Paul to have been so exceedingly changeable ! (See the apt remarks of *Holtzmann*, ut supra, p. 230). Until these difficulties, which tell strongly against the half-critical view of "The Letters of the Imprisonment," are more satisfactorily solved than they have hitherto been, the assertion of Weiss (Neutest. Theol., 2nd. ed. p. 203, foot-note) that the "Letters of the Imprisonment" must stand or fall together will remain an assertion and nothing more.

this community at the time of its composition, while it would be exceedingly difficult to account for exactly this individual colouring in any other writer.[1]

Finally, with regard to the exposition of Paul's original system, the question may be asked, whether the genetic process, as it has been briefly sketched in this Introduction, should not have been made the foundation. The special object of this book, namely, to delineate the organic process of development of the Christian dogma in its commencement in Paul, might seem to require this. But the carrying out of this principle would, in the first place, have led us into far too much repetition; and, secondly, it would have made it much more difficult to survey the foundation of the several dogmas by Paul. For this reason I have preferred first to give in the form of an introductory sketch the organic development of Paul's thought as deduced from its single root, but in the remainder of the work to arrange my materials pretty much under the usual heads, while at the same time I have striven to have regard as much as possible to the position of each dogma in the progressive teaching of Paul. As the result, therefore, of a kind of compromise between these two considerations, the following order was adopted: Sin and the Law, Redemption through the Death of Christ, the Person of Christ, Justification through Faith, Spiritual Life, Communion in Christ, the Completion of Salvation. The transition to the further history of the development and transformation of Paul's system must be made by setting forth the original relation between it and the tendencies of Jewish thought, in the course of which it will be necessary to describe the relations of parties, as they appear in various forms in the Epistles to the Galatians, to the Corinthians, and to the Romans and Philippians.

[1] On the authorship of the Philippians, cf. Hilgenfeld's essays in the Z. f. w. Th., 1871, Part. iii. p. 309 f., and 1873, Part ii. p. 178 f.: on 1 Thess., cf. the same Review for 1862, Part iii., and 1866, Part iii. It is to be hoped that some competent hand will soon give us a handbook of early Christian literature, or introduction to the New Testament, containing the *established* results of modern criticism *well sifted.* This is a want much felt in works like the present, which, though not directly critical, must presuppose criticism, and therefore need standard critical works to refer to.

Part First.

STATEMENT OF THE DOCTRINE OF PAUL.

CHAPTER I.

SIN AND THE LAW.

IN making the doctrine of sin the point from which we start in our statement of his doctrinal system, we are following the systematic logical order observed by the Apostle himself in the Epistle to the Romans, where he (Rom. i. 18—iii. 20) prepares the way for his thesis of righteousness by faith, and supports it *negatively* by proving the *actual universality of sin, both among Jews and Gentiles.* An appeal like this to actual experience forms a most suitable point of departure for an exposition which was to bring home the peculiar teaching of the Apostle to the consciousness of the reader by connecting it with universally admitted truths of experience. But an inductive proof of this kind drawn from experience could neither in itself, nor for the dogmatic consciousness of the Apostle, be the underlying and fundamental principle of the wholly original idea of righteousness by faith; and for this simple reason, that such an inductive judgment of complete universality, drawn from the frequency of a phenomenon, only produces an impression of relative truth, or probability, not the absolute certainty of a dogmatic principle. In this instance especially, the facts of experience on which the proof rests consist from the nature of the case of gross acts of sin which are at once suggested by the survey of general states of morality, and are certainly also indicative of the average character of a mass, of a people, of a generation, and the like, but which are far from justifying the inference of a similar corruption in every individual. On the contrary, the same experience which proves the average moral corruption of the mass, nevertheless always exhibits individual exceptions, or at all events the greatest differences in degree of better and worse,—facts which in themselves may perfectly well be used as negative instances against the inductive inference of the universality of sin, and have in fact often been so used. Thus much at all events is clear, that a proof from experience, as adduced in Rom. i. 18—iii. 20, to show the universality of sin, can only have a *supporting* force for a theory which has been already established without this proof, and rests on a much deeper foundation.

This theory is discussed by Paul principally in two other passages (Rom. v. 12 f. and vii.), both times in connection with, or on the occasion of, a dogmatic explanation of the relation of the saving work of Christ to the law, or to the old pre-Christian economy; from which it is perfectly clear that the real ground and point of support for the dogmatic theory of sin was found by the Apostle in his doctrine of redemption.

Sin as the Principle of the Pre-Christian or Natural Man.

The well-known passage which is the authority on this subject, Rom. v. 12—21, can only be rightly understood by starting from the point of view that the Apostle is not seeking here to establish a doctrine of sin, but rather to support his doctrine of justification, by fitting it into a glorious frame-work of history viewed in the light of the philosophy of religion. The paradoxical notion of an *objective righteousness* (granted by God to man, without regard to the subjective nature of his life, and solely for Christ's sake), which is supported in detail in iii. 21 f., is now in conclusion to be made acceptable, and stripped of its apparently extraordinary and arbitrary character, by a parallel drawn from the philosophy of religion. Its counterpart or anti-type, corresponding exactly in form, though opposite in content, is

found in an equally *objective dominion of sin and death*, decreed
against all through Adam without regard to the subjective nature
of their lives. That this is the intention of the parallel which
opens with the word ὥσπερ at ver. 12, becomes clear from vers.
18, 19, 21, in which the comparison of Adam and Christ, which
had been interrupted by the insertion of the points of difference
in vers. 15—17, is carried out in the formal resemblance of the
effects they produced. The theme of the preceding section is,
that through the obedience of one, namely Christ, many (faithful)
have righteousness imputed to them (are enabled to stand in the
position of righteous men), or that the favour of God, through the
mediation of Jesus Christ, exercises a dominion to eternal life
by means of righteousness. This had before (i. 17) been given
out as the main theme of the letter, and this he here means in
conclusion (for ch. vi. passes on to other thoughts) to recapitulate,
and at the same time to confirm it by the parallel with sin.

It is of importance for the right understanding of ver. 12, with
which the comparison commences, that the object of it, as shown
in ver. 21, which concludes it, should be clearly perceived. Here
we see, placed in opposition to one another, the dominion of sin,
which it exercises through death (being proved to be the power
which causes the death of man), and *the dominion of grace by
means of righteousness unto eternal life:* eternal life is the final
object wrought out by the dominion of grace, but righteousness
is the intermediate cause of this end, and the immediate effect of
grace. The chief force of the entire chain of thought lies in the
fact of righteousness being the immediate proof of grace, in which
the sovereign power of grace first manifests itself. This relation
of righteousness to life corresponds with that of sin to death on
the other side of the parallel. The main point here is, that sin
exercises a sovereign dominion, to which all are subject through
Adam's one act of sin (ἐβασίλευσεν ἡ ἁμαρτία, ver. 21; ἁμαρτωλοὶ
κατεστάθησαν οἱ πολλοί, ver. 19). And sin possesses this sovereign
power in consequence of a divine act of justice (κρίμα, κατάκριμα,
vers. 16, 18), as, on the other hand, righteousness and life have

as their ultimate cause a divine act of grace ($\chi\acute{a}\rho\iota\sigma\mu a$). And as
in the one case life appears as the final object of grace, attained
by means of righteousness as the intermediate cause, so in the
other death is exhibited as the final effect of $\kappa\rho\acute{\iota}\mu a$, and the immediate effect of $\acute{a}\mu a\rho\tau\acute{\iota}a$, which precisely herein manifests its
despotic power. Now although the subject of the preceding
verses (14—17) is only the dominion of *death* in consequence of
Adam's sin, we can see plainly from vers. 19 and 21 that the
main point throughout this section is not this, but the dominion
of *sin*, which is related to the dominion of *death* as the *real cause*
to the external working and manifestation. But just because
the dominion of sin is manifested by the dominion of death, the
latter, as that which is immediately given in experience, serves
as the ground of our knowledge of the former; and the dominion
of death as the ground of our knowledge must necessarily go
first in the logical argument; it being, however, always presupposed that as death in general has sin as its real cause, so likewise the dominion of death from the time of Adam has as its
real cause the dominion of sin which proceeded from the sin of
Adam.

If we proceed, bearing in mind these conclusions drawn from
the context, and especially from the end of the section, to vers.
12—14, which directly concern us here, it is abundantly clear
that $\acute{\eta}$ $\acute{a}\mu a\rho\tau\acute{\iota}a$ (ver. 12) does not indicate a single act of sin, but
sin as a universal thing, which can be the subject of predicates,
such as $\beta a\sigma\iota\lambda\epsilon\acute{u}\epsilon\iota\nu$ (ver. 21), $\kappa\upsilon\rho\iota\epsilon\acute{u}\epsilon\iota\nu$ (vi. 14), $\dot{\epsilon}\pi\iota\theta\upsilon\mu\acute{\iota}a\nu$ $\kappa a\tau\epsilon\rho\gamma\acute{a}\zeta\epsilon\sigma\theta a\iota$
(vii. 8), which is condemned (viii. 3), under which man is sold
(vii. 14), from which (or from the binding law of which) the Christian is freed (vi. 22, viii. 2); briefly, therefore, it is sin as a *universal power, an objective principle,* which, distinct from each man, and
so from all men altogether, is a cause of effects in them, namely,
on the one hand of sinful desires and actions (vii. 8 f.), on the
other hand of their suffering death as the $\tau\acute{\epsilon}\lambda o\varsigma$, the $\acute{o}\psi\acute{\omega}\nu\iota a$ $\tau\hat{\eta}\varsigma$
$\acute{a}\mu a\rho\tau\acute{\iota}a\varsigma$ (vi. 21, 23). Of sin in this objective sense it is said,
that it " *entered into the world*" (the complex of created existence)

"*by one man*" (namely, by the sin of Adam, παράβασις 'Αδάμ, ver. 14); that to this consequently it owes not only the beginning of its appearance, but also of its existence, for previously to that event it had not come into being at all. "*And through sin came death*"—death also being thought of as an objective power which can be said to reign (vers. 14, 17); not, however, to reign in the sense that it was co-ordinate with sin as a sovereign ruler, but as its coming into the world was only a consequence of the entry of sin, so it serves only as the means by which sin exercises and manifests its dominion. "*And so death reached all men, inasmuch as all have sinned.*" Οὕτως, that is to say, in consequence of what has just been said, namely, in consequence of death having once come into the world with and by the sin of one man, it now reached every individual man; the dominion of death, having once entered as an objective power into the world, extended itself immediately over the whole mass of mankind, was absolutely universal, therefore no longer conditioned and called out by the particular act of each individual for himself; but by having *once* entered *into* the world *through one man, Adam*, it was (οὕτως) *at once* established as the power which had dominion over *all*.

But now death altogether is only a consequence and visible manifestation of sin; accordingly, its διελθεῖν εἰς πάντας must also be a consequence of sin, being shared by all. This is expressed by the words ἐφ᾽ ᾧ πάντες ἥμαρτον. But the difficulty here lies in the juxtaposition of two apparently contradictory reasons assigned for the universal dominion of death; on the one hand, the one transgression of one man Adam (οὕτως), and on the other hand, the transgression of all (for both Lexicon and Grammar require that ἥμαρτον should be understood of committing sin, and the aorist shows the verb to refer to a definite historical action). But in this hard and unqualified juxtaposition of these two different reasons is contained doubtless an indication that it was the Apostle's intention that they should be regarded, *not as two different things, but as one and the same;* that, consequently, the *transgression of Adam at once and as such was also the transgression of all.* Of course it is only possible to view the matter thus by supposing that, through a certain moral or mystic identity with Adam as the representative head of the race, all *were made partakers* of his act. Such an identification of what is done or suffered by a number of individuals with that which is done by their head, who is, as it were, their personified unity, is a mode of thinking by no means unusual with Paul, as will be seen by a glance at the two parallel passages, 2 Cor. v. 14, εἰ εἶς ὑπὲρ πάντων ἀπέθανεν, ἄρα πάντες ἀπέθανον, and 1 Cor. xv. 22, ὥσπερ ἐν τῷ Ἀδαμ πάντες ἀποθνήσκουσιν, οὕτως ἐν τῷ Χριστῷ πάντες ζωοποιήσονται. Moreover, the sense just given to the sentence, ἐφ' ᾧ, &c., is required to maintain the coherence of the passage (for the thread of the argument would be severed by any other interpretation), and also by the words which immediately precede and follow it: by those that precede; for if we were to understand the word ἥμαρτον to refer to the personal transgressions of each individual for himself, then this would plainly be the cause of their being doomed to die; but this would be in direct contradiction to the last sentence, according to which death, on the contrary, *so*, that is in consequence of that one act of Adam, passed directly to all. The thought contained in the chief sentence cannot, however, be nullified by the relative sentence joined to it, but can only be more accurately determined: since, therefore, the chief sentence has declared the dominion of death over all to be the immediate consequence of the act of Adam, the relative sentence cannot in contradiction to this make out the dominion of death over individuals to be caused by their personal transgressions, nor even to be brought about indirectly by this means; but it may well define more accurately the idea contained in the principal sentence, of an immediate causal connection of the sin of Adam with the death of all men, by the *intermediate* thought that not only the objective dominion of death over all, but also no less truly, and indeed as its logical antecedent (hence ἐφ' ᾧ), the objective dominion of sin over all had its origin in the sin of Adam. The relative sentence cannot be intended to give a new cause which would destroy the force of the immediate causal connection between the sin of Adam and the suffering of all affirmed in the chief sentence; it can only assign for the doom of death pronounced on all a cause which is already *implicitly contained* in that causal connection, and therefore simply forms an element in this relation of causality. The word ἥμαρτον is certainly ambiguous in itself; it might, if it stood alone, be also understood to refer to the personal acts of sin of individuals, and apart from the context this would be no doubt the more obvious meaning. But the ambiguity which is perhaps still to be found in ver. 12, is completely removed by the reasoning contained in the following verses: *" For until the law, sin was in the world, but sin is not imputed* (that is, as personal guilt and liability to punishment) *where there is no law; nevertheless, death reigned from Adam to Moses, even over them that had not sinned after the similitude of Adam's transgression, who is a type of him that was to come."* It is the object of these sentences to explain how far the death of all is a punishment for the sinning of all, or in what sense the latter is to be understood as the real cause of the universal dominion of death. It is declared that this cause is *not* to be sought in the *personal* culpability of individuals, as is proved by a two-fold evidence of fact: on the one hand, the personal sin of individuals could not be reckoned against them as personal guilt (by God) during the period from Adam to Moses, while there was as yet no law; therefore they could not be subject to the dominion of death in consequence of sins committed at that time, which were not guilty and mortal transgressions like that of Adam; and yet, on the other hand, it is the fact that they were one and all subject to the universal dominion of death. Consequently this dominion of death *cannot* (at least during that period of history, and therefore not in general and for all) be caused *by the personal culpability of individuals themselves*; accordingly—as it is a fixed

axiom that it must in some way be caused by sin—it can only
be caused by that (impersonal) *sin of the mass which was included
in the sin of the one man Adam.* And this was precisely the idea
contained in ver. 12 which had to be proved.

This theory certainly has something in it very alien to the
modern tone of moral reflection. We should, however, be more
reconciled to it if we considered, in the first place, that Paul is
by no means its inventor, but that he took it from the Jewish
theology, and only adapted it to his Christian system; and,
secondly, that in spite of its harshness it has for intelligent
thought a deeply speculative idea as its basis. That death
(that is, of the body) came into the world and became the
universal inheritance of mankind in consequence of the first sin,
was the universal doctrine of the Jews : for instance, it is said,
Wisd. ii. 24, that when God had made man for immortality,
death came into the world through the envy of the devil; and
Ecclesiasticus xxv. 24, "Of the woman came the beginning of
sin, and through her we all die." Other passages are adduced
from Jewish theology by Reiche in his commentary on this
passage; especially worthy of notice is that in which the
death of the righteous is expressly referred to the sentence pronounced on the first man, to which they are subject in spite
of personal freedom from guilt, which is precisely the idea expressed in vers. 13 and 14. But since there is also another
fundamental notion, "Non est mors sine peccato neque casti-
gatio sine iniquitate," the contradiction of these two views can
only be reconciled by regarding the first sin, which was the
cause of the death of all, to be at the same time the sin of all;
and accordingly it is said further, "Eodem peccato, quo peccavit
primus homo, peccavit totus mundus, quoniam hic erat totus
mundus," or "primo homine peccante cuncta corrupta sunt,
nec in statum pristinum restituentur ante Messiæ adventum;"
and the cause of this is elsewhere stated to be, that the first
man "dux erat mundi et radix omnis posteritatis" (see the

quotations adduced by Reiche, Commentary on the Epistle to the Romans, Vol. I. pp. 368—370). We have here unmistakably . the same idea that is expressed in Rom. v. 12.

If we now examine the dogmatic theory which is contained in these passages, two things are equally certain—that it is not the Church's doctrine of original sin, and that it is not the rationalistic theory of the merely personal sin of the individual. The latter is the direct opposite of what we think we have proved to be the only possible sense of the passage ; but on the other hand the passage, strictly taken, says nothing of a transmission by "inheritance" or otherwise of the sin of Adam to the rest. If the sin of Adam was at the same time the sin of all (the act of the race), there is no more need of a transmission of sin from him to the rest, brought about by the intervention of the individual members of the race ; but the whole mass was placed in the position of sinners *immediately* by his act—that is, they were placed in that relation to God which is determined by sin, in consequence of which sin is now the ruling power over all without any personal co-operation on the part of the subject, nay without any reference whatever to the subjective constitution of individual men.

The relation of mankind to God was fixed *once for all* by the *single* act of Adam as the head and moral representative of the race, as that of sinners who are under sentence which is pronounced against them in the form of the dominion of death. We must not lose sight of the *objectivity* of this dogmatic conception of sin, as no mere subjective moral condition, but an objective religious *relation* between God and man, which appears on the part of God as κρίμα, and on the part of man makes itself felt as θάνατος. For this is of the utmost importance for the right understanding of the entire dogmatic system of Paul, and especially of the doctrine of justification. When so regarded, the idea that the relation of the whole of mankind to God has been fixed by that one act of Adam, and that all have fallen together under sentence, has an appearance of great harshness from a *moral* point of view.

But this point of view is here (as everywhere in the writings of
Paul) too narrow, and fails to do justice to the philosophical
spirit which the Apostle brings to bear on religion. The *one*
act of the first man is obviously *not his mere personal,* individually limited act, but, in the view of the Apostle, *at the same
time that of the race.* It is consequently by no means he who
happened to be the *first* man, selected by chance from among the
rest, but *man in general,* man as man, who has placed himself in
the relation of a sinner to God. This at bottom means that the
relation of man to God is, *a priori,* previously to all contingent
individual action, therefore from the beginning and of necessity,
that of alienation and contradiction. This contradiction manifests itself, and we become conscious of it, as a standing under
the wrath of God, and experiencing this wrath in the doom of
death, and it must have so manifested itself in order that at last
πολλῷ μᾶλλον ἡ χάρις καὶ ἡ δωρεὰ ἐν χάριτι τῇ τοῦ ἑνὸς ἀνθρώπου
Ἰησοῦ Χριστοῦ εἰς τοὺς πολλοὺς ἐπερίσσευσεν. According to this
deeper apprehension of the Apostle's idea, the *one man* Adam
is only the personification of the principle of the natural man,
and his act is therefore the manifestation of this principle, the
commencement of the βασιλεύειν of ἁμαρτία and of θάνατος, and
yet at the same time a necessary moment in the divine scheme
of salvation as the condition of the βασιλεύειν of χάρις. Of course
it is not meant that the Apostle became conscious of this thought
in its pure speculative form, but it would naturally assume in
his mind the *form* of the traditional Jewish notion of a *first* sin,
and a *judicial sentence of condemnation* passed on mankind in consequence. It was only under this form and from it that he
developed the deep idea of a universal and purely objective sin,
which as a religious relation once given, as the principle of the
natural man, not dependent on individual moral conduct, but
the root of it, manifests itself in particular acts of sin. But that
this principle also preceded the first act of sin committed by
Adam, as it precedes the personal sins of all other men, is not
to be found directly expressed in the passage we are consider-

ing,[1] and indeed is inconsistent with the obvious sense of the words and the context. For, in the first place, the words, ἡ ἁμαρτία εἰσῆλθεν εἰς τὸν κόσμον, undoubtedly imply the entrance of something new, which consequently did not previously exist at all; and, in the next place, Adam's act of sin, in order to form a parallel with Christ's act of righteousness, must really have the significance of a causal act. We must in both these cases bear in mind that it is Paul's way to conceive the precise historical moment in which a new general principle is originally manifested as the operative cause of that principle. Thus the death of Christ is, in the dogmatic conception of the Apostle, not merely the manifestation of the new principle of the reconciliation, but the operative cause of it; and in the same way he conceives the sin of Adam, the antithesis in the history of the world to the death of Christ, as not simply the first manifestation of the principle of natural sinfulness, but its efficient cause. The universality of the consequences is then in both cases connected with the individual cause by the conception of a judicial act, in the one case a sentence of favour, in the other a sentence of condemnation; and this is in both instances nothing but the complement of that method of conception according to which the general principle was embodied in an individual causal act. These two conceptions, therefore, are inseparable, and both equally belong to the form of the dogma, and neither is to be explained away from the literal sense of the passage. It is quite out of place, therefore, to introduce here the doctrine of the σάρξ as the *natural* principle of sin, for this passage expressly exhibits the principle of sin, *not* as natural, but as *of historical origin.*[2] It can only cause confusion to apply here a psychological mode of

---

[1] With reference to this point, Ernesti ("v. Ursprung der Sünde," &c., Vol. I. p. 135 f.) must be allowed to be in the right.

[2] This is opposed to the view of Lüdemann, "Anthropologie des Ap. Paulus," p. 86 f. His explanation of this passage shows itself to be wrong by its want of clearness and consistency; and this is the consequence of his arbitrarily introducing the notions of σάρξ and πνεῦμα as the foundation of Paul's doctrine, which notions belong to another sphere of thought.

treatment which is quite alien to this passage, whose point of view is purely that of objective dogma, or of the philosophy of religion, and by no means that of subjective psychology or ethics. Equally unjustifiable is it, on the other hand, on the authority of this passage, which enunciates a historical beginning of the principle of sin, to interpret the doctrine of σάρξ to mean that the human σάρξ became the principle of sin at a particular point of time, and was not in itself that principle. On the contrary, we have no more right to think of the σάρξ in connection with Rom. v. 12 f. (where not one syllable referring to it is to be found), than we have in Rom. vii. to think of the fall of Adam as the cause of the sinfulness of the σάρξ. An unbiassed exegesis will rather leave both views side by side, and will not be put out by the fact that as they stand they are certainly inconsistent. In Philo, too, we find the two contradictory doctrines propounded with equal naïveté: (1) the Jewish theological doctrine of the historical origin of sin in the fall of Adam, and (2) the Platonic philosophical doctrine of the defilement of the soul by the gross material body to which it is bound. But if we are compelled to confess that there is a *formal contradiction* between Rom. v. 12 f., and Paul's doctrine of the sinful σάρξ, we are all the more justified in penetrating through the obvious form of the doctrine in Rom. v. 12 f., to the speculative idea embodied in it, which is so plainly suggested by the actual words of Paul where he identifies the act of Adam with the common act of all. So soon as we grasp the thought that it was not in truth the first man as an individual who was the subject of the fall, but man as man, we see the historical beginning to be merely the form which expresses the universality of the principle which has no beginning; and thus the *substantial agreement* of the passage with the line of thought in Rom. vii. is placed beyond doubt.

From the moment when Paul had established the idea of sin as an objective reality, corresponding with an objective righteousness, consequently a state of sin previous to any act of sin, he

must have felt that this result of theological speculation needed
also to be exhibited anthropologically in the nature of man;
and the more so, since with regard to favour (grace) also he did
not remain satisfied with the purely objective "righteousness
before God," but worked out the subjective "life in the spirit"
as the complement of this. When he had once descended in
this way into the sphere of ethical anthropology, the same
antithesis, sin and favour, which had hitherto been apprehended
theologically under the form of a condemning and a justifying
sentence of God, had now to be represented anthropologically
under the form of *Flesh* and *Spirit*.

THE FLESH.

Ch. vii. of the Epistle to the Romans commences (1—13) by
expanding into fuller detail the theme of ch. vi., that man is
freed from the dominion of the lusts of the flesh by faith in the
crucified one; and this idea is here supported by a very peculiar
turn of thought. The bond between man and the law is dissolved
by the death of Christ, and consequently also that between man
and the lusts of the flesh, which worked in his members by
means of the law. But since the point of this argument depends
upon the law and the energy of the sinful lusts being indissolu-
bly bound together, so that the one stands and falls with the
other, it might appear to follow that the law itself is sin (ver. 7).
The Apostle rejects this conclusion. He adheres, indeed, to the
premise, and expands it: the law is the means by which the
energy of sinful lust acts, because by its commandment it gives
the occasion which causes the revival and activity of that sin
which was till then dead. But he goes on to show that the
cause of the law so working as to occasion sin is not to be
sought in the law itself, for it is, on the contrary, holy, just and
good, but in the nature of man, which is such that the law calls
forth in him the opposite of that which was really intended (vers.

13, 14). This brings the Apostle to speak more particularly of the dominion of sin in man, that is, in his "*flesh.*"

When it is said (ver. 18), " I know that in me, that is in my flesh, dwelleth no good thing," and this negative statement is afterwards supplemented by the positive assertion, that the evil which I will not, and yet do, is not really wrought by myself, but by the sin which dwelleth in me (ver. 20) ; and when the words "in me" are more definitely determined (ver. 23) as "in my members," two things are made perfectly clear: first, that *the flesh is not itself sin,* for sin dwells in the flesh, which is therefore the abode of sin, and not sin itself; secondly, *that the flesh is not the entire man,* for the contrary is most distinctly affirmed when the flesh is stated to be the abode of sin, but man's real self to be on the side of the good, of the law ; it is not I myself who do the evil, but sin which dwells in me ; and this expression, "in me," is carefully restricted to the narrower notion, "in my flesh, in my members," it being evidently implied that sin is not the only thing that dwells in me, and "the flesh" is not the only thing which constitutes my nature ; but that looking at me in another relation, something also good after all—a delight in the law of God—has place in me, namely, in my "inner man," or in my νοῦς. This, turned into a positive statement, amounts to saying that the flesh is that side of man which forms the opposite to the "inner man," and which has this in common with the members of a man—that it is the abode of sin. How can we understand this otherwise than that *the flesh is materially identical with the members, that is with the body, as the outer man?* This obvious conclusion is fully established by the fact, that in the same context throughout ch. vi.—viii. the expressions, σάρξ and σῶμα (σῶμα τοῦ θανάτου, vii. 24 ; σῶμα τῆς ἁμαρτίας, vi. 6 ; and σάρξ ἁμαρτίας, viii. 3 ; also, σάρξ and σῶμα as synonymes in viii. 13), are constantly interchanged : the only possible explanation is, that the body of man and the flesh are materially identical. At the same time, it would be carrying this deduction too far to assert that these two notions are absolutely identical, and equivalent in form as well as content. Against this view it has been with good reason urged that certain expressions have been applied to the body which are not applicable to the flesh as the seat of sin. For instance, in 1 Cor. vi. 13—20, where Paul is insisting on the sacredness of the body as an argument against the sensuality of the Corinthians, he says that it belongs to the Lord, it is a member of Christ, the temple of the Holy Ghost, wherefore we should glorify God in our body as well as in our spirit. 1 Cor. xv. 35—50 is especially instructive on this point; here it is said expressly that flesh and blood cannot, inasmuch as they are corruptible, inherit the kingdom of God. Therefore the earthly or natural body, which consists of flesh and blood, and is sown in corruption, must perish, because it is not *the* body that shall be. But the body of the resurrection is composed of different material, that is to say, not earthly but heavenly, not psychical but spiritual, not corruptible but incorruptible and glorious; there are these bodies of flesh and blood, of earthly, corruptible matter, as well as bodies of spiritual, heavenly, incorruptible matter. This brings the relation between the two ideas, σῶμα and σάρξ, into perfect clearness. The σάρξ *is the material of the (earthly) body, but the body is the organized form in which this matter exists as a concrete earthly individual.* It is now plain how far these two conceptions can be interchanged, and in what sense they are, notwithstanding, different. So far as the body has for its material substance the flesh, the earthly, corruptible matter, which is opposed to the heavenly and spiritual, so far can it share the predicates of the flesh, and be designated as the body of death and of sin; but so far as it is, on the other hand, the organ of an ego whose true function is to be governed not by the flesh but by the spirit, and which as Christian actually is determined by the spirit (of God), so far the body can and should be an instrument and temple of the Holy Ghost.

That the *flesh is the material substance of the body, and thus in general what is understood by (living) matter,* is in so many passages the most obvious, not to say the only possible sense, that

E

this meaning could never have been overlooked or disputed, were it not that the moral meaning of the word has constantly been taken erroneously for the point of departure. In the first place, there are the numerous passages in which Paul expresses processes, states, relations of the body and bodily life, by the adjective "fleshly," or by the substantive with a preposition. For instance, "that circumcision which is outward in the flesh" (Rom. ii. 28); the union of the sexes is a union in "one flesh" (1 Cor. vi. 16); birth and blood-relationship is κατὰ σάρκα (Rom. i. 3, ix. 3, 5); the unbelieving Jews are, through their mere bodily relationship to Abraham, while unlike him in spirit, only τέκνα σαρκός (Rom. ix. 8); and similarly Ishmael, who was begotten by the *mere* bodily powers of Abraham, is a son κατὰ σάρκα γεννηθείς; while Isaac, on the contrary, the child miraculously born in consequence of God's promise, is born κατα πνεῦμα (Gal. iv. 29). Then, further, a condition of bodily sickness is called an ἀσθένεια τῆς σαρκός (Gal. iv. 13 f.), σκόλοψ τῇ σαρκί (2 Cor. xii. 7); the mortality of the body depends on the fact that the flesh is mortal, must from its nature fall a prey to corruption (φθορά, 1 Cor. xv. 50; comp. 2 Cor. iv. 10 f. and Rom. viii. 11); and, finally, bodily life is expressed by ζῆν or περιπατεῖν ἐν σαρκί (Gal. ii. 20; Phil. i. 23; 2 Cor. x. 3), which is carefully to be distinguished from εἶναι ἐν σαρκί in a moral sense (Rom. viii. 8 f.), which is equivalent to ζῆν κατὰ σάρκα, or σαρκικὸν εἶναι.

But, further, the living matter which constitutes the substance of the earthly *body* is only a part of the universal matter which forms the *substance of the earthly world*, and by means of which the whole earthly world, as well as the earthly body, has the character of being *visible to the senses*, and therefore also *weak, transient, and perishable* (for the connection of the ideas "visible" and "temporal," see 2 Cor. iv. 18, τὰ βλεπόμενα πρόσκαιρα, τὰ δὲ μὴ βλεπόμενα αἰώνια). Thus the notion of σάρξ obtains a wider extension to everything "*worldly*," in so far as this, as sensuous and transient phenomenal being, is in opposition (though not in contradiction) to the real supersensuous and eternal divine or heavenly being,—a widening of the notion, which, although resting wholly on the primary non-moral meaning of materiality, yet trenches closely upon the moral and dualistic meaning of the word. In this sense earthly goods are called σαρκικά, because they belong to the realm of the sensuous and transient worldly life, in opposition to the higher goods of the spiritual life (Rom. xv. 27; 1 Cor. ix. 11). In this sense masters in relation to slaves are called οἱ κατὰ σάρκα κύριοι (Col. iii. 22), because this social relation affects only the outer worldly life, not the relation of Christian brotherhood. When Paul, according to the practice of his adversaries, will boast κατὰ σάρκα (2 Cor. xi. 18), his boasting refers especially to his bodily descent from Israel (ver. 22), though not to this alone, but also to the other distinctions which mark a legitimate Apostle (xii. 12), all of which, however, belong to the sphere of external sensuous things. When he asks the Galatians whether, after they had begun in the spirit, they will now leave off "in the flesh" (Gal. iii. 3), he is thinking, as is shown especially by iv. 9—11, compared with v. 1 f., of the threatened falling back of the community from the freedom of the gospel which they had already won, into the slavish ceremonial of the heathen and Jewish worship, which hinged entirely upon the sensuous (στοιχεῖα τοῦ κόσμου, iv. 3). In like manner he throws in the teeth of his Judaizing adversaries that their pretended piety moved in the sphere of the σάρξ, inasmuch as they gloried in outward sensuous rites, in circumcision for instance, which, just because it is an external rite, can have no value for the spiritual relation of man to God. Again, when the Apostle assures the Corinthians (2 Cor. x. 3 f.) that he does not strive κατὰ σάρκα, and that his weapons are not fleshly, the context, together with ver. 1, vii. 10, and xi. 6, shows very plainly that he means by this expression such arguments as would impress a mind which looks at the exterior, is influenced mainly by that which it sees through the eyes, and is liable to be deceived by the sensuous appearance of things; such weapons are not at his command, for, as is well known, neither his person nor his speech was impressive; on the contrary, his appearance conveyed the impression of ἀσθένεια, of φόβος and τρόμος, and his preaching had nothing in it of the persuasive power of man's wisdom (1 Cor. ii. 3 and 4), and was on this very account foolish in the eyes of those who were fleshly or worldly-wise (i. 20, 26); but nevertheless, on the other hand, it was wisdom in the eyes of the perfect, namely, the wisdom of God in secret, hidden until that time, but now revealed by the spirit of God (ii. 6 f.). This last antithesis alone is sufficient to show that here too we have to do with the primary meaning of the word; a wisdom is fleshly that keeps to the outside, to the surface of sensuous appearance, while the preaching of the Apostle deals with the hidden secrets in which the depths of the Godhead are disclosed. Finally, this is established by the special application of what has before been said to the concrete case of the Corinthians (1 Cor. iii.). When the Apostle in this passage calls his readers "fleshly" ("carnal"), and "babes," because in their party spirit they gloried in men (iii. 21), that is to say, prided themselves upon the authority of this or that man, as if it alone were valid, instead of placing themselves upon the one foundation, Christ, and judging all authorities thereby, in whatsoever esteem they might be held by men, it is clear that in this case also the reproach of being "fleshly" refers to the fact of the Corinthians determining the greater or less authority of their different teachers and party leaders by the consideration of their external advantages or deficiencies, and thus forming a hasty judgment based on mere appearance, with which the divine and true judgment did not coincide, the result of which accordingly was but empty vanity and self-glorification (iii. 21; compare iv. 3—7).

In all these passages we have as yet no ground for going beyond the common Hebraic notion of σάρξ, according to which it signifies material substance, which is void indeed of the spirit, but not contrary to it, which is certainly weak and perishable, and so far unclean, but not positively evil. And as the Old Testament also called men in general "flesh," and attached to this expression the idea of human weakness and nothingness, but not of positive wickedness, so Paul knows the word in this sense, and repeatedly uses it so (Rom. iii. 20; 1 Cor. i. 29; Gal. ii. 16, and i. 16: σάρξ καὶ αἷμα, equivalent to fallible, weak men). Only one cannot but see that it was naturally the next step, to raise the uncleanness and perishableness of the flesh, in consequence of which it cannot attain to the kingdom of God (1 Cor. xv. 50), to actual sinfulness, since both these notions coincide in expressing something displeasing to God, and contrary to the essential holiness of his nature. In fact, this step in advance had already been made in many passages of the Old Testament, in which the sinfulness of man is referred to his fleshly origin and his fleshly nature (cf. Ps. li. 7, ciii. 10, with 14 f.; Is. xlviii. 8, and especially numerous passages in Job, iv. 17 f., xv. 14 f., xxv. 4—6). But Paul must have been the more ready to take this step of advancing the physical uncleanness and perishableness of the σάρξ to moral sinfulness, since the Messianic πνεῦμα had for him, as we know, grown out of a principle of transcendent physical life into a principle of morally good life. When it is no longer the mere imperishableness and strength of a heavenly substance that is connected with the idea of πνεῦμα, but a morally good spontaneity, its opposite, σάρξ can no longer be a mere earthly perishable substance, but a moral spontaneity must also belong to it, which can of course only be the opposite to that of πνεῦμα, and therefore wicked. Thus out of σάρξ as merely spiritless substance grows a causality opposed to the spirit, out of its merely passive mortality an active tendency towards death, or working of death (τὸ φρόνημα τῆς σαρκὸς θάνατος, Rom. viii. 6; τὰ παθήματα τῶν ἁμαρτιῶν ἐνηργεῖτο ἐν τοῖς μέλεσιν ἡμῶν εἰς τὸ καρποφορῆσαι τῷ θανάτῳ, Rom. vii. 5[1]). But when the σάρξ has once grown out of a mere spiritless substance into an agency opposed to the spirit, its peculiar activity can of course only consist in an ἐπιθυμεῖν κατὰ πνεύματος, and the

---

[1] Lüdemann has aptly commented on this passage in his "Paulin. Anthropologie," p. 30 f.

product of this, its natural activity in the individual, can only be individual ἐπιθυμίαι and ἔργα of a sinful kind. *Thus from the opposition of physically different substances*, as set forth in 1 Cor. xv., *results the dualism*[1] *of antagonistic moral principles.* Gal. v. 17 : ἡ σάρξ ἐπιθυμεῖ κατὰ τοῦ πνεύματος, τὸ δὲ πνεῦμα κατὰ τῆς σαρκός, ταῦτα δὲ ἀλλήλοις ἀντίκειται, ἵνα μὴ ἃ ἂν θέλητε, ταῦτα ποιῆτε. How entirely both these principles are thought to be objective, is shown by the concluding sentence ; they stand over man, who is as it were placed between them as the object of their mutual antagonism, so that when he follows either one of them, he always experiences an opposition from the other.

It is clear what kind of fruit we get from the flesh so con-stituted, when its anti-spiritual ἐπιθυμεῖν gains the victory and transforms itself into action ; nothing but gross sins, first of sensuality, but afterwards also the more spiritual sins of idolatry and witchcraft, and the manifold forms of selfishness (vers. 19—21). That sins of selfishness too proceed from the flesh, has proved a stumbling-block, and has given rise to the opinion that it is necessary to give to the word flesh as used by Paul a strange sense, which is entirely alien to the primary meaning of the word.[2] Only we must bear in mind that when once the material σάρξ has been conceived as an agency opposed to the spirit, it may easily become the *principle* of sin in general, and thus of every individual sin, without its following that the *form of manifestation* of each individual sin must be determined by this

---

[1] It is the merit of Holsten to have been the first to work out energetically the dualistic idea of the Pauline σάρξ, first of all in a remarkable treatise on this idea, published 1855, and afterwards in a work which I have often quoted, "Zum Evange-lium des Paulus und Petrus, Altes und Neues." Agreeing with him as I do in the main, I cannot always follow him in details, and in the inferences which he draws.

[2] Thus *Schmid*, in his "Neutest. Theol.," II. 268, makes out that the σάρξ is proneness to sin in general ; and *J. Müller*, in his "Lehre von der Sünde," says that the σάρξ is the love of the world ! These explanations, which simply set aside the primary meaning of the word, are exegetical caprices which are refuted by the whole of the preceding observations ; we will only refer by way of example to the monstrous absurdity of such an expression as, "In me, that is in my proneness to sin, or in my love of the world, dwells no good thing." A careful exegesis should avoid imputing to the Apostle such unmeaning tautology as this.

materiality, and so can only be sensuous. The form of the individual sins which result from the principle of σάρξ is rather determined in each case by the *organ* which is seized by the impulse of the sinful principle, and becomes subservient to it. If this organ is the body (which has been shown to be by no means identical with "flesh"), then the sins which proceed from the flesh will be of a sensual kind ; but if it is the soul or spiritual faculty, the reason (νοῦς), or the heart (καρδία), the sins also will belong to the thinking and feeling spirit, and so be of a spiritual nature, like those of selfishness and irreligion.[1] This is a point of cardinal importance for the right understanding of Paul's anthropology. Since matter, which the "flesh" everywhere and always is, has been changed from a mere spiritless substance into a principle opposed to spirit, its activity henceforth is not limited to its immediate sphere, namely, the sinful body, but extends over the entire man, so that he now becomes a σαρκικὸς ἄνθρωπος, i.e. one who not only has the σάρξ for his physical substance or basis—that would be σάρκινος—but who has adopted the anti-spiritual ἐπιθυμεῖν, which is the peculiarity of the σάρξ, as the law of his life, whose entire personal life is enslaved under the directing influence of an anti-spiritual principle. Accordingly the σαρκικὸς ἄνθρωπος is by no means merely the sensuous or sensuously-minded man, but he who in his entire personal life, that is in every relation, is guided in opposition to the spirit and to God; but man is this by nature just because he is σάρκινος, i.e. because he has fleshly matter for his substance :[2] from his being physically flesh (σάρκινον εἶναι), it inevitably follows that morally he is fleshly (σαρκικὸν εἶναι), that is to say, in sinful opposition to the spirit. This relation of the two conceptions is made quite clear by Rom. vii. 14, ὁ νόμος πνευματικός ἐστιν, ἐγὼ δὲ σάρκινός εἰμι, πεπραμένος ὑπὸ τὴν ἁμαρτίαν, that is to say, the law is in its substance spirit, I am in my substance flesh, whence it follows inevitably that in the actual moral constitution of my life also, I cannot be in harmony with the law,

[1] Compare Lüdemann, ut supra, p. 72 f.   [2] Compare Holsten, p. 397.

but must be in contradiction to it; or that I am sold as a bond-man to the anti-spiritual principle of sin, and given over to its dominion. In precisely the same way, σάρκινος in 1 Cor. iii. 1—3 is primarily the physical antithesis to πνευματικός, and denotes the Corinthians as persons who (like every other natural man) have flesh as their substance, and so as in the first instance unspiritual, babes (νήπιοι, ib.). But here also this being flesh is taken immediately to involve being fleshly; (ver. 3) ἔτι γὰρ σαρκικόι ἐστε: for from the existence of ἔρις, ζῆλος and διχοστασία among them, it is to be seen that in them the flesh, or the substance of their natural man, still continues to be the guiding principle of their personal character.

From all this it follows very plainly that the ἐπιθυμεῖν τῆς σαρκός has not more in common with that which we call "sensual inclination," or "sensuality," than with selfishness or the self-seeking particular will of the natural self. Nay, we may with strict truth say that the peculiar anti-spiritual activity of the substance of flesh, its ἐπιθυμεῖν, is at bottom no other than *the natural will that is directed towards the finite natural life of the individual*, as it shows itself sometimes as sensual, sometimes as selfish; only while modern psychology takes the individual soul or spirit which animates this material corporeality as the subject of this natural will, Paul takes the animated matter of the body itself,—a distinction which has its origin in the difference between two ways of regarding the universe, but has no important bearing on the *practical* side of the question, with which we have here to do. But it is probable that the misinterpretation of the word σάρξ is a consequence of overlooking this difference between our anthropology and that of Paul. I refer to those who take the word in its specific Pauline sense to mean, not matter in active opposition to spirit, but the passivity of spirit as against matter, or such a direction of life by spirit as allows itself to be determined by matter.[1] This view cannot

---

[1] Thus *Ernesti*, "Vom Ursprung der Sünde nach Paulin. Lehrgehalt," II. 52 f.; also *R. Schmidt*, "Paulin. Christologie," p. 43 f.; likewise *Biedermann*, "Dogmatik," § 207.

be reconciled with an impartial consideration of Paul's statements. Expressions such as κατὰ σάρκα εἶναι, or περιπατεῖν,
would on such an interpretation be astounding pleonasms; it
would scarcely be possible to speak of ἐπιθυμεῖν, or φρόνημα τῆς
σαρκός, since the state of allowing oneself to be determined by
matter could not be the subject of such predicates.[1] Any
attempt to disarm this objection by substituting for this passive
state, or this kind of direction of life, the nature of man so far
as it is found in this condition, the natural human being determined by sense or by the world,[2] would only increase the difficulty on the other side. For how could Paul in that case draw
so marked a distinction between the self and the flesh as the
real abode of sin, as he does in Rom. vii. 18? How could the
ἐν τῇ σαρκί μου of this verse be replaced by ἐν τοῖς μελεσίν μου in
ver. 23, if he understood by it the whole human being as it is by
nature? The νοῦς, though it also belongs to the whole human
being, is here exactly opposed to the μέλη, as the opposite to the
abode of sin, as the abode of the law of God. How could he,
moreover, connect the σῶμα τοῦ θανάτου with σάρξ, as requiring
deliverance, if σάρξ were not just the material of this body, if it
were in fact something entirely different from it, namely, the whole
nature of man? How could he in this case describe, in viii. 13,
the living no longer after the flesh as a mortifying of the πράξεις
τοῦ σώματος? All these passages become clear, without any forced
interpretation, only when we allow to σάρξ in every instance its
primary meaning—which is also the most natural one—of matter.

The main reason why this, which is the simplest and the only
satisfactory view, meets, notwithstanding, with such constant
opposition from so many quarters, is probably to be sought in
its undeniable consequence, that sin, if the animated matter of
the body is its principle, appears unavoidable, and humanity
tainted with sin by nature and of necessity. We can certainly
escape from this difficulty by maintaining that it is not matter

---

[1] Compare on this point *Lüdemann*, ut supra, p. 58 f.

[2] So *Weiss*, "Neutest. Theol.," 2nd ed., p. 244 f.: cf. *Ritschl*, "Entstehung der altkath. Kirche," 2nd ed., p. 70.

as it is in itself that is the ground of sin, but only self-surrender
to it, or empirical human nature so far as the spirit in it allows
itself to be dominated by materiality. Only this is so far from
being the meaning of Paul, that it is exactly the opposite of it.
For it is precisely the object of Rom. vii. to explain the moral
constitution of the empirical nature of man from the flesh, from
the νόμος ἐν τοῖς μέλεσιν, from the ἁμαρτία which was already
latent and potentially present in our members, before any commandment existed, and which is only called into life by the
commandment. If, then, the σάρξ itself were nothing but just
this condition of man's nature which was to be explained, then
the whole of this wonderfully subtle and brilliant deduction
would in truth be nothing but the most wretched argument in a
circle! People would give anything to explain away the idea
of an impersonal principle of sin contained in the nature of man,
that precedes every manifestation of sin, and is the ultimate
cause which infallibly produces it; and yet this is just the pith
of the whole passage. For according to the 7th and following
verses, sin is already in man, even before the law comes to him
and brings it to his consciousness. Sin, then, by no means originates in the ego allowing itself, with consciousness and will, to
be determined by that which is material, but rooted in the being
of this conscious sinner lies as ultimate cause an unconscious
ἁμαρτία in the form of a purely objective power, which as unconscious may be called "dead," because it does not make itself
sensible to the conscience as sin. But this dead, i.e. latent sin,
which is potentially present, is roused to life (ἀνέζησεν, ver. 9) by
occasion of the law, which forbids the hitherto innocent desire,
i.e. it now comes into consciousness as sin, and awakes the feeling of personal guilt and liability to death (ἐγὼ δὲ ἀπέθανον).
And thus becoming conscious, the ego first distinguishes itself
ideally from the sin that dwells in it, and from the flesh as its
principle and abode, and is now further able really to separate
itself, with its personal wishes, its sympathy and antipathy, from
this element of its nature which is opposed to the law, and apply
itself to the law of God, though of course it can do this only in

inward reactions, which lack the power of actually overcoming the law of sin in the members. So completely, then, is the σάρξ – an independent, objective principle of sin, that it was not only sinful in itself from the beginning, as yet *without the willing or the wishing of the ego*, as the subject of the ἐπιθυμεῖν which was by its nature opposed to the law, but it afterwards proceeds still further, *in spite of the better knowing and wishing of the ego*, and in open contest with it, to work out its anti-spiritual activity in real acts of sin which it constrains the resisting but powerless ego to commit.

As a "dead" sin is here spoken of which is roused to life by "occasion" of the commandment, and then first exhibits itself in desires opposed to the law as that which it already was in itself innocently (ἵνα γένηται καθ᾽ ὑπερβολὴν ἁμαρτωλὸς ἡ ἁμαρτία διὰ τῆς ἐντολῆς, ver. 13), so, on the other hand, the potentiality of sin, which was restrained at least outwardly by the bridle of the law, may also find in a false freedom the "occasion" of its release; comp. Gal. v. 13, μόνον μὴ τὴν ἐλευθερίαν εἰς ἀφορμὴν τῇ σαρκὶ, i.e. the Christian freedom from the law ought not to serve as a soliciting occasion to the flesh whereby its hitherto bridled ἐπιθυμεῖν would be released and given over to a life of gross sin. Although the point of view here is very different from that of Rom. vii. 8 f., inasmuch as the question is not here, as in the latter passage, about the first inward awakening of the potentiality of sin and of the consciousness of guilt, but about the breaking out of the inward potentiality into the actual life of sin, yet the presupposition (with which alone we are here concerned) is in both cases the same, namely, that the basis of all actual sin is a natural potentiality of sin, which may be called indifferently ἁμαρτία or – σάρξ (it is called the former in Rom. vii. 7, 8; the latter in Gal. v. 13), because it consists in that ἐπιθυμεῖν κατὰ τοῦ πνεύματος, which is essentially peculiar to the σάρξ, and owing to which the σάρξ is from the first in itself, and by a necessity of its nature, sinful and sin-working.

Thus our conception of the σάρξ of Paul receives confirmation

at all points, over and above the advantage it has on the score of
simplicity, inasmuch as it never loses sight of the original meaning of the word, about which there can of course be no doubt.
The difference between such expressions as, e.g., ζῆν or περιπατεῖν
ἐν σάρκι, Gal. ii. 20, Phil. i. 22, 2 Cor. x. 3, and εἶναι ἐν σάρκι,
Rom. viii. 8 f., seems to us to be only that between different
moments or elements of the same idea: in both cases ἐν σάρκι
means "in the material element;" only in the former instance, as
this forms the substance of the earthly body, it is equivalent to
"in the earthly life of the body;" but in the latter case, since it
constitutes the agency which is opposed to the spirit, it is equivalent to "in the sovereignty of the principle of sin." In every
individual case the context must decide which of these two
moments is to be thought of: in many passages, however, the
moral is fused almost inseparably with the physical meaning, in
so far at least as the negative element of unspirituality and
vanity attaches to the latter, as in those passages of the Corinthians where the writer speaks of "fleshly wisdom," and of the
party-seeking Corinthians being fleshly.

In the notion of σάρξ thus defined we now have again the
objective guiltiness of man previously to any subjective will
and deed on his part, as it has already been presented to us in
Rom. v. 12. In both cases, sin appears as something original,
objective, presupposed as a necessary antecedent of the individual
will. But the difference between that passage and the doctrine
of σάρξ is, that in the former the origin of this general principle
is found historically in the first sin of Adam, in the latter psychologically in the nature of man, in the material of his corporeality. It has often been thought that this discrepancy in
the ground assigned in these two parts of the New Testament
for the empirical sinfulness of man could be reconciled by
regarding the constitution of the flesh, according to which it is
the principle of sin, as the consequence of Adam's sin, so that
before this historical fall the nature of man had been quite
different, and therefore that his flesh had undergone in conse-

quence of this act a complete change of its nature. Only in
Paul himself we find not the slightest trace of such an astounding doctrine. On the one hand, he speaks indeed of the fall,
but without connecting it with a change in the nature of man;
on the contrary, the consequence of it was only the Divine judgment by which all men were objectively set down as sinners, i.e.
placed towards God in the relation of sinners, and therefore, as
objects of the Divine anger, liable to the penalty of death. On
the other hand, Paul traces sin to the constitution of man's
nature, his being flesh; but he not only speaks not a syllable
that would indicate that any past historical change had accompanied this, but, on the contrary, he plainly excludes such a
supposition;[1] he speaks, Gal. v. 17, of the antagonism of the
flesh to the spirit in terms of such wide universality, as necessarily to convey the impression that it attaches to these two
substances by their very nature, and so from the beginning and
without exception; nay, in the very passage (1 Cor. xv. 45—47)
in which he speaks expressly of the first Adam in his relation
to the second, or to Christ, and consequently could hardly have
avoided putting the original better nature of Adam prominently
forward, he is so far from doing this, that he lays the strongest
possible stress on the opposition of the two: the first Adam is
χöικòς ἐκ γῆς, a mere ψυχὴ ζῶσα, not like the second πνευματικός;
with his nature, which consists of flesh and blood, he attains not
to the kingdom of heaven. Now here, although we must regard
these expressions as referring primarily to the physical constitution of the flesh as a corruptible and impure substance, yet
we must not forget that to Paul the unspiritual passive material
is at the same time the active material which is opposed to the

---

[1] Compare *Usteri*, "Paulin. Lehrbegriff" (6th edition), p. 28. "There appears
to be no allusion in the writings of Paul to a change in the moral nature of man, or
of his bodily constitution in consequence of the fall, i.e. of the first actual sin of
Adam; on the contrary, he makes the first Adam (1 Cor. xv.) χöικός and ψυχικός
from the beginning, which he certainly would not wish to be understood of his nature
after the fall and not before it." We must allow *Usteri* to be right here, although
we consider him to have failed in his attempt to reconcile this view with Rom. v. 12.

spirit. If, then, the σάρξ is by its nature and from the beginning the principle of sin, the question of the origin of sin certainly brings us face to face with an antinomy,[1] the deeper solution of which (indicated above, p. 46) does not further concern an exegetical statement. We will only remark here, that the Church's doctrine of original sin resulting from a change in man's nature through the historical fall of Adam, rests on a *combination* of Paul's two modes of representation, but cannot be justified either by the letter or the spirit of the doctrine of Paul.

Certain as it is, however, that Paul regards man as essentially sinful through his fleshly nature, it is as clearly not his view that he is merely sinful, that no better power forms a part of his nature.[2] On the contrary, in the all-important passage from which we started, Rom vii., the σάρξ is mentioned as one part of the whole man, and an essentially different part, the ἔσω ἄνθρωπος, or νοῦς, is distinguished from it. This conception corresponds generally to our " reason," so far as we understand by this both the theoretical and practical faculty of thought. Νοῦς is not, like πνεῦμα, substance, but faculty, the formal capacity of the ego to exert itself in thinking and willing ; in its most universal form, it is simply consciousness or self-consciousness (in this merely formal sense, e.g., in 1 Cor. xiv. 14 f., equivalent to consciously reflecting activity of thought). The νοῦς, as formal capacity of the spirit, can take up into itself contents of opposite nature, drawn either from the divine spirit or from the flesh and the world ; in the latter case, it becomes itself a νοῦς τῆς σαρκὸς (Col. ii. 18), νοῦς ἀνόητος ἀδόκιμος (Gal. iii. 1 ; Rom. i. 28), and as such needs renewal in the strength of the spirit of God (Rom. xii. 2), by which it then becomes a νοῦς Χριστοῦ, a percep-

---

[1] And so we may venture to say that the two parties in this controversy *(Ernesti, Weiss,* on one side, and on the other, *Baur, Holsten, Usteri, Lüdemann)* are both equally right and equally wrong.

[2] This and what follows is in opposition to *Holsten,* who (ut supra, p. 403 f.), erroneously identifying the σάρξ with the whole man (whereas it really constitutes only the ἔξω ἄνθρωπος), makes this latter to be "in its substantial essence ἁμαρτία"—a decidedly un-Pauline, Manichean exaggeration.

tive reason filled and enlightened by the spirit of Christ, a Christian reason, such as is attained by Christians (1 Cor. ii. 16). Yet we must not suppose that the νοῦς is according to Paul a mere empty form of the spirit, indifferently related to each and every content; on the contrary, the νόμος θεοῦ dwells within it, and that not merely as an object of consciousness, but as its own immanent impulse towards goodness (νόμος τοῦ νοός μου, Rom. vii. 23), which wars against the inclination to sin which is in the members, and that with such success that the ego, at least according to the inner man, turns in harmony and sympathy towards the law of God, though its external activity still remains captive under the ban of the law of sin in the members. It is only because man possesses in his νοῦς a not inactive element akin to the divine, that it is possible for him under the influence of the law to free himself entirely from the flesh (with whose sin-working substance the ego in the first stage of its growth is indistinguishably fused), and to arrive, through the consciousness of the discord between his outward action and his inner better will, at the feeling of the need of deliverance, as is so strikingly expressed in Rom. vii. 24.

It is this divine element contained in the νοῦς which manifests itself even in the heathen as *knowledge of God* (Rom. i. 20), and as *law of conscience* (ii. 14 f.). The moral consciousness, as possessed and obeyed even by the heathen, proves that men have the essential contents of the law written in their hearts, and that not as a dead, theoretical knowledge of good and evil, but (as is indicated by the reference to the specific organ, "the heart") as a force working through desire and feeling, which both gives the impulse to action (ἐὰν φύσει τὰ τοῦ νόμου ποιῇ), and also makes itself felt as a guiding authority in the testimony of conscience to itself (συμμαρτυρούσης τῆς συνειδήσεως καὶ μεταξὺ ἀλλήλων τῶν λογισμῶν κατηγορούντων). And the divine relationship of the νοῦς is revealed in the natural knowledge of God, no less than in the moral consciousness; for it is no other than the activity of the νοῦς, the νοεῖν, by means of which the Godhead, which cannot

be perceived by the senses, becomes through its works an object
of intuition to the inner sense ; it is through an intellectual
intuition that the reason recognizes God in the creation (τὰ
ἀόρατα αὐτοῦ ἀπὸ κτίσεως κόσμου τοῖς ποιήμασι νοούμενα καθορᾶται,
i. 20). The undeniable conclusion from all this is, that in following Paul we must not venture to regard man so one-sidedly
as a creature of flesh as to forget that he still has within himself,
united to his sinful flesh, namely, in his reason and conscience,
a higher divine capacity, a natural element of deliverance (i.e.
an element in the preparation for his Christian redemption). In
this well-weighed estimate of man's moral and religious nature,
Paul is as far removed from the Pelagian over-estimation as from
Augustine's depreciation of man.[1]

A question here occurs incidentally, which does not belong
directly to Paul's doctrine of sin, but is only indirectly connected
with it, since it does not refer to the specific Christian anthropology of the Apostle, but to the general views which he held in
common with the Jews. It is the question whether, together with
the σάρξ, a πνεῦμα belongs to the natural man, and in what sense.
An affirmative answer must unhesitatingly be given to the first
part of the question, on the authority of several quite unequivo-
cal passages. The Apostle speaks expressly of the πνεῦμα ἀνθρώπου
in opposition to the πνεῦμα θεοῦ, in 1 Cor. ii. 11, where the context
distinctly excludes the notion of the πνεῦμα ἅγιον of the Christian, since he is dealing with a proposition of the most general
psychological truth. Similarly, in 1 Cor. v. 4, vi. 20, vii. 34,
2 Cor. vii. 1, the πνεῦμα is simply the psychological opposite to
the σῶμα, and indicates the immaterial personality, or the inner
man, in opposition to his material appearance in the body. This
view is also supported by 2 Cor. ii. 12, vii. 13, and 1 Cor. xvi. 18 ;
for although it is the spirit of the Apostle which is here spoken

---

[1] Compare the following striking judgment of *Baur's:* "To allow that not only the
σάρξ, but also the νοῦς, belongs to human nature, and that the activity of the νοῦς
tends to the good, even to the extent that the Apostle admits, is to hold a view essentially different from that of Augustine" (Neutest. Theol., p. 148).

of, and this might therefore be the Christian spirit, yet the context clearly points to the natural human spirit ; for he ascribes to it such states of feeling (ἀνάπαυσις and ἄνεσις) as can be predicated much better of the human spirit, weak and liable to suffering as it is, than of the divine spirit, the active principle of strength and consolation. Lastly, Rom. viii. 16 unmistakably shows that Paul further distinguishes the human from the divine spirit in the Christian, as the receiving from the giving subject.

But the more important question is, What is the meaning of this natural πνεῦμα in the anthropology of Paul ? Has it a higher dignity, essentially related to the Christian πνεῦμα, or not ? We may obtain some significant indications on this point from the passages to which we have already referred. The human spirit is there distinguished specifically, as requiring consolation and rest, from the divine spirit, which is essentially strength, not capable of suffering. But the human spirit may evidently be defiled, and may therefore require purification from all pollution (2 Cor. vii. 1, καθαρίσωμεν ἑαυτοὺς ἀπὸ παντὸς μολυσμοῦ σαρκὸς καὶ πνεύματος) ; it may be an object of Christian solicitude to be holy both in body and in *spirit* (1 Cor. vii. 34), which presupposes that *this* spirit, namely, the natural, might also be not holy. It is in entire accordance with this view that the Apostle, in 1 Thess. v. 23, wishes for his readers, that the God of peace may sanctify them wholly, and that so both their spirit, soul, and body may be preserved blameless : this presupposes, again, that *this* spirit, namely, the natural spirit, is still in need of sanctification through the divine influence, and would not otherwise be preserved uninjured, nay, would more probably be lost. It is no less evident from 1 Cor. v. 5, ἵνα τὸ πνεῦμα σωθῇ ἐν τῇ ἡμέρᾳ τοῦ κυρίου Ἰησοῦ Χρίστου, that there is a possibility of this natural πνεῦμα not being saved, or being lost. All these passages agree in yielding to us the two-fold result, that the natural πνεῦμα is indeed subject to the possibility of suffering, of defilement, and of perdition, and yet that this possibility by no means must necessarily come to actuality ; but, on the contrary, that its weakness can and should be helped, its defilement prevented, and its ruin guarded against, by the strength of the Christian πνεῦμα. According to this, the natural spirit is just as essentially distinguished from the specific Christian πνεῦμα which *cannot* be exposed to all these affections, as from the anti-spiritual σάρξ which must perish by φθορά, because its most characteristic tendency is towards θάνατος (cf. supra, p. 53).[1] Thus the natural πνεῦμα stands indifferently midway between those two opposing principles, as the neutral substratum of personal life, which forms the ground on which those two principles operate. It has no more in common with the supernatural Messianic πνεῦμα which is imparted in baptism, than the universal divine *spirit of life*, which according to the Old Testament view animates all creatures and especially man, has with the supernatural *spirit of revelation* which comes from time to time upon the prophets. As that spirit of life of the Old Testament is essentially identical with the *soul* (since this simply represents the individualization of that universal substance), so also in the language of the New Testament, from which Paul makes in this case no exception, the (natural) πνεῦμα is in fact no other than the ψυχή (the way in which the two expressions are put side by side in Luke i. 46 f., is quite enough to show their essential identity).[2] This is no doubt the reason why Paul, when speaking of the natural man in his moral and religious aspect, so constantly avoids using the word πνεῦμα, and only speaks of ψυχή or σάρξ on the one

---

[1] Compare *Lüdemann*, ut supra, pp. 43, 48. *Baur* had already written in the same strain, ut supra, p. 147 : "Although Paul also speaks of a human πνεῦμα, yet this has no significance in connection with his peculiar notion of πνεῦμα." Also *Holsten*, p. 391, who, however, draws erroneous consequences as to the meaning of the word νοῦς.

[2] Compare *Weiss*, Neutest. Theol. (2nd edit.), p. 245 f. Even 1 Thess. v. 23 appears to me to furnish no argument against this view ; for just as in Luke i. 46 f. the two conceptions are placed one beside the other in a popular rhetorical fashion without being really different, so may Paul, when he wishes to emphasize the completeness of man's being, bring together the different expressions of popular phraseology, without any intention of teaching thereby a philosophical trichotomy, of which we certainly find no trace elsewhere, and shall scarcely, I think, find any in Hebrew thought.

hand, and on the other hand of the νοῦς. The natural man has - none of the πνεῦμα, as Paul understands it in his specific Christian psychology, which forms the dualistic antithesis to the σάρξ: in marked contrast to this πνεῦμα ζωοποιοῦν, he is mere ψυχή ζῶσα, a mere physical principle of life, which as such is no autonomous power opposed to the σάρξ, but, though not exactly identical with it, is only the powerless substratum for its ruling force. The higher, godlike side of man, as distinguished from the σάρξ, - is therefore not his πνεῦμα but his νοῦς, in which we have already recognized the godlike spiritual faculty of reason in the widest sense of the word, which however is only related to the Christian πνεῦμα as the receptive capacity to the effective principle of redemption. The inquiry regarding the relation of the νοῦς to the Christian πνεῦμα cannot be carried out in detail until we arrive at a later stage of our work (Ch. v.), as we cannot till then enter upon the peculiar Christian psychology of the Apostle. The only further question that need be here raised is, how is it possible to suppose a godlike spiritual capacity, like the νοῦς, to exist in men, if the substratum of it, the subject of the personal life, is only such an indifferent πνεῦμα as has just been described? We certainly cannot expect to obtain a solution of this question from Paul, to whose mind pure anthropological questions of this kind were evidently quite alien, and who, therefore, in this case simply followed the popular unreflective mode of viewing the matter which he found current; and our exegesis must accordingly confine itself to indicating this difficulty, which is one only from our point of view.[1]

---

[1] According to our mode of thinking, it appears to me that logical consistency requires that we adopt one of the two following conclusions : either, looking to the πνεῦμα of the natural man, which is indifferent and alien to the moral essence of God, we must deny to him every godlike element, so that his νοῦς too would be a merely indifferent form of consciousness ; or, looking to the godlike element, which according to Paul is present in the νοῦς, we must allow that the substance of personality also which shows itself in νοῦς, the human πνεῦμα, is something related in its essence to the πνεῦμα Θεοῦ, and therefore at least the potentiality of the Christian πνεῦμα, so that this latter is the actuality of the natural πνεῦμα. The former consequence has been deduced by *Holsten*, but with the result, as we have shown above, of placing himself

The Law.

By the expression ὁ νόμος, Paul always understands primarily the *positive Mosaic law,* and that in its *undivided entirety.* Although the idea starting from this point so enlarges itself in his mind, that he recognizes also in the natural moral consciousness a law written in the heart,[1] yet ὁ νόμος, without any further qualification, is always the specific term for the positive Mosaic law, so much so that expressions like οἱ ἐν τῷ νόμῳ (Rom. iii. 29, ii. 12), οἱ ὑπὸ νόμον (1 Cor. ix. 20), are precisely synonymous with Ἰουδαῖοι (Rom. iii. 19, ix.; 1 Cor. ix. 20). Moreover, Paul's view of what is comprehended under this conception is the same as that of all Jews, or Jewish Christians; it denotes primarily the whole of the positive ordinances contained in the Old Tes-

---

in open contradiction to Paul's doctrine of νοῦς, and grossly exaggerating his doctrine of sin. Impressed with this fact, I followed the second course in my article on "The Πνεῦμα of Paul" in the "Hilgenfeld'sche Zeitschrift" (1871, Vol. II.), and this I still believe to be more in accordance with the meaning and spirit of Pauline speculation than the former, which is followed by *Holsten.* But I willingly grant that the way in which I there tried, starting from the νοῦς, to prove that the natural πνεῦμα is also a potentiality of a divine Christian πνεῦμα, is not in harmony with the immediate form of the Pauline doctrine, and is altogether more in accordance with modern than with ancient modes of thought. I wish to explain, therefore, that the essay referred to is a dogmatic attempt to solve, by means of categories of modern thought, the difficulty which exegesis has simply to point out and to leave alone. Moreover, I may remark that the article expressly professes to be "an exegetic and *dogmatic* study:" its error, therefore, consisted solely in not making a sufficiently clear distinction between the dogmatic and the exegetical parts.

[1] This law written in the heart must by no means be confounded with the Christian law of the spirit. Nor is it the meaning of Paul to ascribe to it on account of its inwardness an advantage over the external Mosaic law (comp. Rom. iii. 2 with ix. 4). That inwardness is obviously very far from that in which the law has become the proper content of the will, the subjective determination of the will which constitutes the Christian law of the spirit, but, "from the pre-christian point of view, the law, even where it appears as something inward, exhibits itself as the command of a foreign higher voice, a holy power which man must recognize in opposition to his corrupt will; it remains, therefore, a letter that kills, whether it exhibits itself as the command of an external or internal revelation of God." So *Neander* well says, Gesch. d. Pfl. d. Chr. Kr., p. 568; and to the same purport, *Usteri,* Paul. Lehrb., p. 36; and *Weiss,* Neut. Theol., p. 259: "It was an essential advantage that the Jews possessed the law fixed in writing; it stood before them by this means in unassailable objectivity."

tament, without any distinction between the ethical and ritual
portions; then, further, the whole of the Old Testament as a
divine revelation, without regard to the particular contents
referred to in each single case; for even passages from the
Psalms or Prophets are quoted as declarations of the law
(Rom iii. 19; 1 Cor. xiv. 21); and especially the whole of the
historical part of the Old Testament is included under the νόμος
(Gal. iv. 21; Rom. iii. 21, 31, which passages can only be explained as introducing the proofs from the Old Testament
history which follow).[1] We must absolutely reject the distinction between the ethical and the ritual part of the law, in the
sense that Paul did not consider the latter as belonging to the
revealed law of Moses, but only perhaps to the πατρικαὶ παραδόσεις.[2]
The free position which Paul everywhere assumes with regard
to the ritual law also from the standpoint of the gospel freedom
from the law, is far from being a proof that he ignored the former
as a divine and Mosaic revelation; on the contrary, the pro-
fusion of theological dialectic with which he tries to convince
the Judaizing Galatians of the invalidity of precisely this ceremonial law as well as of the other (circumcision, laws regarding
food, ii. 12, the keeping of days, iv. 10), is the clearest proof
how completely he held the ritual to stand or fall with the
general body of the law. If it had been in his eyes something
which did not at all belong to the law proper, he could have
made his treatment of the matter far easier to himself; for he
could in that case have simply drawn the line of demarcation
between the real and the imaginary law, instead of between the
law and the promise. Moreover, he mentions (Rom. ix. 4) among

---

[1] The interpretation, often favoured elsewhere, which connects the above passages
with the ethical law of the Christian spirit (Rom. viii.), would interrupt the simple
course of the argument in Rom. iii. 21 by an unmeaning digression.

[2] Cf., for example, *Holsten*, ut supra, p. 401; and, on the other hand, for the true
view of the unity of the νόμος, cf. *Usteri*, Paul. Lehrbegriff, p. 34 f.; *Neander*,
"Geschichte der Pflanzung der Christlichen Kirche, durch die Apostel," pp. 507, 569;
Lipsius, "Paulin. Rechtfertigungslehre," p. 54; *Ritschl*, Altkathol. Kirche, p. 73;
Weiss, Neutest. Theol., p. 259 f.

the advantages granted by God to the Jews, between the revealed
νομοθεσία and the likewise revealed ἐπαγγελίαι, the λατρεία, the
service of God, consequently the ceremonial law, which was
something revealed to the Jew by God, and accordingly belonged
to the positive divine law as much as any other part of it.

If it be asked how the Apostle could in that case have said of
the law in general and without qualification, that it was πνευματικός, when the external ritual law also belonged to it, the
answer is, that the law was to the Apostle, simply in consequence of its immediately divine *origin*, something transcending
the realm of earth, and therefore belonging to that of spirit;
consequently that it had also a spiritual character through this
origin, quite independently of its particular content; because it
is in its entire positive shape a revelation of the spiritual will
of God, therefore it is also with regard to its entire contents
something spiritual—that is to say, in the sense that in every part
of the law there must be spiritual *contents* and an essentially
deeper meaning. This allegorical mode of thought, which was
common in Paul's time, did not make it impossible for the immediate *form* to be unspiritual, purely external. So far as this
alone were reflected on, the essence of the law might even be
represented as a service of the worldly (external and sensuous)
elements, and placed on the same level as the heathen worship.[1]
Although, then, the Mosaic law is spiritual as regards its origin
and essential contents, yet it establishes, so far as its outward
form is concerned, a "weak and beggarly" sensuous worship for

---

[1] Gal. iv. 3—9, στοιχεῖα τοῦ κόσμου, can grammatically mean nothing but the
primary materials of the world, the elements cognizable by the senses, since the genitive joined to στοιχεῖα must denote the whole which is composed of the στοιχεῖα.
By these sensuous elements we must understand partly the earthly materials used in
worship, such as sacrifices and offerings of food, partly sidereal powers (the signs of
the zodiac, which used to be shortly designated as στοιχεῖα), which determined the
seasons, and consequently the feast days (ver. 10) ; both these meanings are applicable
to στοιχεῖα also in Col. ii. 20. Compare ver. 16 (possibly also in ver. 8). This,
the oldest, interpretation has been again of late rightly maintained, in preference to
"the rudimentary condition of non-Christian humanity," by *Neander* and *Hilgenfeld*,
with whom *Baur*, *Lipsius*, *Holsten*, and *R. Schmidt* agree.

beginners (νήπιοι), who could not yet bear anything higher—that is to say, the spiritual service in its pure and adequate form of presentation. Thus it is not between one part of the law and the other, the ethical and the ritual, that the Apostle distinguishes, but, if he distinguishes at all, it is *only* between the spiritual content of the whole undivided law and its literal form (γράμμα, 2 Cor. iii.). And though the latter, *taken by itself,* was to him something worldly or fleshly (στοιχεῖα τοῦ κόσμου, Gal. iv. 3, or σάρξ, iii. 3 and vi. 12), yet this distinction, after all, is ordinarily kept in the background, because, according to the habit of allegorizing sanctioned by tradition, the form, that which was literal and external, appeared as the vehicle of the deeper spiritual content, with no independent value of its own. Thus, for example, in 1 Cor. ix. 9, the command, "Thou shalt not muzzle the ox that treadeth out the corn," is, without hesitation, not merely applied as an illustration, but interpreted actually to mean that the gospel workmen were worthy of their hire ; and in Gal. iv. 24, the account of Sarah and Hagar is interpreted as relating to the law and the gospel.

Now we might certainly suppose that, by logically carrying out this typical allegorical interpretation, Paul could have established the abrogation of the ceremonial law, on which the contest with the Judaizers primarily turned, more simply and more mildly than by his harsh and artificial method of exhibiting the law (still regarded as divinely revealed) in a purely negative relation to the scheme of salvation. And in fact we find that Paul's system, as it appears tinged by Alexandrian thought in the Epistles to the Hebrews and the Epistle of Barnabas, has followed that course, and that with the marked approval of the ancient Church, to which this mode of conceiving the relation between the law and the gospel was much more familiar than Paul's own mode. But it is easy to understand how Paul himself did not yet take this course, and could not well have taken it. For we must bear in mind that the Jewish school, to which the allegorical interpretation in Paul's time was

familiar, were far from abrogating the validity of the literal sense
of their historical Scriptures, or those which related to the law,
by ascribing to them a spiritual meaning; on the contrary, the
spiritual deepening of the sense would have had the effect of
contributing to the predominance of the law, and therefore to
the confirmation of its validity as a whole, including its literal
sense; this spiritual content and the literal form of his revealed
scripture were far too intimately united in the mind of a Jew for
him to think of a separation of the two, and the abrogation of
the latter, as even possible. How, then, could Paul have hoped
to attain his object by this method? How could he prove to
the Judaizers the abrogation of the ceremonial law by spiritual
allegorizing, when they thought to glorify and confirm the whole
law—including its ceremonial portion—by this very means? But
Paul's own habits of thought made it impossible for him to think
of doing so, for he himself had by no means arrived by the road
of such allegorizing speculation at the consciousness of the non-
validity of the law for believers in Christ, but by the very different way of the knowledge of the cross of Christ. In this he
saw the radical breach between the old covenant of works of the
law and the new one of righteousness by faith accomplished in
fact; and to labour for the practical recognition of this breach
was the work of his life; *the relation between law and faith* must
therefore of necessity have presented itself to him in theory also
as *a purely exclusive and negative relation;* and hence a problem
of no slight difficulty had to be faced, namely, to reconcile this
their negative relation with the origin of both in the revelation
of the one God. Most of the Apostle's dialectical dissertations
on the law are attempts to solve this problem.

Until, then, the abrogation of the Mosaic law for the Christian
community had been declared as a principle, and partly also in
fact established, by the active energy of Paul, no one could think
of finding a *positive typical* relation also between the law and
the gospel, by systematically carrying out that allegorizing of
the law and the history of the Old Testament which was then

in vogue and had already been used incidentally by Paul himself, and thus making the breach less abrupt, and less oppressive
to the consciousness of the Jews who believed in the revelation
of the law.

We have hitherto seen the Apostle Paul in complete harmony
with the Jewish consciousness as to the apprehension of the
essence (notion and origin) of the law. So much the more difficult must have been his position when he now, proceeding from
this common ground, set forth the *purpose* of the law in diame-
trical opposition to the conviction of the Jews and Jewish Christians. And this conviction rested on the very ground of that
common presupposition with more apparent logical correctness
than that of Paul, who was compelled to employ artificial dialectic in order to prove the logical correctness of his thesis, which
really rested on the knowledge of the cross of Christ. For whereas
the Jews and Jewish Christians believed that the law, as given
by God, being holy, just, and good in its nature, had also as its
object to make man just, good, and pleasing to God, Paul set
against this, first, the *antithesis*, " By works of the law is no flesh
righteous before God;" and, secondly, the *thesis*, " The law came
in (between promise and fulfilment, or between sin and redemption) on account of sin;" that is to say, first, that sin might be
known; secondly, that it might be increased and filled up.

As to the ground on which the first proposition rests, we
must distinguish between the reason or the ground of our knowledge and the real ground or cause of the fact itself. The former
is taken from the Christian consciousness of the significance of
Christ's death on the cross in the Divine scheme of revelation,
and is therefore only convincing to the consciousness of one who
already believes in Christ; the real ground, on the other hand, is
the fleshliness of human nature, which stands a priori in contradiction to the spiritual contents of the law.

Although the latter is the more objective, yet, just in the chief
passages in which he deals with the proof of the abrogation of
the law, Paul has made no use of it, but has drawn his proofs in

a very artificial manner from the Scripture; a very noteworthy
fact, which indicates to us that the Apostle did not arrive by the
method of psychological speculation at his original view of the
purpose of the Mosaic law, and also that his no less original doctrine of the σάρξ is derived not from the presuppositions but
from the consequences of his doctrine of salvation; for on this
supposition alone can we explain the fact that the decisive proofs
of the doctrine of salvation are set forth independently of the
σάρξ doctrine. The Apostle's doctrine of salvation was *immediately* dependent, in its negative as well as its positive aspect, on
the significance of the cross of Christ. This is shown by the
fact that the Apostle thus clearly expresses the decisive *ground
of his own conviction.* "*If righteousness came by the law, then
did Christ die in vain;*" and to the same purport, "If a law
had been given that could make alive, then would righteousness
indeed come by the law," and not from the faith in the crucified;
the death on the cross would have been aimless and fruitless.
According to these passages (Gal. ii. 21, iii. 21), the process of
the Apostle's thought is simply the following: it is impossible
that the death of Jesus as the Messiah upon the cross can be
regarded as an event allowed by God to happen by chance,
without reason or purpose; but its purpose can have been no
other than to produce true righteousness: now if the death of
Christ (i.e. faith in it) be the means of effecting this purpose,
then the significance hitherto attributed to the law, of serving
as the means of righteousness, is by that very fact denied; for
of these two means, the death of Christ and the law of Moses,
which have as little to do with one another as believing and
doing (iii. 10—12), it is only possible that *either* one *or* the other
can be the right means to the end: now if this means be, as
it indubitably is to the Christian, the death of Christ, then it
cannot also be the law, the saving efficacy of which, as a means
to righteousness, is absolutely excluded by that of the death of
Christ. The way in which the Apostle thought out dogmatically
in detail this connection between reason and consequent, does

not belong to this part of our inquiry, but to the doctrine of redemption and justification : here we have only to establish the fact, that the logical ground for his peculiar view as to the purpose of the law, is to be sought in the root of his Christian consciousness, in his faith in the crucified.

But now the *real ground* of the impossibility of righteousness by the law, lies not in the law as such ; this, on the contrary, is holy, just, and good ; nay, it is, although completely void of the strength of the πνεῦμα ζωοποιοῦν, still πνευματικός (at least as regards its essential content, though here the fact is certainly left out of sight that it belongs also to the realm of the worldly and fleshly with respect to its form as γράμμα). The ground of the fact that the law, although πνευματικός, does not attain to ζωοποιῆσαι, lies in the nature of man, in his being sold under sin, in his being fleshly. Because the natural man as σάρκινος (see above) is under the dominion of the material principle, the σάρξ, the spiritual will of God and his revelation finds in the law only a formal point of connection with the νοῦς of man and his ideal power of willing ; but in actual life the claims of the spiritual principle which is external to him are overborne by the real energy of the principle of the flesh which dominates him from within : this does not subject itself to the law, and indeed *cannot* do so, because it is contrary to its nature, whose characteristic it is, ἐπιθυμεῖν κατὰ πνευματός, and also κατὰ νόμου (Rom. viii. 7 and Gal. v. 17). But if we ask further, why the law has not the power to conquer the flesh, and to bring its own spiritual content to the actuality of action in spite of it, Paul's answer would be, Because the material substance of the flesh can be conquered only by the opposite and equally real substance of the spirit when it enters man as a real life-giving power ; the law cannot ζωοποιῆσαι (Gal. iii. 21), because it is not itself a πνεῦμα ζωοποιοῦν, a substantial power of life and real animating principle, not an outpouring of the divine essence, which (like the πνεῦμα) would produce even in man a divine and spiritual vitality, but a mere expression of the divine will, which, as against the real substance of that flesh which is opposed to God, is something unreal and without strength.

Now, for us, with our modes of thought, the outcome of this certainly is, that the law, precisely on account of its *externality*, cannot produce true righteousness, the inward goodness of the will itself, because, as an abstract command, as a mere imperative, it always stands *over against* the concrete will, and accordingly cannot animate it *inwardly*, cannot turn it to inward unity with the good, but at most can move it to outward subjection in external acts (ἔργα τοῦ νόμου), which leave its self-willed desires (the ἐπιθυμεῖν κατὰ τοῦ πνεύματος) unbroken. It comes to the same thing, then, whether we say that the impossibility of righteousness by the law lies in the flesh, or that it lies in the externality[1] of the law, inasmuch as both express the opposition between the subjective will and the objective command, between the natural self-will and the divine determination of man,—an opposition which cannot be overcome by starting from one of the two opposing parts, because their existence is involved in this very opposition, but only from an entirely new standpoint and from an entirely new principle. But however certain it is that we have here the characteristic *idea* and the great and enduring truth of Paul's doctrine of the impossibility of righteousness by law, yet we cannot but acknowledge that the immediate *form* in which this doctrine is presented by him is determined by the peculiar realistic Jewish view of flesh and spirit. The psychological deduction, therefore, given above, though quite consistent with his idea, does not correspond with

---

[1] Only we must be careful not to understand by this *externality* merely the positive form of the Mosaic law, but rather that characteristic which belongs to the law *as such*, and therefore also to the law of conscience, namely, that of standing as an objective power over against, i.e. in opposition to the will, so far and so long as it is purely subjective. This characteristic, which lies in the nature of this ethical relation, although it is strikingly exemplified in the positive law of Moses, is yet by no means exclusively peculiar to it. Consequently what Paul says of that law has its *enduring significance wherever the standpoint is that of law*, recurring constantly, as this standpoint does, in the spiritual development of humanity, so that it may even at times become the predominant type of the whole of Christianity.

the way in which he sets it immediately before us. He nowhere[1] <
refers the impotence of the law to its externality, but always
simply to the resistance of the σάρξ. Even in 2 Cor. iii., the
law is called a "letter that killeth," not with reference to the
psychological relation between command and will, but simply
because it announces to the sinner in a fixed judicial form
(γράμμα) the judgment of death (κατάκρισις) as a penal statute
of positive validity. And with regard to the ἔργα νόμου, his <
meaning is not that they are insufficient for righteousness before
God, because the external law demands merely external ἔργα, so
that the *law* might be satisfied by those ἔργα (external "legality"
prompted by a sensuous motive), but not *God*, who sees the
heart, and who is satisfied only by true "morality." That is a
modern turn of thought[2] which is quite alien to the direct sense
of Paul's doctrine. (But the ἔργα νόμου cannot make righteous,
first, because in that case righteousness by faith according to the
promise would be done away—this is the *logical* and for Paul
the decisive ground—and, secondly, because man as flesh can by
no means be truly subject to the law of God, since the φρονεῖν of
the flesh is by nature ἔχθρα εἰς θεόν, so that consequently the
actual fulfilment of the νόμος τοῦ θεοῦ, or actually perfect ἔργα τοῦ
νόμου, are absolutely impossible.) But it is evident how completely this *real ground* is a merely secondary and derivative
inferential one in the eyes of Paul, from his speaking, when
righteousness by faith has recurred to his mind, quite frankly of
ποιηταὶ τοῦ νόμου, of ἔργα and ἐργάζεσθαι τὸ ἀγαθόν, for which every
man will receive from the Judge the due recompence (Rom. ii.

---

[1] This is in opposition to the view of *Neander*, ut supra, p. 508 f., and p. 573 f.,
to that of *Usteri*, p. 55 f., *Lipsius*, p. 65 f., who introduce the modern psychological
mode of thought too directly into that of Paul.

[2] According to this mode of thought, the whole weight of the unsatisfactory nature
of the ἔργα τοῦ νόμου would fall upon the Mosaic law, as if this were satisfied with
mere external ἔργα. But (this presupposition, incorrect in itself, was very alien to the
mind of the Apostle, who saw in the law a holy and good revelation of the spiritual
will of God.) And so Baur's criticism also of the conception of the ἔργα τοῦ νόμου
does not apply to the actual doctrine of Paul, but only to the rationalizing interpretations of it (*Baur*, N. Test. Theol., p. 179).

6—13). To interpret these expressions, ἔργα, ποιητὴς νόμου, simply of faith, as the only work which is of value in the eyes of God, is a makeshift which may be very convenient to relieve the embarrassment of Protestant commentators, but is utterly unsatisfactory; for ἐργάζεσθαι and πιστεύειν, μισθὸς and χάρις, are, in iv. 4 f., placed in opposition so as mutually to exclude one another. Nor is the attempt to consider those ἔργα as the fruit of faith in any way justified by the context. If we look at the matter impartially, from a historical standpoint, this antinomy (for we have one here and frequently elsewhere in the writings of Paul) can only be explained by supposing that in Rom. ii. Paul adopts the standpoint of *ordinary morality*, and especially of the Jewish law, from which standpoint the impossibility of works of the law and a reward for them did not strike him.[1] If he had arrived by means of psychology at his specific doctrine of the law, it would scarcely have been possible for him to take the view expressed in Rom. ii.; but we can well understand that it everywhere occurred to him again where the logical premises of his altered doctrine of law (the doctrine of grace) were absent from his thoughts, if we suppose the real logical, i.e. psychological, ground of his new doctrine of law to be contained in his Christian doctrine of redemption. Thus our view of the inner genesis of the system of Paul is again corroborated on this point.

But now, if the law is so weakened by the resistance of the flesh (Rom. viii. 3) that it can never produce actual righteousness in man, has it not then been given by God utterly without a

---

[1] Compare *Baur*, N. Test. Theol., p. 181: "Paul speaks in Rom. ii. 6 f. of works as the rule of divine justice, without any embarrassment, as if the possibility of a collision with his doctrine of faith had never occurred to him. It does not occur to him because his doctrine of justification refers throughout only to the relation of Christianity to Judaism, an opposition which, when thought of in the abstract, has to do with general principles, but, as soon as it is applied to the concrete relations of actual life, becomes of itself a mere relative opposition."—What is true in this is, that the doctrine of the insufficiency of ἔργα is founded upon their antithesis to justification by faith, and that this abstract opposition of ἔργα and πίστις allows of and even requires a higher synthesis, which indeed it has found in the writings of Paul himself, in his doctrine of living in the spirit.

purpose? No; it undoubtedly has a purpose, only this is primarily the exact opposite of that which is generally supposed. It has been given, not for the sake of righteousness, but, on the contrary, *for the sake of sin*, τῶν παραβάσεων χάριν, Gal. iii. 19.[1] And this in a double sense; for sin, which as yet is in man unconsciously, *must be brought into consciousness* as what it is; but also at the same time the latent power of sin must be incited *to manifest and develope itself completely by fuller utterance in deeds.*

Sin, indeed, was already present in the world before the law ∠ was given by Moses, and is also present in the individual man before he becomes aware of the command (Rom. v. 13, vii. 7); that is to say, in an objective manner, in the ungodly and anti-spiritual tendency of the fleshly principle which dominates him. But in this merely objective existence of sin, the subjective consciousness that this sinful condition or action ought not to be, is still wanting; the imputing of sin as personal guilt is therefore still wanting, and consequently the feeling of guilt, in which the ego for the first time feels the sting of its contradiction with itself and with·God. And so far this *condition of relative innocence*, when evil is only present objectively, and does not come to the subjective consciousness, and so is not willed as the true act of the ego, nor burdened with the painful feeling of guilt, may be designated in a certain sense as a state of "being alive,"

---

[1] To give to these words the interpretation, "to guard against transgressions," is a gross misapprehension. In the first place, the language itself does not allow of it, for χάριν always implies furtherance, and not hindrance. Then, again, it contradicts the whole of the context, which is intended to prove neither more nor less than this very point of the inability of the law to procure righteousness or to guard against sin. Moreover, it contradicts the plain words of the Apostle in Rom. v. 20 and vii. 13, which remove all doubt that he looked upon the increasing of sin and the multiplying of transgressions, instead of the opposite of this, as the primary object of the law. Besides, it is part of Paul's notion of παράβασις that, as a positive transgression of a command, it presupposes the existence of the law; therefore the law could not have been given in the first instance in consequence of the παραβάσεις, for the purpose of restraining them.—Comp. *Usteri*, p. 64 (who, moreover, like *Baur*, places the purpose too one-sidedly in the consciousness of sin). The right view is given by *Weiss*, ut supra, p. 263; *Lipsius*, ut supra, p. 75; *Ritschl*, ut supra, p. 73; *Hausrath*, Neutest. Ztgesch., II. 473: also the commentaries of *Meyer* and *Hilgenfeld: De Wette* and *Rückert* take a different view.

of unchecked feeling of life, because a state of undisturbed inner
harmony (Rom. vii. 9). Though death, the necessity that the
body should die (v. 14), was already dominant during this
period, yet it also still lacked its painful sting (1 Cor. xv. 56),
so long as the feeling of guilt was absent; for it was felt only
as the natural lot of man, and not as a penalty inflicted in
consequence of sin, and so could not disturb the harmonious
feeling of life in the state of relative innocence which preceded
the law.   But this state can only last in man and in each
individual so long as sin "*is dead*" in him (that is to say, for
his consciousness, consciousness of sin being not yet awakened);
it immediately ceases, therefore, when the law, with its command, μὴ ἐπιθυμήσεις, confronts the man innocently dominated
by the ἐπιθυμία τῆς σαρκός. The immediate result is, that sin,
which was before dead, "*revives;*" that is, in the first place, it
comes to consciousness as that which it is, as contradiction to
the (expressed) will of God, or as *transgression* of the (positive)
command; thereby also it ceases to be unimputable; it is now
imputed as the true conscious guiltiness of the ego.   (Hence
"without the law no παράβασις, no ἐλλογεῖσθαι;" both come only
in consequence of the μὴ ἐπιθυμήσεις; cf. iv. 15, v. 13, vii. 7—9).
The previous state of inward harmony and of undisturbed feeling
of life is at once disturbed by this awakening of the feeling of
guilt, and in its place comes the feeling of discord in one's self
and with God, which is felt as the damning wrath of God, and
destroys the joyous feeling of life (hence, ἐγὼ ἀπέθανον, vii. 10.
The law, κατεργάζεται ὀργὴν—θάνατον, iv. 15, vii. 13).

Now inasmuch as the death of the body acquires its pain and
sting as the punishment of sin, by the entering in of this figurative death, or of the misery of the feeling of guilt wrought by
the law, it may be said of the law, as in Rom. v. 13, without
contradiction, that it gives to sin the power by which it becomes
the sting of death, or briefly, that the letter of the law "*killeth*"
(1 Cor. xv. 56; 2 Cor. iii. 6). The revival of sin by occasion of
the commandment, however, does not consist in this process of

consciousness alone; the actual *increase* of its manifestation is inseparably connected with it. For indwelling sin, the sinful inclination of the flesh, takes occasion from the commandment falsely to represent that which is forbidden as a good worth striving for, and by this "guile" to excite what was before innocent desire, so that now all kinds of concupiscence begin to be awakened, and these incited still further by the goad of the command become wilful lusts, and for the first time acquire the energy (vii. 5, 8) to master and enslave the will, so that the law only calls forth more abundantly the transgressions which it ought to prevent. Thus the law is the incitement which provokes the sin latent in man to put forth its whole energy, the result of which is, that sin appears as sin; nay, more, as "exceeding sinful," and hence, at the same time, its consequences, its having death as its fruit, become more and more sensible (vers. 5, 13).

Now according to the Apostle all this is not only the effect which the law produces in our experience, but the divine *purpose* of it. What was distinctively new, so thoroughly paradoxical and so deeply wounding to the Jewish consciousness, was precisely this doctrine that the law, this revelation of the holy will of God, should have, not merely as its contingent effect, but as its direct purpose, the increase of sin and the working of wrath, instead of the prevention of sin and the working of righteousness. But to the Apostle this was emphatically a cardinal point. By exhibiting the law as a means of sin, the bond that connected it in the consciousness of the Jew, and even of the Jewish Christian, with the end of salvation as a means or condition, was completely sundered; the law was utterly severed from its positive causal connection with salvation (whether as sole or as auxiliary cause), and thus ceased to have any positive significance and validity for the time of the accomplishment of salvation.

But how could the law have only a temporary validity, and yet be a revelation of the *eternal* will of God? And how could

it be a revelation of the *holy* will of God, if it had as its
purpose the increase of sin ?   The Apostle solved these obvious
questions by proving that what he stated to be the proximate
purpose of the law, was again a negative preparatory (not positive causal) *means* to the final end of salvation willed by God,
to redemption by Christ.   Excluded from its positive causal
connection with the scheme of salvation, the law might yet be
incorporated as a negative moment in the process of salvation,
and so remain, if not in immediate yet in indirect relation to
the Divine purpose of salvation, which was identical and consistent with itself through all the various stages of the process.
This, then, is the position which the Apostle assigns to the law
with reference to the scheme of salvation—*it comes in between sin
and redemption, as an intermediate purpose directed to the latter*
(Rom. v. 20).   But in support of this theory, the result of dogmatic reflection on the relation of the law and the gospel (to a
certain extent speculatively constructed out of the Christian
consciousness), he required also a supplementary *exegetical proof*.
This he found in the relation in time between the first revelation to Abraham of the will of God regarding salvation, and the
revelation of the law through Moses.

To Abraham, as is set forth in Rom. iv., Gal. iii., was given the
promise of the inheritance, the foundation of the scheme of salvation, as a *promise of favour* (*grace*), that is to say, in the sense
that it was to be a free gift of the favour of God.   Only afterwards was the law added to the promise of favour which had
already been made 430 years before.   Now if the object of this
law had been, that the obtaining of the inheritance should be
conditioned by the doing of the law, then the inheritance would
have been the wages of service, and no longer a gift of favour,
for the wages of serviceable deeds is a debt and not a gift of
favour.   In this case, then, a previous utterance of the will of
God sanctioned by an oath—the promise of the inheritance as
a gift of favour—would be so essentially changed in its original meaning by the "supplementary ordinance" (ἐπιδιατάσσεται,

Gal. iii. 15) of a condition on the fulfilment of which depended the attainment of that which was promised, that it would be as good as abrogated (ἀθετεῖ, ibid.). Now if such a supplementary alteration or abrogation of an expression of the will, sanctioned by an oath, is not permissible even among men, how much less is it conceivable that the oath of God to Abraham which was solemnly confirmed with reference to Christ, should be again abrogated by the later coming in of the law, i.e. altered in its essential original meaning as a promise of a gift of favour! Accordingly, the only view that remains open to us is, that the law which came in after the promise must have had a purpose of such a nature as to prepare and establish the fulfilment of the promise in its original sense. But the obtaining of the inheritance as *a gift of favour* would be established by proving that every other way of obtaining it was impossible. This is exactly what was done by the law; it had by no means to release men from the bondage of sin, from their imprisonment in the dungeon of sin, and to lead them to righteousness, but, on the contrary, to keep guard over them in this imprisonment, so that they should not in any way seek to deliver themselves; it was to keep them for ever mindful of their bondage in the slavery of sin, so that they might seek to attain salvation by no other way than by the way of faith which was ordained by God, and which alone corresponded to the sense of the promise. Thus the law is the jailer who keeps guard over men shut up in the prison of sin, in order that they may accept the fulfilment of the promise of *favour* as such, in faith, and not strive to obtain it by works; in another figure, the law is the schoolmaster who keeps the boy under restraint, until the time when he will be capable of attaining, by the road of faith which is ordained by God, the right of sonship which belongs to him.

This is the meaning of the passage, Gal. iii. 22—24. There is no question here of the restraining or bridling of the sinful lusts, any more than in ver. 19. The expression, συνέκλεισεν ἡ γραφὴ τὰ πάντα ὑπὸ ἁμαρτίαν, can, according to the context, and according to the very similar parallel passage, Rom. xi. 32, have no other meaning than that God has (according to the testimony of Scripture) given all men as prisoners under the dominion of sin; and in this imprisonment they are guarded by the law, inasmuch as it never allows them to escape from the conscious-ness of their impotence by which they are fettered.[1] But the same thought is also expressed in the other figure of the παιδαγωγός: in this character the law, by the constraint of discipline, presents the consciousness of the right of sonship from arising until the goal is reached, at which the promise of the υἱοθ εσία has attained fulfilment; with this the submission to restraint and the yoke of service imposed by the schoolmaster came to an end, and was superseded by the right of sonship (vers. 25, 26). Accordingly this conception of the law as a schoolmaster does not, any more than the other figure, directly point to the awakening of the desire of salvation as a positive preparation for the redemption; the obvious thought is only that of a *bondage* which forbids the striving after salvation in one's own might, by any other than the pre-ordained way of faith, in order that the fulfilment of the promise should be imparted *to all* simply as the result of faith (ἐκ πίστεως, ver. 22), and that so a part (the Jews) should not seek to obtain the promise by the private road of ἐργάζεσθαι κατ' ὀφείλημα, instead of κατὰ χάριν.

The law, according to this explanation, is only the negative means, which is to cut off at once and render impossible any other way than that of faith. But as to the means by which faith itself comes into existence, the passage in question con-tains no direct intimation. It is true that the negation with which we have been dealing contains also indirectly the affir-mation that the law, in bringing to consciousness the impossi-bility of a subjective self-won righteousness, calls forth the

---

[1] The right explanation, in the main, is given by *Meyer* and *Hilgenfeld*, Comm.; *Lipsius*, p. 79 f.; *Weiss*, p. 264; *Usteri* (not without some vacillation), p. 65 f. *Holsten* truly remarks that it is not quite correct to say that the awakening of the need of redemption by the law is to be found directly in the passage under review, p. 316.; and *Hausrath*, ut supra, p. 474, follows him.

desire for the means of salvation ordained by God himself.
In this sense, the complement of our text on its psychological
side is found in that passage, Rom. vii., where the struggle
between the law and the flesh forces from the writer the cry,
"O wretched man that I am, who will deliver me from this
body of death?" Here again, then, in the case of the law,
as before in the case of sin, we have the same two modes
of viewing the matter,—the objective theological and the subjective anthropological,—at times running parallel to each other,
and at times indistinguishably intertwined. According to the
former, the several moments of the development of man, or the
history of religion,—sin (Adam), promise (Abraham), law (Moses),
redemption (Christ),—are fused together only in the objective
unity of the Divine counsel, the fulness of whose wisdom is
unfolded precisely in the manifoldness and relative opposition
of the ways to the one goal (Rom. xi. 33 in connection with
32). But according to the latter, these moments proceed as
phases of an immanent process of the spirit of man and of
humanity, the one preparing for the other, the one bringing
itself about by means of the other.[1] The former determines the
course of the discussion in Rom. xi. and Rom. v. 12—21, and
especially in Gal. iii.; the second is found in Rom. vii., and
with a somewhat different turn in Gal. iv., inasmuch as the
figure of the schoolmastership of the law in this passage leads
to the thought of a childish stage in the development of
humanity, which precedes the freedom of sonship as a natural
preparatory step, in which the bondage of the law appears, not
as a positive institution of the Divine counsel with a view to the
revelation of favour, but as the natural consequence of the imma-
turity of man in his first stage of development. Yet here, again,
the end of the period of tutelage is conditioned, not by the occur-
rence of natural maturity, but by Divine predetermination (προ-
θεσμία, ver. 2); and, conversely, in Rom. xi. the succession of the

---

[1] Compare on this the similar observations of *Holsten*, ut supra, p. 317, note, and
p. 419.

moments of the history of religion, determined by the Divine counsel, is again brought about psychologically by means of the belief and unbelief of the Jews or Gentiles. Thus the objective and subjective modes of viewing the scheme of revelation, i.e. the religious development of humanity, easily run into one another, as is natural, since they are in fact only two sides of the same process, which is at once divine and human.

Finally, we may ask whether and to what extent Paul has attained his object, of reconciling his peculiar doctrine of the law with the belief in its immediately divine origin, and making it acceptable to the believers in revelation, to the Jews and Jewish Christians, who took their stand on the ground of the theocratic history of the Bible. And here, while we cannot but admire the keen intellect of the Apostle, who sought to render possible what was impossible, to incorporate the ideal truth of the new and deep views of the world and of history with the letter of the historical religion of Israel, we must at the same time in fairness allow that the Jews and Jewish Christians were really in the right, from the positive standpoint of the letter and of history. However deep and true, from the standpoint of Christian speculation, that relation is which the Apostle established between the law and the salvation willed by God, and however masterly each step of the reasoning by which he seeks to prove this relation, in Rom. iv. and Gal. iii., by the position of the law relatively to the promise, yet it is not to be denied that all this was altogether alien from the *historical* intention of the giving of the law, and is wholly without ground in the *letter* of the law. It is simply self-evident to the mind of any one who takes his stand on the historical ground of the Old Testament, that the law was not given with the object of increasing sin by its non-fulfilment, but in order to be fulfilled, and by this means to lead to righteousness. It could never occur to one in that position that this purpose of the law stood in any way in contradiction to the promise made to Abraham, as Paul argued; it would, on the contrary, appear self-evident that God, in the covenant which he made with Abraham, only gave the promise of blessing for the seed of Abraham on the understanding (no matter whether expressed or not) that the seed of Abraham should devote itself on its part to obedience to the Divine will, and therefore to the fulfilment of the law which was to follow: with this, therefore, as the conditio sine qua non, the fulfilment of the promise to Abraham would appear to him to be inseparably connected; how else could it be a covenant, if performance on the one part did not correspond to performance on the other? And although the law, which was the obligation of Israel to do its part corresponding to the promise, certainly followed 430 years after the promise, yet the covenant obligation on the part of Abraham was at once entered upon by the acceptance of circumcision, from the first, as the seal of the covenant; and accordingly the promise was from the beginning attached to a performance on the part of man as its indispensable conditio sine qua non; and thus the law by no means came in between promise and fulfilment as something foreign to them both, but is the necessary complement of the promise; and the doing of the law is not the mere temporary, but the permanent and still valid condition of the fulfilment of the promise. Against such obvious objections of his Judaistic opposers, Paul might assert ∠ that the promise of God to Abraham was established beforehand with reference to Christ (προκεκυρωμένην εἰς Χριστόν, Gal. iii. 17, comp. 16), inasmuch as the exact words of the oath, τῷ σπέρματι (and in an oath the exact words must be taken), could only apply to one man, Christ. But, in the first place, this kind of proof, if not inadmissible, could certainly not be convincing even for that age; and, secondly, even on the assumption that this proof was valid, the conclusion which Paul drew from it was more than his opponents would allow. For they could always say, even supposing that in the promise to Abraham reference was made to its fulfilment in Jesus Christ, this would not exclude their conceiving the fulfilment of the promise in Jesus Christ as attached from the beginning to the fulfilment of the covenant-obligation

of obedience to the law, as the corresponding performance on
the part of the children of Abraham. The argument urged by
Paul against this was, that in that case the fulfilment of the
promise would no longer be κατὰ χάριν, but κατ᾽ ὀφείλημα, as
μισθὸς for the ἐργάζεσθαι of man (Rom. iv. 2—4, 13—16, xi. 6;
Gal. iii. 18). But on what ground was he really justified in
making this exclusive disjunction of these two ideas? What if
the Jewish Christians had a conception of Christian salvation
to which that dilemma was in no way applicable; which, on the
contrary, included within itself ἐργάζεσθαι and μισθὸς on the one
hand, and πιστεύειν and χάρις on the other, as two mutually com-
plementary moments, in which conception, therefore, righteousness and life were *both* gifts of Christ, *and also* consequences of
man's own act? To this Paul had only one answer, but that
the weighty one, ἄρα Χριστὸς δωρεὰν ἀπέθανεν!

> It is quite clear that the Jewish Christians were right from
the historical exegetical point of view, but that Paul was right
dogmatically; the former had on their side the literal interpretation, judging by which the world would pronounce them to be
in the right; the latter had only the divine right of the higher
idea, which must always submit to be regarded by the men of
the letter as a falsification of the word of God and an invention
of individual caprice (2 Cor. iv. 2, 5); and that for the simple
reason, that the truth of the higher idea must ever remain unintelligible, in spite of the best intentions, to those who cannot
free themselves from the bondage of the letter; how much more
so to those whose clearness of vision is darkened by malignant
prejudice and suspicion, and the self-conceit of infallible authority! (ibid. vers. 3, 4). But the position of Paul was all the
more difficult, because he also fully shared the assumption of
his opponents,—the irrefragable authority of the letter as the
immediately revealed word of God. Consequently he could not
have recourse to the modern historical point of view, of an
advance from a lower to a higher stage of the development of
the spirit of man, according to which the earlier stage, for all its

relative truth, evidently loses its authority in presence of the
higher stage. It is true that he does in many passages show a
tendency towards this point of view, especially in Gal. iv.; only
the strictly supernatural groundwork of his thought does not
allow this to become a ruling principle; even though he at
times considers the law as πτωχὰ καὶ ἀσθενῆ στοιχεῖα τοῦ κόσμου,
yet it still remains in his eyes the immediate literal expression
of the holy and eternal will of God. In this difficulty Paul had
recourse to that method which has at all times assisted thinkers
who have been fettered by supernatural presuppositions to fill
up the gulf between the old and the new; he has thrust back
the new into the place of the old—nay, behind it as the oldest of
all. The evangelical principle of faith was the ruling principle
in the foundation of the scheme of salvation long before the
giving of the law by Moses, namely, in the promise to Abraham,
and a means of salvation was even then contemplated, such as
was manifested in Christ, as a revelation of righteousness through
God by faith without the works of the law. As this could not
of course be demonstrated by the letter of the Old Testament,
he was obliged to have recourse to the traditional *allegorizing*,
the "spiritual interpretation of Scripture," by means of which a
mind which formally believes in the letter, but has substantially advanced beyond it, has been able, from the time of Philo
to our own age, to conceal from itself the inward contradiction,
and by a gentle violence to force the opposing letter to bend to
the power of the higher idea.

For our modes of thought of course an exegetical method of
this kind has no authority, and its arguments carry no conviction.
That the singular τῷ σπέρματι must refer to Christ (Gal. iii. 16);
that the driving out of Hagar with her son Ishmael, in favour of
Sarah and Isaac, means the abrogation of the covenant of the
law in favour of the gospel freedom of sonship (Gal. iv. 21—31);
that the dissolution of the marriage bond by the death of the
husband represents the dissolution of the covenant of the law
by the mystical death of the body of Christ (Rom. vii. 7); that

the transitory luminous appearance in the face of Moses had indicated to Moses himself that the law was a merely temporary institution, and that he had veiled his face from the Israelites in order to veil from them the knowledge of this fact (2 Cor. iii. 7—13),—all this appears to us to be quite arbitrary subjective interpretation, without any objective power of conviction, and we cannot blame the Jewish Christians if they did not feel in the least degree refuted by such arguments, but, on the contrary, rather confirmed in their view of what they regarded as Paul's boundless caprice. Completely justified, however, as the Jewish Christians might be, from *their* positive historical standpoint, in urging this objection against Paul, and especially against his exegetical mode of arguing, yet when viewed from the *higher* ideal historical standpoint, the objection is very weak. For we must bear in mind that, in the first place, allegorizing was at that time the established method of all really independent and intelligent study of the Scriptures; and, in the next place, that the allegorizing of a Paul, compared with that of a Philo or of the Rabbis, stands infinitely higher, because with him the caprice, after all, lay only in the form, while the substance, which he invested with authority by means of this arbitrary method, consisted of operative ideas full of the deepest objective truth, and was not the mere play of a subjective fancy; and, finally, that it is true of all times (including our own) that there is no other means of reconciling faith which is still formally steadfast to the unconditional truth of the old letter, with the ideal conviction which has in substance advanced beyond it, than this very "artifice of the idea" by means of which the religious spirit veils its new developments from itself, until the fruit has grown strong enough to dispense with the protecting shell of the old, and allow it to fall off.

CHAPTER II.

REDEMPTION BY THE DEATH OF CHRIST.

WE have seen how Paul regards man as *a prisoner in a two-fold sense :* first, inasmuch as he is under the law as his task-master and jailer, which holds him fast in the fetters and the curse of the consciousness of guilt, reveals to him the wrath of God, and is consequently for him the letter that killeth, or delivers over to death ; and, secondly, inasmuch as he is sold under sin itself as the power dwelling in his flesh, subjected as a slave, without a will of his own, to its dominating desires. Now with this two-fold imprisonment the Apostle connects redemption by Christ—that is to say, by his death. For it is impossible to doubt that in his eyes the *death* of Jesus, the Messiah, is not merely the principal, but the exclusive means of salvation. We have already seen (Introduction, p. 7) how the whole of his gospel is comprised in the "word of the cross," in the knowledge and preaching of Christ Jesus as "the crucified." We shall see more fully later on how far salvation could for Paul be based, κατ᾽ ἐξοχήν, precisely on this death, as an external fact by itself, and quite apart from the life[1] of Jesus, which

---

[1] Rom. v. 19, διὰ τῆς ὑπακοῆς τοῦ ἑνός, furnishes no argument against this, for we must understand by this expression, not the whole obedience of the life of Jesus, but his one act of obedience (δικαίωμα, ver. 18), in opposition to Adam's one act of disobedience (παράπτωμα, ver. 17). The words here made use of are evidently to be explained by their opposite. The view so much favoured in modern times that it was only as the culminating point of his moral life that the death of Jesus had this high significance for Paul, is part and parcel of the rationalizing misinterpretation of the whole of Paul's doctrine of redemption.

preceded it. Corresponding to the two-fold imprisonment from which the death of Jesus redeemed mankind, the idea of this redemption has also two separate sides to be distinguished. The *first* signification (both in origin and importance) of the redeeming death of Christ is connected with the sentence of guilt, by which man, as the object of the wrath of God, was placed under *the curse of the law*, subjected to death as the punishment of sin. Man is ransomed from this disastrous state of punishment in that the demand for his punishment is satisfied by the death of Christ as a vicarious *expiatory sacrifice*. Through this ransom the death of Christ is the cause of the appeasing of the wrath of God, or of the manifestation of his love, and thus it is a purely *objective* act of God on Christ *in our behalf*, for the purpose of our rescue. But, *at the same time*, the death of Christ frees us from the *power of sin* which dwells in the flesh, for this principle of sin is destroyed, first in Christ himself, and then in us through our mystical communion with him. From this point of view the death of Christ as a *mortification of the flesh* is the commencement of a *subjective* ethical process, which goes on and completes itself *in us*. Here also then, in order to do justice to all Paul's utterances, we must distinguish between the same two essentially different points of view as in the doctrine of sin, namely, the *objective theological* and the *subjective anthropological*. According to the former, the death of Christ is the principle of a new *religious relation* of humanity; according to the latter, it is the principle of a new *moral behaviour*.

THE DEATH OF CHRIST AS AN EXPIATORY SACRIFICE.

We must unquestionably take as our starting-point that passage in which Paul, in the course of the systematic development of his doctrine, first expressly discusses the Christian principle of "the righteousness of God," and traces it back to its objective ground, in the redemption by means of Christ (Rom.

iii. 24—26). After having shown in the preceding part of the letter that righteousness is not in fact attained by means of human action through fulfilment of the law, the Apostle now shows how it must proceed from the favour of God and come to man as a gift, and has been wrought out by God himself through the scheme which is completed in the death of Christ. This scheme is described by the Apostle in the following unmistakable language: *"God has set forth Jesus Christ as a propitiation through faith* (as a propitiatory sacrifice which becomes subjectively operative through faith), *by means of his blood* (by the shedding of his blood, i. e. by a violent death, as a bloody sacrifice ; and that) *for the purpose of declaring his* (God's) *righteousness,* (which was necessary) *because of the remission* (the overlooking, leaving unpunished) *of sins that are past,* (which remission was only possible) *through the forbearance of God; for the purpose* (he resumes) *of declaring his righteousness at this time,* (and, further, this proof of his righteousness was given in this way, namely, in the expiatory death of Christ instead of the death of all men, with the two-fold intention) *that He might be* (seen to be) *just Himself, and* (at the same time) *the justifier of him* (who takes the determining principle of his religious life) *from faith in Jesus* (an intensive expression for the believer)."

Let us now expand the thoughts contained or indirectly presupposed in this passage. Sin during the period which preceded Christ was not only not prevented, but was in fact increased by the law; nor had the particular manifestations of the wrath of God against sin availed to suppress it; on the contrary, they had still further aggravated it (compare i. 24 f.), and could not, therefore, be regarded as an adequate punishment of human guilt, such as should prove God a just Judge. Consequently, the relation of God to sin on the whole, in spite of all particular instances of punishment, was essentially that of forbearance and remission, of indulgent non-observance. But in this way the Divine justice which demanded punishment was not satisfied; it had no adequate proof by facts, and might, therefore, appear to have no existence. This required a tangible proof that avenging justice, although hitherto (relatively) latent, nevertheless really existed. This proof could only be given by filling up the measure of punishment, that is to say —since death is the wages of sin—by a bloody penal death. Were this to be accomplished, however, in the person of the guilty, the justice of God would indeed be shown, but not his favour. God would appear as just or righteous Himself, but not as also justifying the unrighteous. In order to attain, therefore, this *two-fold* end, in order so to demonstrate the justice which required punishment, that favour should at the same time be shown, God, instead of inflicting the full penalty of death, as his avenging justice required, on all who had deserved it, inflicted it on one who had not deserved it; and thus set forth this one in his blood that was shed, as the victim who suffered (vicariously) the punishment due to others, and so expiated their guilt; and this He did in his own interest ($\pi\rho o\acute{\epsilon}\theta\epsilon\tau o$ in the middle voice), in order to cause the recognition of his own justice, which recognition had been endangered by the previous impunity of sin; though, of course, at the same time in the interest of men, who found themselves by this means redeemed (ransomed—$\grave{a}\pi o\lambda\acute{v}\tau\rho\omega\sigma\iota\varsigma$, from $\lambda\acute{v}\tau\rho o\nu$) from guilt, or from the avenging justice of God, which hung over them like the sword of Damocles, requiring the exaction of the penalty.

It cannot be denied that this explanation is equally in accordance with grammar and logic; nor that it is strikingly in harmony with the presuppositions of the Jewish idea of God and sacrificial ritual. As regards the *"justice of God,"* which is proved by the death of Christ, nothing else is to be understood by it than the justice which judges—that is to say, which punishes; this is clearly shown by the context, according to which the proof of justice appeared to be necessary "on account of the previous overlooking"—that is to say, impunity of sin, in connection with which it is evident that only the justice which punishes could be called in question. Moreover, this view[1] is the only one which accords simply and naturally with Jewish notions, according to which justice consists in the exact requital of actions, and consequently the punishing of every instance of guilt; but in whose person the guilt was punished, whether in that of the guilty person himself, or vicariously in that of another, was of no immediate concern; all that was required was that the penalty should be inflicted, and the punishment of even the third and fourth generation for the sins of their fathers was quite conceivable. The Jewish mind was especially familiarized by the rite of sacrifice with the idea of an expiation of guilt by a vicarious atonement. But we are plainly directed to this train of thought by the use of the word ἱλαστήριον in the text. The primary meaning of the word is certainly only "means of propitiation," but in connection with ἐν τῶ—αἵματι and προέθετο, according to which it was a means of propitiation set forth through the shedding of blood, the means of propitiation can only be thought of in the concrete as a "propitiatory sacrifice." But the Hebrew consciousness[2] (like that of the ancient

---

[1] Among the different interpretations which have been suggested in modern times, that of *Hofmann* has found much favour, namely, the "consistency of God," which agrees with that of *Ritschl*, who says, "God has proved his justice in Christ, in that He has acted according to his essential nature in justifying the believer, and yet having no communion with sinners without an atonement" (Altkath. K., p. 86). But we must remark that Paul always refers the justification of believers by God solely to the Divine favour, and not to the justice of God, which, on the contrary, requires the punishment of the sinner. *Ritschl's* view evidently arises from his confounding the divine quality of righteousness or justice with the righteousness which proceeds from God as a gift conferred by his favour; but these are two entirely different ideas, both as to their origin and meaning. The interpretation which *Lipsius* has given to the text in his work, "Paulin. Rechtfertigungslehre," may be passed over, as he has himself abandoned it.

[The English language has two different words, "justice" and "righteousness," to express these two ideas, while the German "Gerechtigkeit," like the Greek δικαιοσύνη, covers both; but "justification" of course means "making righteous."—*Trans.*]

[2] *The idea of expiatory sacrifice,* as expressed in Lev. xvii. 11, is, that the (shed) blood of the sacrifice, by means of the soul or life contained therein, is to "serve as a covering" for the souls of those who bring it. This does not mean that the unholiness

world in general) associated with this idea the thought of vicariously giving up a living thing to death, in order to redeem by
this means another life which had been forfeited to the Deity;
the wrath of the Deity, aroused by sin, demands expiation by
death; the life of the guilty person himself is first of all forfeited
to this demand; but this forfeited life may be rescued, if another
is given up in its place to the death demanded by the wrath of
God. This is only so far "vicarious punishment," that one life,
which had incurred the penalty of death, is set free through the
vicarious suffering of death by another, without this other one,
who suffers death vicariously for him who is worthy of death,
suffering this penalty *on his part also as a punishment;* the penal
character of the expiatory suffering ceases through the vicarious
quittance of the penalty. We should therefore be going beyond
the biblical idea of expiatory sacrifice if we were to imagine
Christ to be a personal object of punishment inflicted by the
wrath of God. He only experienced in himself, in his person,
the suffering which the guilty had incurred as a punishment due
to themselves, the infliction of which was demanded by the
Divine wrath; but as an innocent person who only suffers
vicariously, he experienced suffering, not as a punishment, but
only as externally allotted to him. According to biblical ideas,
therefore, there is no such thing as a "vicarious *punishment* of

of the man is to be screened from the sight of God, by placing between them the holy (!)
life of a beast (this would be a strange notion !), but that the souls which have
become liable to punishment through sin, and subject to the avenging justice of God,
are covered, i. e. protected and rescued from the wrath of God, which would otherwise
strike them, inasmuch as his claim to a life which has become forfeited to Him, is
satisfied by the substitution of the life of the beast. This meaning of the Hebrew
word is made very clear by one of its derivatives, which signifies "redemption through
a substitute tendered for the real debtor, *ransom,*" λύτρον. Compare Ex. xxi. 30 ;
Num. xxxv. 31 ; and Is. xliii. 3, which is quite conclusive: "I have given Egypt Cush
and Sheba, λύτρον ἀντί σου." For how could these unclean Gentile nations serve as a
"covering" for Israel in the sense of screening their uncleanness from the holy eyes of
God ?   But they might well serve as a vicarious substitute or ransom, by which Israel
is redeemed from the curse of God's avenging justice, under which he would otherwise
have irrecoverably fallen, inasmuch as the Divine wrath, which demands the punishment that is due, now finds the satisfaction of its claims in those heathen nations
which are substituted for Israel itself.

Christ," inasmuch as vicarious suffering is the negation of punishment, is expiation *instead* of punishment.

It will be conclusively proved by other passages that Paul applied this idea of propitiatory sacrifice, which is found in the Old Testament, to the death of Christ; or rather that he adopted this view, which had already been enunciated by Jesus himself (Matt. xx. 28), and which was prevalent in the primitive community (compare ἀρνίον ἐσφαγμένον in the Apocalypse). In this sense alone must we understand Paul when he says, 1 Cor. vi. 20 and vii. 23, ἠγοράσθητε τιμῆς, " Ye are bought with a price," which God, as it were, allowed it to cost Him, by giving up his Son for your redemption, and which Christ has paid by his vicariously given life, in order to rescue those who were otherwise lost, and thereby at the same time to win them as a possession for God. The same idea is still more distinctly contained in 1 Cor. v. 7, τὸ πάσχα ἡμῶν ὑπὲρ ἡμῶν ἐτύθη Χριστός : if Christ was sacrificed for us *as our Passover*, then this sacrificial death was an *expiatory* sacrifice ; for vicarious atonement is undeniably the fundamental conception of this primitive rite, the Semitic " ver sacrum," in which the first-born, who was devoted to God, was released by the vicarious sacrifice of a lamb, and his exemption thereby purchased ("exemption" is the meaning of the Hebrew, "release" of the Arabic name of this rite).

Essentially similar is the thought contained in Rom. v. 8—10, in spite of the apparent contradiction that the death of Christ is in iii. 24 f. stated to be a proof of the justice of God, but in this passage a proof of his love. It is in reality both of these in both passages : that death follows sin as a punishment, is a proof of his justice, but that Christ undergoes the penalty instead of the guilty, is a proof of the love of God, who has ordained this scheme which reconciles his justice with his love, of his own free will (τῇ αὐτοῦ χάριτι, iii. 24). The words ὑπὲρ ἡμῶν, which occur here and are repeated in many other passages, signify primarily indeed simply "for our good;" but the connecting thought, both in this and the other passages, is that of a

H

vicarious act (compare especially 2 Cor. v. 21). This is also
indicated by the *effect* of the death of Christ as described in
ver. 9 f.; this consists in two things—first, in the already completed *fact* that we ἐχθροὶ ὄντες κατηλλάγημεν τῷ θεῷ διὰ τοῦ
θανάτου τοῦ υἱοῦ αὐτοῦ; and, secondly, in the *hope* which is founded
on this, that we σωθησόμεθα δι᾽ αὐτοῦ ἀπὸ τῆς ὀργῆς, that is at the
last judgment. As this hope is derived from the completed fact,
the future hoped for must be the completion or the definite confirmation of the same work of salvation, which as past is expressed by ἐχθροὶ ὄντες κατηλλάγημεν τῷ θεῷ: καταλλαγῆναι τῷ
θεῷ must therefore contain a declaration about our position with
regard to God, or concerning our faith which is dependent on
God, just as this is evidently contained in σώζεσθαι ἀπὸ τῆς ὀργῆς.
But in that case, καταλλαγῆναι τῷ θεῷ cannot express a change in
our voluntary behaviour towards God, our disposition and moral
attitude towards Him, for that would be of course dependent
upon ourselves, and not, like σώζεσθαι ἀπὸ τῆς ὀργῆς, upon Him;
no conclusion could therefore be drawn from the former to the
latter, and least of all the conclusion clearly drawn with so
much confidence in ver. 10, from the greater to the less. Because
we had changed our hostile feeling towards God, it would by no
means follow with certainty that *God* also would from that
time have given up his anger against us, and that we should be
saved from its disastrous consequences; the merely subjective
wish to be henceforth at peace with God would not suffice to
justify the objective certainty that God also on his part was
at peace with us. But the future salvation from the wrath of
God might be hoped for with all the more certainty, on the
supposition that the greater thing had already been done by
God; that we, while as sinners we were objects of his wrath, had
nevertheless been reconciled to Him by the death of his Son,
which had been ordained by Himself, as the palpable proof that
his love towards us far outweighed his anger. Accordingly, καταλ-
λαγῆναι is a change of our relation to God proceeding from God
himself, not a change of our behaviour towards God proceeding

from us ; and ἐχθροὶ ὄντες therefore does not denote[1] an active enmity on our part against God, but our passive condition under the curse of the Divine anger. In this sense alone is the text consistent with itself, and with Rom. iii. 25, and 2 Cor. v. 18; it declares that the death of Christ was a pooof to us of the Divine love, inasmuch as by it we have become reconciled to God, instead of being hated by Him, and so the anger of God which oppressed us is removed from us—in short, the death of Christ was a conciliation of God's anger, ordained by his love.

The same thing is said in Gal. iii. 13. That which is expressed in the previous passage as " propitiating the enmity of God," is here called " *redemption from the curse of the law.*" The law is the expression of the Divine will, therefore the curse of the law is the expression of the wrathful will of God, of his avenging justice. From this curse which oppressed us, Christ has " redeemed us *by being made a curse for us,*" that is, by giving himself up as a ransom to the death which the Divine wrath demanded. The abstract expression κατάρα is probably not applied here merely in recollection of the words used in the passage quoted from the Old Testament, but also because it really expresses the thought more accurately than any other : Christ was not personally accursed, but only came to stand in the place of such an one before God, inasmuch as he suffered the accursed death as a vicarious expiatory sacrifice, and by this ransom redeemed our life, which as cursed was forfeit to our

---

[1] This follows necessarily from a right understanding of the meaning of καταλ-λαγῆναι. If we understand this to refer to the doing away with the anger of God against sinful humanity, and ἐχθροὶ ὄντες, nevertheless, to refer to our hostile attitude towards God, there is certainly a "want of clearness of thought" (*Rückert*), only it is not the Apostle who betrays it. *Ritschl* is more consistent, who (Altkath. K., p. 87) not only understands ἐχθροὶ in an active sense of "the sin of mankind in its quality of enmity against God," but also denies that it has any reference to an expiation of the wrath of God, because Paul always connects the wrath of God with the ἀπολλύμενοι, but in no case with the σωζόμενοι, who on the contrary, so far as their former condition as sinners is concerned, are only put under favour. And yet Paul says σωθησόμεθα ἀπὸ τῆς ὀργῆς ; if we require to be *saved* from the wrath of God, then we must surely at one time have lain under it.

wrathful God.   Thus this passage also agrees exactly with the ancient notion of expiatory sacrifice.[1]

The same may be said finally of 2 Cor. v. 21 : *"God hath made him to be sin for us, who knew no sin* (by personal experience), *that we might become the righteousness of God in him."*   Here also we have the abstract word ἁμαρτία, as in Gal. iii. 13, κατάρα, not without good reason—for Christ was not personally sinful; the relative sentence expressly denies it; but he was put in the objective relation of the sinful world towards God,[2] so that, although really in his own person not sinful, yet he passed ideally for a sinner in God's regard and dealing, was esteemed as such; exactly in the same way as we, conversely, by reason of what was done to him, come to stand towards God in the objective relation of the righteous, to pass ideally in the regard and the dealing of God as righteous, although we are not so really in our own persons, but, on the contrary, are sinners.   We have here neither more nor less than an *exchange between Christ and us,*— he takes from us the part of sinners, we receive from him that of the righteous ; sin and righteousness appear on both sides as purely objective characters, separable from the person, and transferable, of mere ideal validity in themselves, but involving very real consequences—on the one hand death, on the other hand life.   This is a mode of looking at the matter which will not so much surprise us after what we have seen in chap. i. of the

---

[1] The dogmatic objections urged by *Al. Schweizer* (Stud. und Krit. 1858, p. 436 f.) can have no weight against these simple facts that exegesis yields.   Not that they are therefore groundless : we shall in a later portion of this work bring forward the very same considerations ; only they ought not to be introduced directly into the exegesis.

[2] The interpretation of this passage given by *Holsten*, ut supra, p. 437, and accepted by *Hausrath*, that God placed him, who in his previous existence was absolutely sinless, in a condition of being really affected with sin, by sending him into sinful flesh, is wrong, first, because in the whole context there is no reference to Christ becoming man, but throughout, and therefore also in ver. 21, only to his *death ;* and, secondly, on account of the analogy with our δικαιοσύνη θεοῦ, by which, according to Paul's use of the word, and according to the context (compare especially ver. 19, μὴ λογιζόμενος —αὐτῶν), imputed, ideal righteousness alone can be understood ; consequently that which corresponds to it, the ἁμαρτία of Christ, must also be only imputed and ideal.

objectivity of Paul's notion of sin, and what we shall have to say of the objectivity of his notion of righteousness in chap. iv. ; although it must appear in the highest degree perplexing to a mind accustomed to think of morality as subjective.

One can hardly help further giving to ὑπὲρ ἡμῶν in this passage the meaning, "in our stead," especially as the words ὑπὲρ Χριστοῦ, which occur twice previously, can scarcely be rendered otherwise than in Christ's stead; ὑπὲρ is thus precisely equivalent to ἀντί. This makes it still less possible to suppose that the text refers to a deliverance from the power of sin ; not only do the analogies drawn from other passages which we have mentioned point rather to exemption from guilt, but ver. 19 does the same, when taken in connection with the passage we are here discussing, inasmuch as the reconciliation with God, completed by God in (that is by means of) Christ, is here further elucidated by the words, μὴ λογιζόμενος αὐτοῖς τὰ παραπτώματα αὐτῶν. This reconciliation, therefore, does not consist in the fact that sin is no longer operative in man, but in the fact that it is no longer imputed to him by God as guilt which deserves damnation, that consequently man is no longer on its account an object of the Divine anger. And in this way the whole passage contains the thought, which fully agrees with all that has gone before, that the redemption of mankind from guilt is brought about by Christ's vicariously suffering the penalty which man had incurred through sin, and that this exchange of parts between the guiltless and the guilty has been ordained by God himself from love to us.

And here one cannot avoid asking the question, what necessity was there that this incurred penalty should be suffered at all, when the Divine willingness to show favour already existed before this expiation, and indeed was necessary in order to render it possible ? What need was there that the love of God to sinners should attain its realization in this round-about way ? Since it was God himself who ordained the reconciliation of the sinful world, how could this same God, who so abounded in love, be on the other hand one who required an expiation, whose avenging wrath must be satisfied, before his love could show itself as such? This question it is, probably, which has consciously or unconsciously hovered before the mind of commentators with a confusing influence, and hindered an impartial apprehension of the simple grammatical meaning of the passages we have quoted (which may be classed amongst the most misinterpreted texts of the Bible). Nor can it be denied that this question involves no small difficulty, and that not merely when regarded from a modern point of view, or one otherwise alien to that of Paul, but quite as much so when we start from Paul's own position. It may indeed be said that the real answer to the question just propounded is perfectly simple and obvious. Redemption from the curse of the law by a vicarious endurance of it was necessary, because the law, this irrevocable expression of the holy will of God, had once for all assigned death as the punishment of sin. Simple and lucid, however, as this conclusion may appear, and completely satisfactory as it may be to ecclesiastical and orthodox commentators, yet it has no slight obstacle to encounter in the presuppositions of Paul himself. Let us only recollect for a moment what this very Apostle has taught about the law, its meaning and its purpose in the Divine economy. The law is to him, as we have seen, by no means a thing that is valid, unconditionally and eternally, and therefore also in reference to Christ, but it has only come in as a temporary intermediate purpose, between promise and fulfilment, in order to increase sin, and to awaken mankind, who were all enslaved and impotent under its bondage, to faith. Now how can this law, which from the beginning was only destined to a mere temporary dominion, as a means subservient to Christ, raise against Christ, its originally predestined Lord, after he had appeared, such a claim as could only be satisfied by his bloody expiatory death? Is not a claim which was originally established only for a certain period of time, extinguished of itself at the expiration of this period, without the necessity of any other release ? And this question remains with equal force if we turn from the law to the Divine justice which reveals itself in the law. How is it possible that its claims for the punishment of sin should be unconditional, and valid with regard to Christ, when it was God himself whose sentence had subjected all to sin, with the distinct purpose of showing mercy on all through favour ? (Gal. iii. 22 ; Rom. ii. 32). If the avenging justice were from the beginning ancillary to the will to save, as a subordinate moment, in the same way as the law is an ancillary moment or temporary stage in the scheme of salvation, can it (the avenging justice) in that case make so unconditional a claim to satisfaction, that without it the will to show favour can in no way be realized ? If this were so, would not that which should only be a moment, be raised into an independent and co-ordinate, if not a predominant, factor ? All these questions undeniably bear hard upon the Pauline system, and add to the difficulty of understanding it. But that only binds us the more, as scientific expositors, impartially to establish this inconsistency in Paul's system and to make its origin intelligible. In fact, the contradiction to which we have drawn attention, is very simply explained by the genesis of the system, and is a most instructive point, giving us a deep insight into the structure of the dogmatic thought of Paul.

For thus much is clear—if Paul's notion of the law, its insufficiency in a religious point of view, and its merely temporary significance, had been his original view, from which he started and on which his system was founded, then he could by no possibility have conceded that the claims of the law, which he ranked so low, could only be satisfied by the accursed death of the Messiah, as a vicarious expiatory sacrifice; but the law would have been for him (as it was in the eyes of John) a lower preparatory stage, which disappeared of itself on the manifestation of favour and truth in Christ; and the death of Christ would have had no relation whatever to the extinct claims and threats of the law.　But in fact it is just the reverse in the case of Paul.　The law was from first to last to him, as much as to every Jew, the unconditional decree of the Divine will, and its validity was unlimited.　Its abrogation by the death of Christ, which opened a new way of salvation, could therefore only take place in such a way that the claims of the law should at the same time be recognized and satisfied, and thus an adjustment or compromise should be established between the new principle of favour and the legal principle of justice, such as we found in the expiatory death of Christ.　Proceeding from this point, the abrogation of the law by the expiatory death of Christ being now established, he came upon the further task which awaited him—to reconcile this conditional and temporarily limited solidity of the law with the unity and unchangeableness of God. We have seen how Paul did this, by deducing from the temporary establishment of the law between promise and fulfilment, the inference that it had also in the Divine intention from the beginning only the character of a conditional intermediate purpose, not that of an absolute final end.　Thus Paul, starting from his initial hypothesis of the indestructible validity of the law, and still influenced by it in his view of the death on the cross as an expiatory sacrifice, was ultimately driven, by the logical consequences of the doctrine of the cross itself, to a conclusion regarding the law which completely destroyed his hypothesis.　This striking discord between the conclusion reached through manifold dialectic arguments and the original premise (regarding the law), might easily be concealed from the mind of its author—the experience of all times furnishes similar examples: on the other hand, it was probably the main reason that the system of Paul could not be taken up by others without undergoing a change, nor be retained in its original sense in the Christian community, and least of all by those who accepted its essential conclusions.　Inasmuch as these took their stand at once on the conquest and degradation of the law, to which Paul could only have attained after a violent conflict with the law, they had no longer any ground for regarding the work of Christ, after Paul's manner, as an escape from the demands of the law, a redemption from the curse of the law, a manifestation of the avenging justice of God, and the like. In their eyes, therefore, the ethical significance of the appearance of Christ, and especially of his death (which significance was not overlooked indeed by Paul, but held a secondary place in his thoughts), must have occupied the foreground and formed the cardinal point of their system and of their preaching. This was the simple and inevitable consequence of the direction already taken by Paul himself in his new doctrine of the law; but with Paul the new doctrine of the law, which resulted from his doctrine of redemption, produced no reflex influence on the form of the doctrine of redemption itself, and it is this which has given to the dogmatic teaching of Paul its peculiar character, which combines and blends together the Jewish form and the Christian idea. *Paul's doctrine of redemption was thus the way of overcoming the religion of the law, still put in legal forms, a compromise between grace and the law, in terms derived wholly from the law.*

By this historical mode of considering our subject, we shall arrive at the solution of another question, which has ever been much vexed by dogmatic writers, although it is remarkable that it was never raised by Paul, because it lay quite out of his path, in the psychological genesis of his system, and it is this : How far was the death of the one victim, Jesus, an expiation satisfactory to the justice of God for the sin of humanity, or an equivalent ransom in place of the death of all? It is commonly thought that the ground of the absolute sufficiency of the death of Christ as an expiation is to be found in 2 Cor. v. 21, where it is stated that it was the death of one who was personally *sinless.* But certain as it is that personal sinlessness forms the *conditio sine qua non* of the possibility of vicarious expiation, it is no less certain that it does not follow hence that this could be a sufficient ground for the unconditional expiatory value of one death in the place of all. *One* undeserved death is obviously in reality only the equivalent for *one* deserved death, but not for the death of the countless numbers who have deserved it. Nor does the passage quoted say that it is; in the words, τὸν μὴ γνόντα ἁμαρτίαν, it only states the condition on which alone the expression ἁμαρτίαν ἐποίησε could have been applicable—on which alone, therefore, a vicarious suffering could take place; but it says nothing to show what it was that gave to this its absolute expiating power. In the other passages that have been quoted, it is simply stated that redemption has taken place through Jesus Christ, through the death of the Son of God, that Christ has redeemed us, without a word of explanation to indicate what gave this expiatory value to the death of Christ. That there is no reference in the mention of the "Son of God" to a divine nature, the partaking of which has made this one death sufficient (according to the views of Anselm and Luther), is self-evident, for a divine nature of that kind was utterly alien to Paul's Christology, as we shall presently see. The fact from which we must start rather is, that Paul prefers to speak of the death or cross of *Christ*, i. e. the Messiah. And this reminds us of the source from which this whole theory has sprung. The death of the Messiah on the cross would in itself be an inconceivable contradiction, if it had not been ordained by God as the means of producing the Messianic righteousness by the expiation of guilt: for this reason, that is for no real reason, but for consistency's sake only, it is to be regarded as the absolute means of expiation. We have only to realize in our minds this psychological account of the doctrine of the expiatory death of Christ, in order to understand clearly how it might well happen that the question of the *possibility* of such a vicarious satisfaction never arrested Paul's attention, any more than that of its *necessity*.

Let us now abstract from that which we must regard as the Jewish and legal form of Paul's doctrine of the atonement, and there still remains, as the ideal religious substance of his thought, *the contemplation of the reconciling love of God,* which raises man out of the discordant relation to God in which he finds himself by nature, and places him in the unity of fellowship with God in love (Rom. iii. 24, χάρις; v. 8, ἀγάπη τοῦ θεοῦ εἰς ἡμᾶς; 2 Cor. v. 19, θεὸς ἦν ἐν Χριστῷ, κόσμον καταλλάσσων ἑαυτῷ; Rom. viii. 31 f., ὁ θεὸς ὑπὲρ ἡμῶν, ὅς γε τοῦ ἰδίου υἱοῦ οὐκ ἐφείσατο ἀλλ' ὑπὲρ πάντων παρέδωκεν αὐτόν), and which can only be met on the part of man by a grateful confidence, and believing acceptance of God's willingness to show favour. As it is no less certain that this, which is the core of the Pauline doctrine of reconciliation, contains the fundamental idea of genuine evangelical piety, than that its form is derived from genuine Jewish thought, we can easily understand from this antagonism why Christian piety at one time accounts this doctrine a treasure, and at another time finds it a rock of offence. But there is another point which is hereby rendered intelligible. This variance between the Christian idea and the Jewish form places in God himself an opposition between reconciling love and wrath which is irreconcilable because it insists on punishment,— an opposition of motives which dogmatic thought has striven in vain to harmonize, because it is in fact only to be explained by its psychological genesis. In such cases the religious imagination has recourse to the simple expedient of separating the opposing motives, and attributing them to different subjects as influenced by them and representing them, and then regarding the reconciliation of them as the action of these opposite characters. And so it has happened here. The *love* of God, the motive of the work of reconciliation, naturally found its representative in him who gave himself up in self-sacrifice as a willing organ of its counsel of grace, that is to say, in *Christ*, the historical Mediator of reconciliation. But the *wrath*, which through its inexorable demand of punishment made a vicarious expiation necessary for the work of reconciliation, found its representative in that form in which the religious consciousness of the Jewish nation had long ago personified the avenging

justice of God, namely, the *devil*.   Love and wrath, whose working together in God, like the diagonal of two opposing forces,
produced the atonement by means of vicarious expiation, were
thus respectively attributed by the religious imagination to
Christ and the Devil; and consequently the atonement itself
naturally became a dramatic action, struggle, or judicial process,
between these two representatives of opposing motives in God.
Naively as this idea was at a later period worked out, and
widely as it departed from the elementary form given to it by
Paul, yet no one who is familiar with the character and processes
of religious imagination will see anything else in this than a
perfectly natural, nay necessary, development of Paul's doctrine
of reconciliation, with its antagonism of love and anger in God,
of the Christian and the Jewish idea of God.   In the original
system of Paul, it is true that this substantiating, in the person
of the devil, of that wrath which requires expiation, is not yet
completed; although the personification of the curse of the law,
from whose claims the sinful world must "be redeemed," or of
the dominion of the law from which we are released, being
"accounted righteous through the death of Christ," approaches
very closely to this substantiation, and prepares the way for it.
But in the earliest form of Pauline doctrine, immediately subse-
quent to the time of Paul himself, namely, in the Epistles to the
Colossians and Hebrews, we already find the death of Christ
brought into relation with the Devil and the Satanic kingdom
(Heb. ii. 14; Col. ii. 15; compare Chap. ix. of this work). On the
other hand, it was more obvious to *envisage the reconciling love of
God in him who brought about the reconciliation as a human act of
love*, and to return it to Him with grateful responsive love. Here,
in this kindly element, the doctrine of the atonement has from
the first thrown off the hard dogmatic husk, and has become a
growing germ of pure and simple piety. This was the case in an
extraordinary degree with Paul himself; through all his dogmatic reasoning on the knowledge of the cross of Christ, the
dominant mood is grateful love to him who loved him and gave

himself for him. And it is the intensity of this simple and morally true feeling which became in Paul the root of a new and most significant mode of regarding the death of Christ.

THE DEATH OF CHRIST AS LIBERATION FROM THE DOMINION OF SIN.

This view has not, as would appear from some of the later commentaries, sprung from scholastic reflection on the relation of the death of Christ to the nature of the flesh. The theological idea of the destruction of sin in the death of Christ is, on the contrary, the last dogmatic precipitate from a religious experience, the source of which lies in the simplest characteristic of Christian piety, in the thankful giving up of the heart to the Mediator who has given himself up for us, in the consciousness of the duty of entirely devoting our whole life to him, to whose act of love we owe our higher life of union with God. Gal. ii. 19 f. and 2 Cor. v. 14 f. are the passages which afford us a glimpse of the psychological genesis of this train of thought, of the religious birth-place of that mystical union with Christ, in which Christian piety in the mind of Paul discovered the power of sanctification, of the new moral life and freedom from the servitude of sin, at the same time with the blessedness of reconciliation. "If one died for all," says this passage in Corinthians, "then are you all dead; and in truth he died for all, in order that they who live might henceforth not live for themselves, but for him who died for them and has risen. Therefore, if any one is in Christ, then is he a new creature; the old has passed away; behold, all has become new." This passage starts unmistakably from that view of the death of Christ which we have hitherto been considering, viz., as a vicarious suffering *for us* (and it thus agrees with the passage above mentioned, v. 19—21), but it no less plainly goes further, and gives to Christ's dying *for* us an application which makes it a (moral) dying of all *with*

Christ.[1] But this turn of thought is brought about simply by the subjective reaction which the objective fact of a death endured for us was calculated to produce in our *sense of gratitude*; if we owe our rescued life to Christ who has rescued us by his vicarious death, then this rescued life can no longer be held by us at our own disposal, but it must belong to him to whom we owe it; but as such it is no longer the old life, which consisted in our living only for ourselves, but it has become an entirely new life, as belonging to Christ and devoted to him, namely, a life bound up in communion with Christ (ἐν Χριστῷ), kept within certain limits by his love, of which he gave proof by deed in dying for us (ver. 14, ἡ ἀγάπη τοῦ Χριστοῦ συνέχει ἡμᾶς); accordingly, if we compare this new life of obligation to Christ and through him with our former life of selfish freedom from obligation, or of obligation to the law, we cannot but come to the conclusion that we who are in possession of the love of Christ are altogether on our side also dead with Christ (as to our former life); his death therefore was at the same time our death.   Thus

---

[1] We may certainly call this also a vicarious relation, only in another sense; thus *Baur*, N. T. Theol., p. 159, and in *Hilgenfeld's* Ztschr. f. w. Th. 1859, p. 241: "It is possible to take the place of another in two different senses; first, in such a way that he whose place another takes does not do that which another does for him; secondly, so that he whose place another takes likewise makes that which this other does for him into his own act. We may call the first the *real*, the second the *ideal* vicarious act; in the former, one person stands only externally beside another person; in the latter, each is not merely beside and outside the other, but each is in a spiritual, inward fashion in the other." And p. 243: "The idea of this passage (2 Cor. v. 14 f.) is that of a union of Christ with us, brought about by the principle of love, by means of which that which he has done for us is the same thing as if we ourselves had done it; as he identifies himself with us in his death, and has set himself in our place as dying for us, so must we also think of ourselves as in his place, and regard ourselves as dead with him.   This unity as a being in each other, in which one lives in the other, in which we are crucified with Christ because he has been crucified for us, we live in him because he lives in us (Gal. ii. 20), is the true Pauline notion of vicarious action." This latter passage says too much. For the original notion of vicarious action, and that which alone corresponds to the dogmatic theory of expiation, is rather that which *Baur* in the passage quoted above calls the "real," or which might also have been called the legal notion.   But the text we have quoted certainly shows how easy it was for this "real" to pass over into the "ideal," the legal into the mystical notion, and how decided from the very beginning was the *tendency of Paul's own mind to gravitate in the latter direction.*

regarded, therefore, the death of Christ is seen to be the common
death of all who believe in Christ, by which they cease to exist
according to their "old man," and begin the life of a new man.
But the Apostle himself tells us in the plainest language whence
this view sprang; it is founded on *reflection upon a fact of
inward experience*—the fact, namely, that he whom Christ's love,
as shown in deeds, has rescued, has become devoted to Christ, and
thereby a new man (ἡ ἀγάπη τοῦ Χριστοῦ συνέχει ἡμας, κρίναντας τοῦτο,
ὅτι εἰ εἷς, &c.). We find precisely the same idea in Gal. ii. 19 f.
Here also the being crucified with Christ, through which Christ
becomes the principle of life in man instead of the old self, is
traced back to the *inward fact* of "belief in the Son of God, who
loved me and gave himself for me"—an explanatory sentence,
which plainly enough describes this belief as precisely that
frame of mind which is presupposed in the passage from the
Corinthians above referred to, namely, that of grateful obligation and self-devotion. In this passage also, it is the sense of
being bound up with Christ in the feeling of a grateful return of
his love, which makes the faithful partakers in the death of
Christ, or makes this death to be the common death of all
believers. Gal. vi. 14, δι᾽ οὗ ἐμοὶ κόσμος ἐσταύρωται κἀγώ τῷ κόσμῳ,
will be seen to point to the same view, although the emotional
process which engendered the idea cannot so directly be traced
here as in the two passages last mentioned; yet even here there
is an intimation of it in the word καυχᾶσθαι, which is an expression of joyfully exalted feeling. Gal. v. 24 declares further (οἱ τοῦ
Χριστοῦ τὴν σάρκα ἐσταύρωσαν), that the mortification of the flesh
of the old man is already accomplished in principle in those
who belong to Christ's family, and this by the very fact of their
having entered that family through faith and baptism: but that
the killing of the flesh in a purely objective sense, apart from
this subjective act, has been once for all accomplished by the
death of Christ, is not only not stated in this passage, but is a
notion that is expressly excluded by the use of the active verb,
ἐσταύρωσαν, according to which the killing of the flesh is referred

to the personal act of each individual in becoming a Christian, and consequently depends again on self-devotion to Christ.

Thus we see that, according to these earlier letters, the death of Christ effects the putting away of our old man and the beginning of a new moral life, in no other way than by the *psychological means* of our grateful devotion to him who died for us. But the teaching of the Epistle to the Romans goes further by connecting this effect *directly*, overlooking the psychological means by which it was attained, with the bodily death of Christ. This, however, is an advance, not so much (as has strangely enough been generally thought in later times) in the dogmatic deepening of the knowledge of the death of Christ, as in the dogmatic formalization, and at the same time externalization, of a fact of religious experience, which is in itself purely inward and of psychological origin.[1] It is probable that the motive for this is to be found in the fact that, considering the immoral consequences that might be deduced from the doctrine of favour, the Apostle was most anxious to prove that for Christians to remain in sin was a logical impossibility, by reason of an actual objective breach with sin.   With this aim he recurs in Rom. vi. first of all to Christian baptism unto the crucified, in which the believer, by his mystical communion with Christ, had made the death of Christ his own death, so that he himself was also crucified as to his old man.   The train of thought connected

---

[1] By overlooking this, and making a conception like that of Rom. viii. 3, the direct source of Paul's doctrine of salvation (as, *e.g.*, *R. Schmidt* does in his "Paulin. Christologie"), the theological dogma is cut off from its roots in the religious consciousness, and nothing remains but a dry scholastic theory; in which form one cannot conceive how it can ever have produced any impression on the religious mind.   Reuss also (Histoire de la Theol. Chrét. &c. II. 165 f.) holds the mystic doctrine of redemption based on Rom. vi.—viii. for the only one, and rejects that of vicarious atonement in face of the historical facts; but at any rate he traces back this, which he supposes to be the sole doctrine, to its true source in the mystic faith of Paul.   To see in this a " hazy mysticism," which "leaves an utterly unreasoned residuum in the very heart of Paul's view " (*R. Schmidt*, ut supra, p. 63, note; cf. *Weiss*, Neut. Theol., p. 205, 2nd. ed.), is an utter mistake ; so much so that the truth is rather the very opposite ; it is just the would-be scientific attempt to ignore the mystic faith of Paul, in which the dogmas most peculiarly his own all have their root, that makes these dogmas an " utterly unreasoned " and utterly unreasonable scholasticism.

with this idea had not yet been worked out in the passages
before quoted from the Epistle to the Galatians and the second
to the Corinthians. But now the Apostle endeavours to ground
this "being dead to sin," given for the believer as an ethical
fact in baptism, upon a deeper, and as it were a still more objective fact; thus that which in the baptism to the death of Christ
(therefore generally in the union with Christ through faith) was
accomplished in the individual as a spiritual fact,—namely, the
dying to sin, or the death of the old man of sin,—now comes to
be represented as a fact accomplished externally, and to the
senses, in that very death of Christ: the purely sensuous fact of
the violent putting to death of the fleshly body of Christ becomes
in his eyes not only a symbol, but an essentially homogeneous
type and beginning of the putting to death of the old man in
us: ὅ γὰρ ἀπέθανε, τῇ ἁμαρτίᾳ ἀπέθανεν ἐφάπαξ—οὕτω καὶ ὑμεῖς
λογίζεσθε ἑαυτοὺς νεκροὺς μὲν τῇ ἁμαρτίᾳ ζῶντας δέ, &c. (ver. 10 f.).
We must not fail to note here that the relation of these two
sentences in the *logical* argument, as they were used by the
Apostle for his hortatory purpose, proves absolutely nothing as
to the succession of these thoughts in their *psychological* genesis;
in the latter, their relation to each other is precisely reversed;
just as they who have been baptized unto Christ have to regard
themselves as dead to sin, just so, and for that same reason, we
have to regard Christ as one who himself also died to sin in his
own (bodily) death: proceeding from the former thought, which
was given as the immediate principle of Christian consciousness,
the Apostle was led on to the latter conception simply by that
habit of thought which connects a spiritual principle with a
fact of sense, and envisages it as immediately given in that fact;
only on the ground that the principle is made one with the
external fact, is it possible and necessary that the practical
consequence included in the principle be deduced as a moral
demand from the fact (οὕτω καὶ ὑμεῖς λογίζεσθε, &c.).

This conception of the death of Christ can only be understood by means of this its psychological Genesis; in itself it is

I

anything but simple, and presents the greatest difficulties; for, if one thinks of it, there is but very little, if any, real homogeneity between the physical extinction of the bodily life of Christ on the cross and the ethical annihilation of the old man in devotion to Christ. An allegorical analogy is the utmost that is suggested here, according to our mode of thought; but this is by no means all that the Apostle means; he affirms a thoroughly real parity between the two proceedings, and so in particular a perfectly real dying of Christ to sin—that is to say, ceasing from all relation to it; for the whole force of his argument depends entirely on this parity, and accordingly he makes the dying of Christ to sin to be directly and inseparably connected with his actual death.[1] But now how can it be said of Christ, the sinless (2 Cor. v. 21), that he has really died to sin, ceased through his dying to have any relation to it? For does not this suppose that he previously stood in relation to it, partook of it, in the same way as we partake of it according to our old man? Here, however, the Pauline notion of the σάρξ intervenes as a medium through which alone the comparison of the death of Christ with the death of the old man in the Christian becomes possible in thought. In the passage we are considering it is true that this notion is still in the background, from which fact it may be concluded that this doctrine of the death of Christ has not grown out of the doctrine of the σάρξ; but it comes into prominence in chap. viii., where the whole argument, which commences in chap. vi., is now brought to a pregnant dogmatic conclusion.

The Apostle had in the previous chapter described how in the natural man the law, in spite of its holiness, and in spite of the consent of the ego itself, was impotent, could not guard against concupiscence, nay, could only increase it, on account of the

---

[1] Consequently *Meyer's* interpretation, " that Christ died to the power of sin, so that he had henceforth no more to suffer from it (namely, human sin)," is quite opposed to the context, for it entirely does away with the comparison between ἀποθανεῖν τῇ ἁμαρτίᾳ in the case of Christ and in that of Christians. The translation given by *Schmid* (Neutest. Theol., § 80), " for our sin " (dativus incommodi), is of course grammatically inadmissible.

greater power of sin which dwelt in the flesh. This state of
inward conflict had forced from him the despairing question,
"Wretched man that I am, who will deliver me from this body
of death?" The Christian answer to this is contained in viii. 3,
" *That which was impossible to the law, because it was weakened by
the flesh, that has God done, after He had sent his Son in the form
of sinful flesh* (in a shape or form of existence taken from the
element of sinful flesh and belonging to it), *and for sin He condemned sin in the flesh.*" Κατέκρινε, if we look at the immediate
context and at chap. vii., with which this passage is also connected, can have no other meaning than the above; it cannot
mean, "He set forth sin as deserving damnation," for the law
has in truth already done this sufficiently; neither can it mean,
"He cancelled sin by the atonement," for that could never be
regarded as the intention of the law; it was not for the accomplishment of this that the law was too weak through the flesh,
but it was too weak to break the power of sin, to destroy its
dominion over man. This, therefore, *the doing away with the
power of sin,* was that which God did in Christ; but how? The
expression κατέκρινε (referring back to κατάκριμα, ver. 1) primarily indicates a judicial act; accordingly the destruction of the
power of sin must be regarded as an "actual sentence of condemnation" or *judicial execution;* sin was "*condemned*" in the
flesh. Now in what other way can this "condemnation of sin
in the flesh," accomplished by God in Christ, have taken effect
than through the bloody death of Jesus?

The other favourite interpretation is, that God deprived sin of
its ruling power by sending his Son in the flesh—that is to say,
by means of the whole sinless existence of Jesus on the earth,
inasmuch as he (morally) overcame sin in the course of his life
in the flesh.[1] But this interpretation comes into collision, in the
first place, with κατέκρινε, which implies a destruction by a single
judicial act, not a moral overcoming, extending through a whole

[1] So *Weiss*, ut supra, p. 308; *Ritschl*, Altkath. Kirche, p. 85; *Reuss*, Histoire,
&c., II. p. 80 f.; *Meyer*, in his commentary on this passage.

life; and besides, God would not properly be the subject of this predicate in the latter sense, but Christ.[1] But, in the second place, this interpretation contradicts the view which the Apostle consistently maintains through every other part of his writings; for he never grounds the work of salvation on the life of Jesus, but always on his death (compare the beginning of this chapter). Finally, it does not accord with the expression ἐν τῇ σαρκί, to which, as every one must admit, the same meaning must be given as to the σάρξ, which twice precedes it in the same verse. Now it is proposed to translate the word in each of these instances by the general notion, "human nature." But the word σάρξ nowhere has this meaning at all (see Chap. i.), and here especially it is plainly shown in the two former instances to mean the principle of sin in man, both by the expressly added explanation, σάρξ ἁμαρτίας, and by the assertion that the σάρξ makes the law impotent. It would be a most unwarrantable caprice, therefore, to substitute, when the word occurs for the third time, the indefinite notion of human nature. If, then, for all these reasons, that sense is inadmissible, our interpretation is established—namely, that God has condemned sin in the flesh by the death, and not by the life, of Christ; that is to say, in the sense that by *putting to a bloody death the body of Jesus, which consisted of flesh, sin, which had its abode in the flesh, was put to death with it.*[2] But it could only be killed with the body, if it were actually within it; therefore the σάρξ of Jesus, in order that it might be killed as the principle of sin, or that sin might

---

[1] The combination, "God has condemned sin to subjugation through Christ" (*Weiss*), is quite arbitrarily introduced, and is inconsistent with the emphatic position of ὁ θεός, which makes it plain that a direct causal act of God for the destruction of the power of sin is intended.

[2] Up to this point we are in accord with *Usteri, Baur, R. Schmidt.* The inference that inevitably follows, as it appears to me, from these premises, was first drawn by *Holsten* (p. 436), who is followed by *Overbeck, Hausrath, Lüdemann,* and others; on the other hand, *Baur* has suggested, but left unanswered, the question, "How this right of ἁμαρτία over the σάρξ can be done away with in the σάρξ of Christ, if the σάρξ of Christ were not itself a σάρξ ἁμαρτίας?"—a question to the solution of which *R. Schmidt's* attempt (p. 100 f.) appears to me to contribute nothing.

be killed in it, must in truth have been the same principle of sin as the σάρξ in general from its very nature is, and must really have had the same sin dwelling in it. We shall see from the exposition of Pauline Christology in the next chapter, that this is really implied by the passage, " God sent his Son *in the form of sinful flesh.*" At present we shall only add, that the force and meaning of the whole of the context of this passage is destroyed if this interpretation be rejected. The question was, How can we wretched men obtain deliverance from this body of death, this body in whose members sin, which causes death, dwells, because its substance is that of sinful flesh? The answer is, God has already executed judgment on sin in the flesh of his Son, whom He has sent for that very purpose in the form of sinful flesh. Now, if our deliverance from sinful flesh is to be completed, it is here manifestly presupposed that that which has had judgment executed upon it in the death of Christ was identical with that from which we are to be delivered; consequently that it was precisely the general human substance of flesh, with the quality of sinfulness which is inseparably attached to it, that was destroyed by the death of Christ. The idea that that death was in itself, and directly, the destruction of the principle of sin for all, depends entirely upon the identity of the σάρξ which was made into the body of Christ with our own—an idea certainly in which great difficulty is involved, since the destruction of the flesh in the person of Christ has quite a different meaning from its destruction in Christians : in the former case, it is the flesh as the natural material of the body; in the latter, the flesh as the moral principle of sin; and thus the subject is the same in both cases, but it is regarded from two widely different points of view. In reality, then, this intermediate idea of the σάρξ only gives apparent help towards the removal of this great difficulty, namely, that, as we have already remarked, the bodily death of Christ is in the course of this argument made absolutely identical with the ethical dying of the old man in Christians. We shall, however, find the solution of this difficulty in the psycho-

logical genesis of the dogmatic idea, in that immediate or unreasoned mystic faith, which feels that in devotion to the
crucified "the old has passed away, and all has become new."
On this basis of immediate religious emotion the dogmatic
difficulties of the theory of expiation, as well as of the destruction of the flesh, are resolved, and, at the same time, these two
coalesce into unity; it is one and the same revelation of the
love of God in Christ which becomes, to the believer who grate-
fully gives himself up to it, at once the peace of reconciliation
and the strength of the new life.

The Resurrection of Christ.

The resurrection of Christ presents itself to the Apostle's
mind, not as a new and special source of salvation, but as the
inseparable reverse side to Christ's death.   And accordingly he
takes it up from different points of view, corresponding to the
different modes in which the whole work of salvation may be
regarded.

In the first place, the rising from the dead of the crucified
Jesus, as delivered to him by the tradition of the Christian
community and confirmed by his own visions, is the ground of
his belief in the death of Jesus as a Messianic death of expiation ; the rising from the dead had to his mind the force of a
divine announcement that the crucified was the Messiah.   This
accords so entirely with the nature of the thing, with the course
of thought which pervades the apologetic writings of the primitive Church, and with Paul's own account of his conversion, that
it scarcely needs to be confirmed by the express words of the
Apostle.   He says (1 Cor. xv. 17), "If Christ be not risen, then
is your faith void ; ye are yet in your sins ;" that is to say, the
faith that his death serves to redeem us from our sins would in
that case be groundless and worthless.   Inasmuch as the resurrection of Christ is, according to this passage, not indeed the

means of redemption, but the ground of the belief in the redeeming power of the death of Christ, Paul's Christian faith in
redemption may be accurately designated as faith in the resurrection of Christ from the dead (Rom. x. 9); not because this
formed the *real substance* of his believing consciousness—this
must rather be sought in the religious idea of the doctrine of the
atonement—but because it formed for him the *logical ground*
of the possibility of believing in the crucified,[1] as from the
Jewish point of view is quite natural. The same line of thought
serves to explain Rom. iv. 25, "*Christ was given over* (to death)
for our transgressions, and raised again for our justification," i. e.
the objective expiation of our transgressions is completed by the
death of Christ; but as this expiatory means can only lead to
the justification of individuals through faith (Rom. iii. 25,
ἱλαστήριον διὰ τῆς πίστεως), and faith can only come into existence
on the ground of the resurrection, therefore the resurrection was
the necessary means for the justifying work of salvation performed by the expiation through his death, and was consequently
the intermediate cause of subjective justification, while his death
was the direct cause of the objective cancelling of sins. Accordingly we have here also, not two co-ordinate causes of salvation,
each with its separate effect, but one and the same effect of
salvation, which has in the death of Christ its real cause, and in
his resurrection the logical ground of the possibility of its subjective appropriation by faith.[2]

¹ This distinction ought to be borne in mind in deciding the question of the *permanent dogmatic significance* of belief in the resurrection, more than it usually is by
apologetic writers of the present day, who represent the inseparability of belief in the
resurrection from belief in Christ—self-evident as this is from the Jewish point of
view—as an unconditional and permanent postulate of Christian faith. This is a very
superficial and short-sighted way of dealing with the question, and one which ends in
very serious injury to their own position. It is one of the most painful signs of the
times, that in such matters—simple as they really are—a calm and clear insight is
rendered impossible by the prejudices of ecclesiastical party spirit. A great part of
the blame is undoubtedly due to clerical journals like the "Neue Evangelische," which
immediately drag every question of objective science into the arena of their ecclesiastical party warfare, to the discredit alike of science and of the Church.

² This explanation is supported by most of the commentators. The other, which
refers δικαίωσις to sanctification (according to Catholic commentators, and recently

Still Paul regards the resurrection of Christ, not merely as this indirect means of becoming a believer, and therefore of the subjective appropriation of salvation, but also as a direct element of the work of salvation itself, namely, as the exaltation of the crucified as the Lord of the Christian community.   Phil. ii. 9, "*For this* (i. e. as a reward for his obedience unto death) *has God also exalted him, and given him a name that is above every name, that at the name of Jesus every knee should bend, of those who are of heaven, and those who are of earth, and those who are under the earth, and every tongue should confess that Jesus Christ is Lord, to the honour of God the Father.*"   But this exaltation simply coincides in the mind of the Apostle with the raising from the dead, as he never mentions the ascension, but rather understands the Lordship of Christ always as the immediate consequence of his resurrection.   Thus Rom. xiv. 9, "*Therefore has Christ died and risen again, and become alive, that he might be Lord both of the dead and of the living.*"   To the two-fold state of abasement and exaltation correspond the two classes of his subjects, the dead and the living: and as the latter are again divided into earthly and heavenly, the triple realm of Christ's dominion comes out more clearly as described in the passage quoted above from the Philippians, which is so far from going beyond the sphere of Paul's ideas, that it only expresses more accurately the sense of Rom. xiv. 9.   Now as we saw above that the dying of Christ for all transformed itself in the Apostle's mind into a dying of all with and in Christ, in the same way and in connection with this idea the resurrection of Christ as Lord over all becomes *a rising of all with and in Christ*, their life for him or in his *service* becomes a life in mystical communion with him or in his *spirit*. As Christ at his resurrection passed over into a new state of existence as contrasted with his life on earth—that of pure spirit —so a new life begins for the believer with his entrance into the

again *R. Schmidt*, ut supra, p. 74, "Entrance upon a new state of life no longer conditioned by the flesh"), is inconsistent with Paul's use of the word δικαίωσις, which in Rom. iv., if anywhere, means imputed justification, and nothing else.

possession of Christ at baptism; he becomes a new creature who has the same spirit which forms the life of the exalted Christ, as the determining principle of his life; he therefore obtains a personal share in the life of Christ risen, which thus becomes the common life of the Christian community, which is the mystical body of Christ. Thus the resurrection of Christ has no longer for the religious intelligence the significance of a merely single external and individual event, but becomes the beginning of a continuous creative process in the community, and of the working of that life-giving principle which the community has in common with Christ, the πνεῦμα ζωοποιοῦν. From this point of view it is no longer a question of the mere holding of the truth of an external fact as a miraculous exertion of the power of God, but of the *practical* γνῶναι τὴν δύναμιν τῆς ἀναστάσεως αὐτοῦ, Phil. iii. 10; of the συνεγερθῆναι διὰ τῆς πίστεως, Col. ii. 12; of the σύμφυτον γενέσθαι τῷ ὁμοιώματι τῆς ἀναστάσεως, Rom. vi. 5; in short, of the *real* συζῆν αὐτῷ, ζῶντας τῷ θεῷ ἐν Χριστῷ Ἰησοῦ, ib. vers. 8, 11. The details of this subject belong to the doctrine of the πνεῦμα, chap. v.: we will only observe here in general terms how completely the exalted Christ coincides in the religious consciousness of the Apostle with the πνεῦμα Χριστοῦ sent by God; for the only function which he ascribes to the latter during the whole interval until the coming again of Christ, *intercession with the Father for the faithful* (Rom. viii. 34), is ascribed in the same Epistle (ver. 26), and in precisely similar terms, to the Holy Spirit; but neither the sending of the Spirit nor the organization of the community by the distribution of offices and gifts is ever referred by Paul to the exalted Christ, but only to God himself (it is otherwise with the later author of the Epistle to the Ephesians).

Finally, the Apostle constantly brings *the resurrection of Christ into the closest connection with that of Christians;* partly in the sense that the certain warrant of our hope, or the ground which religion supplies for our belief in our own resurrection, lies in the raising of Christ, as an effect of the Divine favour which sealed the work of redemption; but partly also in the sense that we have the spirit of Christ's life, and therewith the real operative principle of our own resurrection, dwelling in us through the mystical communion with the risen Christ. As a matter of history external to us, the resurrection of Christ is the ground of faith: through the communion of faith with him who has risen, it is the real ground of our own resurrection, or of the completion of the work of salvation, of our eternal life. But these two points of view so completely interpenetrate each other, that they cannot be sharply separated: compare Rom. viii. 11, vi. 8; 1 Cor. xv. 13—22; 2 Cor. iv. 10—14. The further discussion of this subject will be resumed in the chapter on the completion of the work of salvation.

CHAPTER III.

THE PERSON OF JESUS CHRIST.

IT is now becoming generally acknowledged that the teaching of Paul regarding Christ is not founded on a historical knowledge of the details of the life of Jesus. This is proved in part *indirectly* by the silence of the Apostle in cases where the recollection of the life of the historical Jesus would most naturally have been suggested by the context; partly by his *direct* declarations regarding the nature and the origin of his idea of Christ. With respect to the first, the way in which the Apostle impresses on his readers the self-sacrificing love of their neighbour by the example of Christ is significant: of the many instances which might have been drawn from the public ministrations of Jesus to enforce this, not one occurs to him, but he calls to mind either Christ's having suffered death, in general terms (2 Cor. v. 14), or, when he would exhibit it in greater detail, he refers not to historical circumstances, but to a passage of the Psalms, which he interprets as a typical foreshowing of the fate of the Christians and of Christ (Rom. xv. 3); or, finally, he takes as the example of self-sacrificing love the act of becoming man, in which he who existed before the worlds "became poor for your sakes," or "emptied himself," ἑαυτὸν ἐκένωσε (2 Cor. viii. 9; Phil. ii. 7). It is more than probable that one who had so far to seek for an example of self-sacrificing love, had no precise information regarding the circumstances of the historical life of Jesus which lay much nearer to hand.

This view is confirmed by the direct declarations of the Apostle. When he says in Gal. i. 11 f., that he had received his gospel, not from man, but by revelation from Jesus Christ, his meaning is primarily, that the peculiar way in which he understood and proclaimed the message of Christ did not depend upon the authority of man, but on the direct authority of God. Now although this does not directly exclude the possibility of any information regarding the historical Jesus conveyed in the way of ordinary experience, yet it certainly implies so much as this, that whatever information of that kind might have reached him was not of essential import for his religious intuition of the personality of Christ. For in this case alone could he so distinctly aver that the authority of the community, highly regarded as it was, had contributed nothing to that perception of evangelical truth which he derived from a revelation of God (ii. 6). And when he writes to the Corinthians that he determined to know nothing among them but Jesus Christ " *and him as the crucified*" (1 Cor. ii. 2), does he not plainly say, that for his dogmatic teaching concerning Christ, the one fact of the death of Jesus on the cross, apart from all the other circumstances of his historical appearance and life on earth, was all that he regarded ? But this dogmatic indifference to the historical life of Jesus really presupposes a lack of historical knowledge of that life, and was only possible at all on this ground. An attempt has certainly been made to prove the contrary from 2 Cor. v. 16 ; but it happens that this passage, in the first place, affirms once more that Paul had acquired his present Christian perception of Christ quite independently of any previous knowledge whatever of the historical Jesus; so far, therefore, it is at all events a confirmation of the essential point with which we are here concerned, namely, that the dogmatic teaching of Paul regarding Christ did not depend on historical knowledge of Jesus. But, further, it could hardly be inferred from this passage that he ever had such knowledge at all, for the abstract hypothetical sentence, εἰ καὶ ἐγνώκαμεν, &c., by no means necessarily refers in the concrete to Paul himself, but in all probability (for more details on this point, see below, Chap. viii.) only to his opponents. We have no reason, then, beforehand to expect in the teaching of Paul as to Christ anything else than a *free Christian speculation regarding the contents of the Christian consciousness*, which expresses the essence of the Christian principle of salvation in the form of declarations regarding the person of Jesus.

THE SON OF DAVID AND THE SON OF GOD.

The ideas which form the groundwork of Paul's Christology are indicated by the pregnant sentences with which he opens the exposition of his doctrine in the Epistle to the Romans, i. 3 f. He designates as the substance of the gospel of God which had been announced beforehand by the prophets in the Holy Scriptures, " *his* (God's) *Son, who* (on the one hand) *was born of the seed of David as regards his flesh, and who* (on the other hand) *was destined* (or instituted) *to be the Son of God with power as regards the spirit of holiness, after his resurrection from the dead* (then putting both these sides together), *Jesus Christ, our Lord.*" Thus much at least is clear in this passage—the redeemer, who is the object of the message of salvation, is indicated *at first in general terms* as the *Son of God*, who was announced beforehand by the prophets in the Holy Scriptures, i.e. as *the Messiah*. His readers could have understood the idea here conveyed to them (before further details were added) in no other sense, and in this sense they were also meant to understand it; for in the mind of Paul himself the saving power of the name of Jesus the crucified was simply contained in his Messiahship (attested by his rising from the dead). But, taken in this sense, the idea had many meanings, and was to a certain extent indefinite; for the word "Messiah" indicates primarily nothing more than a mission, vocation, and dignity in the Divine economy of salvation, without any statement as to the nature of the personality, or the function of its distinctive dignity. For this reason the general

description at first put forth required a more particular specifi-
cation, which, together with the statement of the essential peculiarity of the person, should at the same time contain the ground
of his mission as Messiah, and should thus add the material
characteristics to that indefinite and formal title. Now the
Apostle states this more precise definition in a very skilful
manner, giving to the general notion put forth in a formal sense
a two-fold foundation and a two-fold meaning; one is, that side
of the Messiah's personality which was in the eyes of the Jewish
Christians the essential, but in the eyes of Paul the subordinate
side; the other is, that which to the Jewish Christians was an
accident, but to Paul the substance. On the one hand, Jesus was
the promised *son of David;* this Judaistic material definition of
the divine sonship of Jesus is not denied by Paul, but put
forth as held in common by him with his Judaistic readers : but
that which was in the eyes of the latter the whole, or at least
the essential part, of that idea, is to Paul only one element in it,
and in fact only the external and unessential element—κατὰ
σάρκα. It is only in the flesh, only in its physical external
aspect, that the person of Jesus has that advantage of the sonship
of David which is regarded by the Judaizers as the chief thing;
which is as good as saying that this does not exhaust the
Messianic *divine sonship.* On the contrary, he goes on to say,
the true essence of it consists in the spiritual inner side of the
personality of the Messiah, in so far as this has as its characteristic the spirit of holiness. The expression, κατὰ πνεῦμα ἀγιωσύνης,
is purposely chosen; κατὰ πνεῦμα by itself only forms the opposition to κατὰ σάρκα as (anthropologically) indicating the
immaterial inner side of the personality, opposed to the material
outward side of the body; but the addition of the qualitative
genitive ἀγιωσύνης shows that the spiritual inner side of *this* personality has a spiritual nature specifically distinct from ordinary human nature, namely, a holy nature, in no degree influenced
by the sinful principle of the flesh, and that it is just this that
forms the essential ground of the divine sonship. If we con-

sider this carefully, we shall find that it involves a quite essential difference between the definition of Paul and that of the Jewish Christians. According to the latter, the anointing with the Holy Spirit was communicated to the son of David by baptism (for the supernatural begetting was not suggested till after the time of Paul), and as a specific endowment of his Messianic office with divine strength, according to the analogy of institution to the prophetic office, by which the personality, which was in itself purely human, was gifted with strength for its divine functions. According to Paul, on the contrary, the spirit of holiness is that which originally constitutes the person of the Messiah (not something which afterwards comes to it from without), the principle which forms the person, consequently *the very essence of the personality of the Messiah*, and not a mere accident of it. Only thus is it possible, even according to the presuppositions of the Pauline anthropology, that the personality of the Messiah should be really sinless, i.e. only if from the very first it not merely possessed a spiritual capacity (νοῦς), which is powerless in presence of the fleshly substance, but was in its own substance spirit of God's spirit, holy spirit; but if it were this from the very beginning, then a difference is at once expressed between this and every ordinary human person, which extends beyond the realm of ethics into that of metaphysics. The commencement of the essential spiritual being of this person presupposes an existence of this spiritual essence before that commencement, a pre-existence of the spirit which constitutes the person. Although this *presupposition*, which is proved by other passages, is not expressly dwelt on in the passage we are considering, because its point of view is taken from the historical Christ (with reference to his exaltation), yet it is so far from being excluded by the statements here made, that it rather forms the background which completes and explains the whole passage; though of course what the writer is here directly concerned with is what followed rather than what preceded the life of Christ on earth.

The divine sonship attaches to the earthly person of the Redeemer in its spiritual inner aspect indeed from the very beginning, inasmuch as it has the spirit of holiness as its constituting principle, but not yet in complete actuality, since it does not yet attach to it in its outward aspect as manifested on earth; for being the son of David evidently did not exclude debasement and weakness according to the flesh. It is probably this physical element only in the notion of σάρξ that we have to bear in mind here, since on it alone rests the opposition of the earthly existence to that of Christ risen again ἐν δυνάμει. But such a state of contradiction between the inner and outer is inadequate to the complete notion of the divine sonship, which requires not only an inward holy essence, but also an outward existence ἐν δυνάμει. The discrepancy is only resolved in the resurrection, in which the holy spiritual essence obtains a corresponding heavenly spiritual body, and thus the entire person, inward and outward, spirit and body (now no longer "flesh") begins now to lead a life of pure spirituality, to which the full declaration of his power as "Lord" over all externally corresponds. This passage, therefore, does not say of the person of the Redeemer simply that he was the son of God as regards the spirit of holiness, because that notion was not as yet, during his existence in the flesh, completely realized; but it says more accurately that, as regards the spirit of holiness (in virtue of which he was already from the first *potentially* the son of God), he was *instituted* (or destined) to be son of God *in power from the time of his resurrection from the dead;* that is to say, that what he already was from the beginning in himself, but in inward fashion only, and not in outward manifestation, that he became in the complete actuality of an existence in power, no longer hampered by any weakness of the flesh, from the time of his resurrection, which clothed his pure spiritual inward part with a corresponding body formed of a supernatural substance. Thus the resurrection of the Redeemer was his *actual institution into the full possession of the divine sonship,* inasmuch as this required not

only a holy spiritual existence inwardly, but also outwardly an
existence in power and heavenly Lordship; but that inner side
was nevertheless from the beginning the real ground of that
divine sonship, which was, as it were, still latent and immanent,
until it was externally realized after his resurrection. Accordingly we must not weaken the force of the word ὁρισθέντος by
supposing that it merely indicates a proof or evidence for the
perception and recognition of men; ὁρίζειν nowhere has this
meaning, but it is always an actual making of something, by the
intervention of an act of the will, whether the effect of this act
takes place at once, or not until some future time: in the former
case it is equivalent to instituting, in the latter equivalent to
destining to something; either of these meanings is equally applicable in this passage, and both, in fact, result in the same sense;
yet inasmuch as in any case the effect of the act of the Divine
will with regard to the person of the Redeemer is connected with
the moment of the resurrection, the latter forms the intermediate
cause (and not only the logical ground of perception) of the
realization of a divine sonship. But we must be equally on our
guard against so far exaggerating, on the other hand, the force of
ὁρισθέντος—ἐξ ἀναστάσεως, as to understand by this expression,
that the person of Jesus was in no sense, that is to say not even
inwardly, during his life on earth, the son of God, and that this
idea refers only to the external establishment of the power of
Christ when exalted to his heavenly Lordship. If it were so,
the passage would certainly stand in glaring and unintelligible contradiction to the clearest passages in other parts of the
Apostle's writings, as we shall shortly see, in which the divine
sonship indicates a characteristic of the person of Jesus inherent
in it from its (pre-existent) origin, and therefore a metaphysical
characteristic of its essence, and not merely the establishment
of his theocratic power. But this limitation of the meaning of
the divine sonship is not only contradicted by these other passages, but also by the words κατὰ πνεῦμα ἁγιωσύνης in the passage
before us; for these words plainly declare that the (external)

K

institution of the Redeemer into the full possession of the divine
sonship from the time of the resurrection, had its real ground in
a principle of divine sonship which already inwardly existed
before this time, namely, in the spirit of holiness, which, according to what has been stated above, we must conceive in no
merely ethical sense, but as a spiritual entity, which was actual
from the beginning in the sense of pre-existent. The decisive
words ὁρισθέντος—δυνάμει, therefore, can only be rightly understood, if each of the more definitive expressions, κατὰ πν. ἁγ. and
ἐξ ἀναστάσεως, be allowed its due force, the former as indicating
the inner real ground, the latter as a statement of the external
means to the complete realization of the divine sonship; or, in
other words, the one exhibiting the essential and original *principle* of the divine sonship, which consituted the pre-existent
personality of Christ, the other the beginning in time of its outward manifestation.[1]

Since, according to the foregoing view, the Pauline Christ is
in his essence spirit, to which essence his existence in the supra-
mundane sphere alone completely corresponds, the more precise
consideration of this Christology must, in accordance with the
Apostle's view, start from the *heavenly* condition of Christ, on
the one hand as the exalted one, and on the other hand as
existing before the world, and pass from this to his *earthly*
life.

---

[1] The explanation of this passage here given is essentially the same as that of
Weiss, p. 291 ; *R. Schmidt*, pp. 119, 157. *Baur*, p. 189, still adheres to the older
rendering of ὁρισθέντος = "proved." *Holsten*, p. 426, and note on p. 181, thinks
that the passage contains essentially the Christology of the Jewish Christians (though
with traces of that of Paul), and consequently finds a contradiction between this and
the other teaching of Paul, and a concession to the ideas of the Jewish Christian
reader. This is, however, a very hazardous supposition, and, as I think has been
shown, one that is by no means demanded by the passage. *Meyer's* exposition here
has a dogmatical bias ; he too understands ὁρισθέντος ἐξ ἀναστ., contrary to the
meaning of the words, as the logical ground of knowledge, instead of the actual institution : lastly, it is an utter mistake to suppose that the πνεῦμα ἁγ. is the human
πνεῦμα as containing the holy Logos which became flesh in him, and that so the "spirit
full of holiness" = filled with the holy God or Logos !

CHRIST IN HEAVEN.

That the Apostle held the true nature of Christ to be not realized until his exaltation by means of the resurrection, is proved especially by the important passage, 1 Cor. xv. 45 f. For there can be no doubt that ver. 45 at least does not refer to the mode of Christ's existence in the world or before the world, but to that condition of the exalted Christ which began with the resurrection. This interpretation is supported above all by the context, for in it the nature of the body which is raised is discussed, and in the very preceding verse the spiritual body of the future life is contrasted with the "natural" (i. e. animated) body of the present earthly life. This qualitative difference between the present and the future body is here referred to their respective authors and originators. Our body in this life is animated by a soul, because it is of the same essence with that of Adam, the father of the race, who was made (at the creation) a living soul only; but our future body will be a spiritual one, because it will be of the same essence with that of Christ (not of course the earthly Christ, but Christ glorified by the resurrection), who was made a quickening spirit. The word ἐγένετο, which is understood in the second clause, must necessarily refer to the point of time at which the genus of the spiritual body, or the body which was raised, came into actual existence, as the ἐγένετο of the first clause relates to the point of time at which the genus of the human animated body came into existence; and as the latter was the creative act of God, by which Adam became a living soul, so the former was God's act of raising from the dead, by which Christ was endowed with a spiritual body, and thereby placed in a position to become for humanity also a life-giving principle, the originator of the heavenly humanity. This rendering (and no other) explains how it can be said in ver. 46 that the "natural" was the earlier, and the spiritual the later; both refer to the mode of the existence of the body of men (in this life

after the manner of Adam, in the future life after the manner of
the risen Christ) ; whereas, if the reference were to the being of
Christ in itself or in its pre-existence, we should require the
contrary statement, that the spiritual (the pattern of humanity)
was before the natural (earthly humanity). This *qualitative*
difference between natural and spiritual humanity is, however,
referred in ver. 47 to their different *origin;* the former is earthy
(fleshly), because derived from the earth, the latter is spiritual,
because derived from heaven. As Adam, and men descended
from Adam, could only become living souls because they had
their origin in the unspiritual, un-godlike essence of earthy
matter, so was the last Adam qualified to become a quickening
spirit for humanity because he had his origin in the sphere of
the spiritual divine life, in heaven. Here, however, we cannot
avoid thinking of the origin of the person of Christ from a
heavenly pre-existence ; for as ἐξ οὐρανοῦ in this verse is given
as the *ground* of the second Adam having become spirit (ἐκ γῆς
supplying the ground of the first Adam being earthy or natural),
so it cannot refer to that condition of the exalted one of which
the resurrection was the ground, but must refer to a heavenly
condition which *preceded* the resurrection, and consequently his
whole earthly life, therefore to the condition of the heavenly
pre-existence. Christ was enabled by his resurrection to become
the second Adam, and the originator of a spiritual humanity,
because he had always in himself been so, because he did not
owe his origin to merely natural humanity, but brought from
heaven and put into it the quickening spiritual principle which
had hitherto been wanting to it ; in short, because he was essentially and originally (and not only from the time of his resurrection) a heavenly man. This shows how exactly this passage
agrees with that which was before mentioned (Rom. i. 3 f.), and
completes it, inasmuch as here also the realization of the πνεῦμα
ζωοποιοῦν is, on the one hand, connected with the moment in
time of the resurrection (ἐγένετο, ver. 45) ; while, on the other
hand, this becoming in time is referred to a being before all time

as its real ground (ἐξ οὐρανοῦ, ver. 47).[1] The peculiarity of Paul's Christology consists precisely in the holding together of these two points of view. At the same time, the passage before us shows that it is from the conception of the exalted one that he starts, and that pre-existence is a secondary idea, to which he is led on by the need of finding in a timeless being the ground of the existence in time.

This is confirmed by Rom. viii. 29 : God predestinated his elect to become συμμόρφους τῆς εἰκόνος τοῦ υἱοῦ αὐτοῦ, εἰς τὸ εἶναι αὐτὸν πρωτότοκον ἐν πολλοῖς ἀδελφοῖς. This being conformed to the image of the Son of God, to which Christians are predestinated, must be the same as that which is indicated in the next verse by the word δοξάζειν as the final end of the divine act of favour, that is, the being glorified in the heavenly state of existence ; and similarly, according to ver. 23, the υἱοθεσία which is still to be waited for, will come with the ἀπολύτρωσις τοῦ σώματος ἡμῶν—that is to say, with the putting off of the fleshly and putting on of the heavenly body, or with the resurrection. With this is connected also the divine purpose, that Christ should become "the first-born among many brethren." As Christians attain to the υἱοθεσία (in the absolute sense which is not yet realized here) through their resurrection, so they become by this means later-born brothers of the first-born; thus Christ is the first-born Son of God, as having gone before to lead the way for the others in the resurrection from the dead ; as ἀπαρχὴ τῶν κεκοιμημένων, 1 Cor. xv. 20; as πρωτότοκος ἐκ τῶν νεκρῶν, Col. i. 18.

---

[1] Compare *Weiss*, p. 293. His exposition entirely agrees with that which has been given here, with one exception : he conceives the words ὁ δεύτερος ἄνθρωπος ἐξ οὐρανοῦ to indicate that the second man as to his origin is from heaven, but not also that he had already been there *as such* (man). This he considers an arbitrary assumption, while it appears to me to be an inevitable inference : on this subject more will be said hereafter. Therefore *R. Schmidt* (ut supra, p. 116 f.) appears to me to argue more consistently than *Weiss* when he declares that there is no reference at all in ver. 47 to the origin of the person of Christ from a heavenly pre-existence ; but *Weiss* agrees with me in showing that this is contradicted by the context. I agree, again, with both these commentators that this passage contains no reference to Philo's doctrine of ideal humanity, which likewise cannot be inferred from my view of ver. 47, but, on the contrary, is quite alien to the entire context of the passage : of this more below.

Thus in him also the *completion* of the υἱότης is connected with his resurrection, in the same way as for the Christians the completion of their υἱοθεσία follows upon their resurrection.   But, as in the case of the latter, at least the ἀπαρχὴ πνεύματος, and indeed πνεύματος υἱοθεσίας, is already in them during their earthly life of faith (ver. 23 compared with 15), so also Christ by no means became by his resurrection for the first time υἱὸς θεοῦ; he was always so in himself (κατὰ πνεῦμα ἁγιωσύνης); but only by his resurrection did he become the operative principle by which men are converted into children of God, and thus the first-born among many brethren.

That the exalted Christ is the pattern for Christians to copy, and at the same time the operative principle of their formation after that pattern, is also said in 2 Cor. iii. 18: "We are changed to the same image from (his) glory to (our) glory (since it comes to us from him), as might well be expected from the Lord, who is spirit." The most pregnant expression for this essence of the exalted one, in himself and in his relation to the community, is to be found in ver. 17, ὁ κύριος τὸ πνεῦμά ἐστιν; his Lordship depends on his being spirit, which is also the very essence of his sonship.   Because he is exalted by his resurrection above all earthly limitation and weakness, and instituted into the pure ideal existence of an ἄνθρωπος πνευματικὸς or ἐπουράνιος, of a υἱὸς θεοῦ ἐν δυνάμει, so by the same means he has obtained the dignity and dominion of a κύριος over the Christian community, and under God over the whole creation.   Although his κυριότης extends primarily over the community, whose head he is, yet all other creatures, both those in heaven and those on the earth, and those under the earth, must do him homage (Phil. ii. 10 f.); for we know that all things must work together for good to the community of them that love God (Rom. viii. 28), and the hope and the longing of the whole creation is to obtain a part in the freedom of the glorified children of God (ib. ver. 21). 1 Cor. x. 26 may also be quoted in support of what has been said, in which passage, although τοῦ κυρίου is a translation of the Jehovah of the Old Testament, yet it is without doubt applied here to Christ. This connection of ideas is exhibited in 1 Cor. iii. 22 f., πάντα ὑμῶν ἐστι, ὑμεῖς δὲ Χριστοῦ, Χριστὸς δὲ θεοῦ.

But the exalted one is the *pattern of the community* only because he is at the same time, as pure πνεῦμα, the perfect *image of God;* and he is *Lord of the world* only inasmuch as he is the perfectly obedient *instrument of the Father.* As the faithful are changed into the image of Christ by the reflection of his δόξα on their πρόσωπον (2 Cor. iii. 18), so Christ is εἰκὼν τοῦ θεοῦ because the δόξα τοῦ θεοῦ appears on his πρόσωπον (iv. 4, 6). Because the brilliant light which is everywhere the manifestation of the πνεῦμα (2 Cor. iii. 8, and above), and forms a special attribute of the majesty of God, belongs to Christ the exalted one, the essence of God himself, so far as it is capable of manifestation, is revealed and made visible in him, and the knowledge of Christ obtained by means of the gospel thus becomes at the same time knowledge of God. But this being the very image of God is so far from being equal to Him, that, on the contrary, Christ's Lordship over the community and the world implies his unconditional subordination to God. As we are Christ's, so Christ is God's (1 Cor. iii. 23); as he is head of the community, so God is κεφαλὴ Χριστοῦ (xi. 3). By God he is exalted to be Lord, to the honour of God he exercises his Lordship, and into God's hands he gives it back at last (Phil. ii. 9, 11; 1 Cor. xv. 24, 28).

Thus Christ as the exalted is, in the eyes of the Apostle, essentially the Lord who is spirit, spiritual or heavenly man, and as such the pattern of Christian humanity; at the same time, the very image and Son of God, spirit of his spirit, and light of his light; finally, Lord and head of the community, in the service of God the Father. But certain as it is that this picture of Christ was originally taken from the conception of the risen and exalted one, it is no less certain that it did not remain thus confined. *The picture of the exalted one threw back its reflection,* not upon the earthly existence (which was rather, as existence in the flesh, externally the exact opposite to the condition of the exalted one, being a condition of humiliation and weakness), but rather into the blank vacuity of his timeless existence in supra-mundane regions before his appearance in time; *that which was brought into being at a certain point of time by the exaltation required, in order to become fixed in the Christian consciousness as unconditional certainty and necessity, a deeper foundation in the timeless being of the heavenly world, in pre-existence.* There ought never to have been any doubt that this was Paul's teaching, for it is contained, sometimes directly, sometimes indirectly, in various passages of *every one* of the Epistles.

When it is said in Rom. viii. 3, Gal. iv. 4, " God sent his Son in the likeness of sinful flesh, born of a woman and placed under the law," the explanatory words indubitably prove that the writer is here speaking, not of the sending of the earthly Jesus in the discharge of his office, but of the sending forth of a being who up to that time had not been an earthly man, but who, in consequence of this sending, took upon him the form of sinful flesh by being born of a woman, and was placed under the law, and who therefore pre-existed up to that time in a state of fleshless or spiritual being, and of lawless or son-like relation to God. What can be meant by these explanations, which would have been quite superfluous if applied to an ordinary man and a Jew, if they do not here refer to a subject regarding whom the statement of them would not be superfluous—to a subject, therefore, who had pre-existed in another form of being before he was born? It is, however, a real subject, a concrete personality, which enters upon these different conditions, and not a mere abstract principle which is only real in the Divine thought, without subsistency of its own.[1]   For how could it be said of a

---

[1] This view is opposed to *Beyschlag*, Christologie des N. T. (p. 243); he thinks "the heavenly man as pre-existent could only be a second person by the side of the Father, a personality independent of God the Father, if Paul ascribed to him in his pre-existence all that belongs to a real man, therefore πνεῦμα and σάρξ (!), and a development of life dependent on both these; but this would be so absurd a concep-

principle, that it was sent in sinful flesh, and born of a woman, and placed under the law? Was it the principle of spiritual quickening which was made subject to the laws of material being and growth (and if so, of course also to the law of death)? Or was the principle of divine sonship and of freedom subjected to the restraint and curse of the law? These are evidently predicates which cannot possibly be affirmed of an ideal principle, but only of an empirical subject who is limited by individuality.

The two passages which declare the appearance of Christ on earth to have been his own act and deed, by which he gave up a higher existence which had preceded it, point to the same conclusion, 2 Cor. viii. 9 and Phil. ii. 6. (Of the latter more will be said hereafter.) The former treats of Christ's work of favour, " *That he who was rich, became poor for your sakes, that you might be made rich by his poverty.*" It is impossible to refer this to the self-denial of the historical Jesus; the aorist ἐπτώχευσε alone would show this, for it denotes an act done once for all, the ceasing of the condition indicated by πλούσιος ὤν, and cannot refer to

tion, that no one would ascribe it to the Apostle, even if it were not expressly excluded by the statement that the Son of God took upon him σάρξ at the time of his earthly birth. Now if Paul conceived the pre-existent to be a heavenly man, and if he could not have conceived the heavenly man to be a real man, then the only alternative is, that he conceived him to be an ideal man." Of course this ideal man must have been a real thought of God, in whom God thought Himself as an *alter ego;* "only it must be understood that this mental reality by no means yields us an independent personality over against God (for where is there any basis for its existence for itself independently of God?), but simply the real principle of one, by the implanting of which in the σάρξ the real personality first comes into being." So says *Beyschlag.* That no personal subsistence is possible without matter (σάρξ) is a very bold philosophical thought of the most modern stamp, for the inquiry into the correctness of which this is no place; but how in the world comes a "believing" commentator to make so modern a dictum of philosophy into a canon of his biblical exegesis? And to think of quietly ascribing it to Paul, as if he had never spoken of σώματα ἐπουράνια and πνευμάτικα, and of the incompatibility of this very σάρξ with the kingdom of God, of his future ἐκδημῆσαι ἐκ τοῦ σώματος, and even of an earlier momentary εἶναι χωρὶς τοῦ σώματος (xii. 3)! The fact is, that nothing could be more utterly at variance with Paul's mode of thinking and that of his whole age, than to attribute to him the notion that personal subsistence depends on fleshly existence. And especially with reference to the Christology, it is precisely *that identity of the principle and the concrete person, so confidently denied by Beyschlag, which is the salient point of the dogma of Paul, and of all its further development.*

a state which continues contemporaneously with πλούσιος ὤν. This πλούσιος, again, is evidently to be taken in the same sense as ἵνα ὑμεῖς πλουτήσητε: now since the latter undoubtedly refers to the heavenly dignity which is to be attained by means of Christ, so also the corresponding expression, the being rich of Christ, which is opposed to his becoming poor, relates to the possession of the heavenly dignity which he gave up by entering into the form of flesh. This is the only interpretation which makes the passage agree with its context, without doing violence to either; for it is plain that the Corinthians were not meant to lay to heart the absence of needs to be satisfied, or virtuous poverty, but the duty of self-sacrificing love is to be impressed upon them by the example of Christ, and thus it is not Christ's natural condition of poverty which is to be exhibited here, but a voluntary act of becoming poor, or of *offering up a possession which he had before held;* but this can only be understood with reference to the giving up of the pre-mundane dignity.[1]

This passage contains at the same time an indication of the manner in which the Apostle may have represented to himself the condition of Christ in his pre-existence, viz., as a being rich, that is to say in heavenly dignity, in that δόξα which is the attribute of Divine Majesty, and the final end to which the elect children of God are destined (Rom. viii. 30). As the exalted Christ, by means of the possession of this δόξα, is said to be εἰκὼν τοῦ θεοῦ (2 Cor. iv. 4, 6), so it is perfectly intelligible that the pre-existent Christ also, with reference to this form of appearance in the image of God, is described as ἐν μορφῇ θεοῦ ὑπάρχων (Phil. ii. 6). This by no means implies that he himself was also God (θεὸς ὁ λόγος); on the contrary, the Pauline notion of being in the image of God, as we have already seen, distinctly includes within itself that of being the pattern of hu-

---

[1] *Köstlin* takes a different view, Johann. Lehrbegr., p. 310; he translates, "though he was rich (in spiritual treasures), he became (at the same time materially) poor." The right view will be found in *Räbiger,* de Christol. Paulina, p. 38 f. *Weiss,* Neutest. Theol., p. 296; *R. Schmidt,* Paulin. Christol., p. 144; and *Meyer's* Commentary.

manity.[1] Paul certainly sees the actual pattern of Christians rather in the exalted than in the mundane or the pre-mundane Christ, but only for this reason, that for him the pattern is not a mere passive ideal, but an operative principle, a pattern which forms the copy of itself, and Christ became such for the Christian community for the first time at his exaltation (see above). But as certainly as he who became at his resurrection the "first-born" among the sons of God, was yet for that very reason *in himself* from the beginning the son of God, and as such was sent here from heaven (Gal. iv. 4, comp. Rom. viii. 29), so certainly may he who at his resurrection became a "heavenly man" and the pattern of heavenly humanity, for that reason also have been *in himself* from the beginning a heavenly man, and as such have come here from heaven. And this is exactly what the Apostle says in the plain words, ὁ δεύτερος ἄνθρωπος ἐξ οὐρανοῦ, 1 Cor. xv. 47. For it has already been shown that these words must be referred to the heavenly origin of the person of Christ; but if this be the case, then we cannot without violence reject the idea that this human person who had his origin *from* heaven, had also pre-existed *in* heaven *as man*, that is to say, as "*spiritual man*," as the *same subject*, and in the *same form of existence*, as that in which he continues to live again in heaven as the exalted one; so that the pre-existent may be indicated by the same name as the post-existent ὁ δεύτερος ἄνθρωπος, ὁ κύριος Ἰησοῦς Χριστός (1 Cor. viii. 6). The attempt to avoid this by supposing that Christ is only called the second man from heaven inasmuch as in coming down from heaven he took upon him human nature as an additional element to the

---

[1] Compare Phil. iii. 20 f. "Christ will change our body of humiliation into one made like to the body of his glory." What else can we understand by this σῶμα τῆς δόξης αὐτοῦ than that very μορφὴ θεοῦ in which the exalted one as well as the pre-existent was clothed ? But in that case this μορφὴ θεοῦ also contains nothing which lies outside of the notion of the εἰκὼν τοῦ υἱοῦ θεοῦ, Rom. viii. 29, or that of the δεύτερος ἄνθρωπος ἐξ οὐρανοῦ, whose image we shall all one day bear (1 Cor. xv. 47—49).

divine nature which he had before, is evidently unsatisfactory;[1]
for in that case the subject "man" would not be that which
came from heaven, but only that which came from the earth
and was united to that which came from heaven; the difference
between that which derived its origin ἐκ γῆς and that which
came ἐξ οὐρανοῦ, would in that case relate not to the first and
second man, but to man on the one hand (to Adam as well as
to the humanity of Christ), and on the other hand to God; but
this would give to the whole passage an entirely different meaning from the only one which the words of this verse and the whole
context admit of. We abide, then, by the conclusion that Paul
conceived Christ as a spiritual man not less in his pre-existence
than in his post-existence. And the way in which he came
so to conceive him becomes quite plain to us if we look at the
source whence the whole idea of the pre-existence is derived;
it is the reflection back into the past of the mental image under
which the exalted and glorified Christ was presented to the
imagination of Paul and the whole Christian community as now
living in heaven.

The explanation of these doctrines, then, does not require us
to drag in fragments of Jewish and Alexandrine philosophy, such
as that of the "heavenly ideal man" or "Adam Cadmon." If it
cannot be denied that this idea has a certain relation or similarity to that of the Pauline doctrine regarding Christ, it can as

---

[1] *Räbiger* appears to understand the passage in this sense, ut supra. p. 34 f. The
whole of his argument, not only here, but throughout what is in parts a very careful
and instructive investigation of Pauline Christology, is infected by the fundamental
error of applying categories which are wholly alien to the dogmatic thought of Paul.
Where does Paul speak of "divine nature," or "human nature"? He speaks of
spirit and of flesh, of the son of God, the image and form of God, of the form of the
flesh and of man, of the first and second Adam, the earthy man that is of the earth,
and the heavenly man that is of heaven; but of all these conceptions, which are quite
consistent with each other, not one coincides with the later categories of "divine and
human nature." This argument holds good also against *Grimm*, who finds the divine
nature of the pre-existent taught in· Phil. ii. 6—11 (Z. f. w. Th., 1873, p. 51),
because θεός and ἄνθρωπος form a direct opposition. But the opposition is rather
formed by μορφὴ θεοῦ and ὁμοίωμα ἀνθρώπων, denoting not the essential nature, but
the form.

little be proved that the latter was in any way influenced by it.[1] The passages which are commonly relied upon for this purpose really say nothing to the point. 1 Cor. xv. 45 must, as we have seen, be referred to the resurrection, by which Christ became a quickening spirit and the originator of a new humanity, not to a primitive coming into existence, of which Paul never speaks at all; besides, Christ is here called the "last Adam," the "second man," whereas, according to the Jewish theory of the "heavenly Adam," he ought, on the contrary, to be the first ("Cadmon"). If we look into the matter more closely, we shall see that the meaning and origin of this description of Christ is in Paul's mind something very different from that philosophic notion. It is the historical significance of Christ as the originator of a new spiritual development of humanity, in which righteousness and life bear rule instead of sin and death, and the determining principle of which is no longer the natural and sensuous, but the divine and spiritual. The significance of Christ as the originator of this new spiritual humanity is pregnantly expressed by the name of the "second" or "last Adam." The name, therefore, does not denote an essential characteristic of his personality; neither in 1 Cor. xv. 45, nor in Rom. v. 14, is this directly contained, though it is indirectly implied certainly, inasmuch as the principle of generation of the new humanity appears personified in its originator. But because this new humanity owes its realization to the historical Christ, to his death and resurrection, therefore the name taken from this historical fact belongs *primarily* to the historical Redeemer, not to the pre-existent. It was not until the origin of the historical Redeemer had been ante-dated and thrown back to a period previous to his beginning in time, that, in consequence of the identity of the two subjects, the designation of the historical was extended also to the pre-existent Christ, so that ὁ δεύτερος ἄνθρωπος

---

[1] In this I agree with *Weiss* (p. 294) and *R. Schmidt* (p. 118), in opposition to most of the later commentators (*Beyschlag, Hilgenfeld, Hausrath, Holtzmann, Holsten,* and others).

came to be also the designation of him who came ἐξ οὐρανοῦ, and so of him who was ἐν οὐρανῷ (ver. 47); just as the purely human name Ἰησοῦς is also without hesitation transferred to the pre-existent by whom, under God, all things were created (1 Cor. viii. 6). As it is impossible that a being intermediate between God and the creation, derived from Philonic speculation, should have been endowed with the name of a historical human individual, so it is equally impossible that the name of a " second man" or "*last* Adam," which can only be explained by the *historical consideration of Christ*, should have any meaning when applied to the ideal man of Philonic speculation. On this ground alone we will venture to believe that this designation of Christ by Paul was an original product of his own Christian speculation. It is still possible that he may have combined this independently formed conception, in a supplementary way at least, with that of the ideal man of the Jewish schools of Alexandria. Only no distinct indications of his doing so are forthcoming. Apart from the fact that in this tenet of Alexandrine philosophy there is no suggestion of the entrance of the ideal man into historical actuality, and thus the very essence of the Pauline Christology is wanting, there are no points of contact of any definite kind between the pre-historical Christ and the ideal man of the Alexandrine philosophy. While Paul, extending the designation of the historical Christ to the pre-existent, thinks of this latter also as discharging the office of Mediator of the divine revelation, no agency of this kind is anywhere ascribed to the ideal man of Philo. The part of Mediator is here, on the contrary, assumed by the Logos. *This* notion—and only this—could therefore suggest itself to Christian speculation as a help towards the fixing of the Christological idea in a philosophical form. *After* the time of Paul, this soon happened; but Paul himself draws his Christian ideas from the originality of his own Christian spirit, not from the dicta of an alien philosophy. It is certain, at least, that the proof of the foreign origin of his ideas has still to be found.

It remains that we notice those passages in which Paul ascribes mediative functions to the pre-existent Christ. The operations of Christ did not commence, according to Paul, when he was sent in the flesh; but the Son of God who was destined to fulfil the purpose of the Divine decree of salvation, was, before the time of his appearing on earth, the Mediator and instrument of the divine revelation to Israel. Of this an indication, though certainly a somewhat obscure one, is to be found in 1 Cor. x. 4: the Israelites drank in the desert from a spiritual rock which followed them, "*but this rock was Christ.*" The explanation that the rock only represented Christ is inadmissible, for in that case ἐστί and not ἦν must have been used; and, moreover, by the epithet "spiritual" both rock and water are declared to be objective supersensuous realities, so that we cannot think of a natural rock, to which a typical significance could only be applied by the subjective contemplation of it. We cannot doubt the meaning of the Apostle here to be, that the proofs of the Divine favour were conveyed to Israel by the pre-existent Christ (who as spirit was united to no definite form of flesh); but it is useless to ask how this was effected.

But the part of Mediator was ascribed to the pre-existing Christ, not only in the historical revealing of salvation, but also in the creation of the world itself. This is distinctly stated in 1 Cor. viii. 6: "*We have one God, the Father, from whom all is, and we* (are created) *for Him, and one Lord Jesus Christ, through whom all is, and we through him.*" The words δι' οὗ τὰ πάντα cannot be limited to the sphere of redemption, because they must have the same meaning in the second clause as in the first, where this limitation would be very forced; and because, moreover, through the addition of καὶ ἡμεῖς δι' αὐτοῦ, the sphere of Christian redemption is represented as a particular and a narrower one within the general sphere of creation (τὰ πάντα), from which it follows that the latter is applied to the world in the metaphysical sense. But this juxtaposition certainly shows at the same time that the idea of Christ's agency in the creation of the world did not grow

out of metaphysical speculation in the Apostle's mind, but was
simply an extension of the mediatorial position held by Christ
as the Redeemer in the scheme of salvation.   For the Christian
consciousness, Christ is the one Lord over all, to whom all
things, even the powers of the invisible world (gods and lords
of the heathen, ib. ver. 5), are subject; and this *religious* conviction (the same as that which is expressed in other words in
Rom. viii. 37—39) finds its expression in the theological doctrine of the agency of Christ in the creation of the world.
This contains also the inference, which was self-evident to the
Apostle, but is only too often overlooked by commentators, that
the instrument of creation is precisely the same subject as the
instrument of redemption, namely, "*the one Lord Jesus Christ*,"
the self-same personality of Christ which, as it appeared in the
flesh, was Jesus the son of David, the historical Redeemer, and
who again through his resurrection became a pure spiritual
man, and the son of God with power.   By the application here
of the two predicates, δι' οὖ τὰ πάντα and δι' οὖ ἡμεῖς, thus
directly and in equal measure to the *one* subject, Jesus Christ
(the two-fold name also here deserves attention), any separation
between the pre-existent son and agent of God in the creation,
and the historical redeemer and mediator of the atonement, is
distinctly precluded.   It is just the identity of the person which,
for the dogmatic conception, forms the thread on which to string
the various predicates and bind them together into a single
picture of the salvation ; although the unity of this picture must
of necessity part asunder again for intelligent thought, since the
predicates which it presents together are in themselves quite
heterogeneous, that is to say partly ideal, relating to the absolute principle of salvation, partly empirical and capable of being
directly predicated only of the historical Mediator of salvation.[1]

---

[1] It is clear from the above analysis of this passage that *Weiss* and *Baur* are both
mistaken in presupposing the incompatibility of the two predicates, heavenly man and
instrument of creation, and consequently eliminating the former (Weiss) or the latter
(Baur) from Paul's conception of the pre-existent Christ.   It is only necessary to pay

If we compare the passage just noticed with the Christological declarations of the *Epistle to the Colossians*, i. 15—19, we shall find that the difference is not so great as it has been often repre- sented. In the latter, Christ is called the "first-born before every creature," through whom all things in heaven and on the earth, visible and invisible, especially all the powers of the in- visible (spirit) world were created; but this is just the meaning of 1 Cor. viii. 6; and even the pointing out of the spirit world especially as a sphere created by Christ, and entirely subordi- nated to him, has a certain analogy to the passage in the Corinth- ians, inasmuch as in the latter, by the connection between verses 5 and 6, the unique position of Christ as the instrument of creation is asserted with special reference to the θεοὶ καὶ κύριοι of the heathen, and so to the realm of demons. In other points, however, the passage in the Colossians certainly goes beyond that in the Corinthians; the world, according to the former, has not only been created by the agency of Christ, but "*in him and for him,*" which seems to imply that Christ was the world's centre, the point from which the powers and the development of the world originated, and to which they return as their end. But this is not agreeable to Paul's older doctrine, for only of God himself does he say ἐξ αὐτοῦ καὶ δι' αὐτοῦ καὶ εἰς αὐτὸν τὰ πάντα (Rom. xi. 36); even the Lordship of Christ is not, according to him, an end in itself, but is to serve to the δόξα of God, which is exclusively the final end of the universe (ib., Phil. ii. 11); nay, it is at a future time to be given back again to the Father, in order that God may be τὰ πάντα ἐν πᾶσι. The expression εἰς αὐτὸν (Χριστόν) τὰ πάντα ἔκτισται in the Colos- sians can hardly be reconciled with this strict assertion of mono- theism by the unconditional subordination of Christ to the Father. But verse 19 in particular diverges most decidedly from the Pauline Christology. The expression πᾶν τὸ πλήρωμα is, according to the parallel passage, ii. 9, the fulness of the God-

attention to the psychological genesis of the whole conception, in order to be convinced that those predicates are quite compatible with each other for such a mind as Paul's.

L

head, the concentration of all the powers which constitute the Divine nature. Paul never says that these dwell in Christ, not even in Phil. ii. 6, where the μορφὴ θεοῦ refers only to the form of his appearance, the σῶμα τῆς δόξης (see above); but that this fulness of the Godhead should have taken up its abode in the *earthly* Christ (for so we must understand Col. i. 19, on account of its connection with ver. 20), is directly contradictory to that which we shall shortly see to have been the older Pauline view of Christ's becoming man. And since in the very *last* letter of Paul, namely, that to the Philippians, the view of the earthly life of Christ as a condition of emptiness and humiliation is insisted upon with the greatest distinctness, we cannot here have recourse to the conclusion that Paul himself developed and expanded his Christology in the direction of John's teaching. Now if we are unwilling to pronounce the Epistle to the Colossians altogether spurious, there appears to be scarcely any other way out of the difficulty than to suppose that this, as well as other passages of this Epistle, was tampered with at a later period. We shall therefore recur to this at a future time.

THE APPEARING OF CHRIST IN THE FLESH.

As the pre-existence of Christ was in the mind of the Apostle only a secondary conception, being but the reflection of his intuition of the exalted one, and assumed as a background for that intuition, we cannot wonder that he teaches us so little, in any definite shape, regarding the passage from it to the earthly life of Christ. All that we can lay hold of consists of a few indications only. According to Rom. viii. 3, Gal. iv. 4, it is God who, after the completion of the time (of preparation), sent his son in the form of sinful flesh, which was done by means of his being born of a woman. According to 2 Cor. viii. 9 and Phil. ii. 7, it is Christ himself who becomes poor, empties himself of his possessions, in order to descend from the condition of

being rich, of possessing a heavenly Lordship, of being in the
form of God, to a condition of poverty, and humiliation, and of
existence in the visible shape of man, and the form of a servant.
These two passages contain essentially the same idea, only it is
more expanded in that from the Philippians; and both alike
were written with a hortatory object (not in the interest of
transcendental Gnostic speculation); in one, the Apostle impresses on the Corinthians the duty of self-sacrificing love, by
the example of Christ, who became poor for our sakes; in the
other, he impresses on the Philippians the duty of humility and
self-forgetfulness, which seeks not its own, but that of others;
and as an example of this humble, self-forgetting disposition,[1]
he holds up to them the example of Christ, "*who, being in the
form of God, thought it not robbery to be equal with God, but
emptied himself in taking on him the form of a servant, that is to
say, he was born in the likeness of men, and was found in the condition of an* (ordinary) *man.*" It has been already remarked on
the words ἐν μορφῇ θεοῦ ὑπάρχων, that they mean nothing else
than the εἰκὼν and δόξα θεοῦ. The only difficulty is in the words
οὐχ ἁρπαγμὸν ἡγήσατο τὸ εἶναι ἴσα θεῷ. It is the first canon of all
sound criticism that a passage must be explained first of all by
itself and the context, and then by the views contained in other
parts of the author's writings; and only when both these re-
sources have failed, by external references and allusions. Let
us set aside, therefore, all explanations of these words drawn
from foreign theories, whether from Gnosticism or from the Old
Testament history of the fall,[2] and endeavour to explain them

---

[1] *Hinsch*, in his article entitled "Untersuchungen zum Philipperbrief" (Z. f. w.
Th., 1873, p. 77), makes the groundless assertion that the view taken in this
passage of Christ's becoming man is un-Pauline, because it is made to "appear
as a voluntary resolve on the part of Christ, the primary object of which was a
purely personal one." And yet the sole aim of the whole passage is to recommend
unselfishness, the not τὰ ἑαυτῶν σκοπεῖν, by the example of Christ, who in the free
(but not therefore arbitrary) act of becoming man, gave the greatest example of unselfishness. It is not easy to understand how any one can find anything un-Pauline in
this view, which is exactly that of 2 Cor. viii. 9.

[2] The former, as is well known, is the explanation of *Baur*, the latter that of
Ernesti. I consider it needless to attempt a fuller refutation of either of these, for,

from the context alone. They are opposed to ἐκένωσεν ἑαυτόν, that is, to the self-sacrificing mode of action, of which Christ is held up as an example; accordingly, ἁρπαγμὸν ἡγήσατο τὸ εἶναι ἴσα θεῷ, if Christ had done it, would have fallen under the category of τὸ ἑαυτῶν ἕκαστον σκοπεῖν; it would have been an act of selfish arrogation (opposed to ταπεινοφροσύνη and τὰ ἑτέρου σκοπεῖν, vers. 3, 4). But this is just the obvious meaning of the words ἁρπαγμὸν ἡγήσατο :[1] they express in a figurative manner the disposition and mode of action of one who in selfish arrogance only τὸ ἑαυτοῦ σκοπεῖ; for it is of the essence of robbing and the robber not to trouble oneself about the welfare of any one else, but with inconsiderate selfishness to seek one's own advantage. What Christ might have striven after in this selfish, grasping manner, if he had wished it, is expressed by the words τὸ εἶναι ἴσα θεῷ; they must therefore indicate something beyond and

according to my principles, the ground of such attempts at explanation vanishes as soon as it is shown that the passage can be explained from itself. Compare *Räbiger*, ut supra, pp. 77—85 ; *Hilgenfeld*, Z. f. w. Th., 1871, 194 f. ; *Grimm*, ib., 1873, 45 ; *Schmidt*, p. 176.

[1] The literal translation of the words is rapinam, i. e. rapiendum putavit, did not consider the being equal with God a thing to be seized by an act of robbery ; but the expression ἁρπαγμὸν ἡγήσατο is used instead of ἥρπασε, in order to show that the essential point here is the mode of thinking, the disposition, of which Christ gave an example. The objection that ἁρπαγμός is not equivalent to ἅρπαγμα, that which is robbed, but to ἁρπάζειν, robbing, would, if it were valid, alter the literal translation, but not the general sense of the passage. In that case, the being equal with God would be not the object of the robbery, but the means to it, which Christ possessed in virtue of his μορφὴ θεοῦ ; and thus τὸ ἴσα θεῷ εἶναι would come to have the same meaning as ἐν μορφῇ θεοῦ ὑπάρχειν. The object of the robbery would then be the sovereignty on earth, the recognition by men of the dignity of the Messianic kingship. The sense would be as follows : Christ would not, as he might have done had he chosen, use the power, which he possessed in an equal degree with God, as a means of usurping a position which was destined for him indeed, but which, according to the intention of God, he was to attain by the path of humiliation and of suffering. I formerly adopted this explanation of *Meyer's* (see the article on Pauline Christology in *Hilgenfeld's* Z. f. w. Th., 1871, p. 520 f.), principally on the supposed ground that ἁρπαγμός could only be taken as equivalent to actio rapiendi, not to res rapiendæ. But the possibility of taking ἁρπαγμός as equivalent to ἅρπαγμα is established beyond doubt by many analogies (compare *Grimm* on this subject, Z. f. w. Th., 1873, p. 38 f.) ; and thus the necessity of this explanation disappears. But I have come to regard it as highly improbable, especially because Paul, after what he has said elsewhere, can hardly have ascribed to Christ an actual εἶναι ἴσα θεῷ.

above that which he had already had, the μορφὴ θεοῦ; and this can only be the dignity of supreme Lordship and equality with God, the absolute, perfect sovereign Majesty, which belongs to God alone, and to no other, not even to the Son who was the very image of Him as regards the form in which he appeared. If this is so, these words contain an indirect confirmation of that distinct subordination which we have repeatedly remarked as a pervading feature of the genuine Pauline Christology. The sense therefore is, that the heavenly Christ was so far from wishing to usurp like a robber, that is to say, in selfish arrogance, the dignity of supreme Lordship and equal sovereignty with God, that he, on the contrary, never thought of doing so, but did the opposite to this—he emptied himself (instead of coveting that which was greater and higher) of that which he (justly) possessed (namely, of the μορφὴ θεοῦ), and by so doing proved his self-forgetting humility, in laying aside the form of God, and taking upon him the form of man, i. e. of a servant. The transition, then, from the pre-existence to the life on earth consisted negatively in giving up the form of God (ἐκένωσεν ἑαυτόν), and positively in taking upon him the "form of a servant;" this is the general expression for the condition of abasement on which Christ entered; it indicates the contrast between the δόξα of the free Son of God, which he had given up, and the lowliness of the earthly appearance which he had assumed, which was so far from according with the nature of a Son of God. But the means by which this transition was accomplished are stated by the following passage: ἐν ὁμοιώματι ἀνθρώπων γενόμενος, "being born in the likeness (outward form) of men," which was proved by the fact that he henceforth "was found in fashion as a man" (as every other ordinary man). The words ἐν ὁμοιώματι ἀνθρώπου γενόμενος have the same meaning as is expressed in Gal. iv. 4 by γενόμενον ἐκ γυναικός, and in Rom. viii. 3, by πέμψας ἐν ὁμοιώματι σαρκὸς ἁμαρτίας. For the outward form (ὁμοίωμα) of man, the external fashion (σχῆμα) which marks an earthly man, is, according to the general Pauline view of things,

no other than the σῶμα τῆς σαρκός, the material or earthly corporality of the ἄνθρωπος χοϊκὸς ἐκ γῆς, which is opposed to the
spiritual corporality (the σῶμα πνευματικόν or τῆς δόξης, 1 Cor.
xv. 44; Phil. iii. 21).[1] The passage of the Philippians, therefore,
does not, any more than the other two, contain the doctrine of the
Docetists in the strictly dogmatical sense; it does not mean to
say that Christ's appearance as man was a mere empty shadow;
on the contrary, it consisted, according to this passage also, of a
real human body of earthly σάρξ; only this fleshly corporality
was in the case of Christ merely the form in which he appeared,
only the element which constituted the outer side (the σχῆμα,
the ἔξω ἄνθρωπος), not the essential and dominating principle of
the entire personality; for this, as well *after* as *before* its appearing in the flesh, was πνεῦμα.

Hence it is plain that the Son of God who appeared in the
flesh, or the historic Jesus, is precisely the same personality as
that of the Son of God in heaven who was to be sent. A personality did not come into being for the first time by means of
the "sending" (the sending would in that case be really equivalent to calling into life or creation); nor was the heavenly person of Christ the spirit thereby united to the earthly person of
Jesus the son of David, in such a way that the historical person
of Jesus the Messiah came into existence by their union.[2] We

---

[1] This interpretation essentially agrees with that of *Weiss*, p. 426, and *R. Schmidt*,
pp. 163—179. And I especially endorse the opinion of the latter that we "certainly
are not justified in describing the expressions made use of in the Epistle to the Philippians as impossible from the genuine standpoint of the Apostle, or as *essentially* going
beyond the substance of the declaration in 2 Cor. viii. 9." But in that case I do not
understand why this declaration of the Epistle to the Philippians, which is essentially
identical with the genuine Pauline Christology, is separated from that declaration and
joined to that of the Epistle to the Colossians, regarding which *Schmidt* himself allows,
that "here the conceptions of Paul have certainly undergone a further development"
(p. 197). And how does this rightly observed relation between the dogmatic Christology of these two Epistles agree with the hypothesis, supported (though not very
decidedly) by *Schmidt*, of the genuineness of the Epistle to the Colossians, which, if
genuine, must be older than that to the Philippians?

[2] The former is the view of *Beyschlag*, which has already been mentioned; the
latter the opinion of *Holsten* (ut supra, p. 423), which is also thrown out as a conjecture by *Meyerhoff* (Epistle to the Colossians, p. 66).

have, on the contrary, already proved from 1 Cor. viii. 6 that the pre-existent, who is designated by the full name of the historical " Jesus Christ," must also be identical with the latter as to his entire personality, and is consequently neither a merely virtual personality, nor merely one half of the historical two-fold person Jesus Christ. Moreover, in Rom. i. 3 f., it is the *one* person of the υἱὸς θεοῦ that is, not split into two personalities, but only regarded under the two aspects, which are to be distinguished in it as in every human person, namely, flesh and spirit. The identity of the subject being thus complete, it is only the *form of existence* which can have been changed by means of the sending, the σῶμα τῆς σαρκός took the place of the σῶμα τῆς δόξης. The question how this took place is inadmissible, because it is one on which Paul never reflected, and because it would be impossible to answer it a priori. At best we may perhaps, without going beyond the range of the Apostle's conceptions, find an analogy in the change of the earthly body into the resurrection body. As in this case τὸ φθαρτὸν καὶ θνητόν is laid aside, and ἀφθαρσία and ἀθανασία is put on, so the converse takes place on the entrance of the pre-existent into the flesh; we have in both cases a miraculous metamorphosis, which evades any intelligible analysis. It is, however, further to be remarked that the body of flesh assumed by Christ was produced, according to Paul, by *natural procreation;* for not only does he nowhere allude to a supernatural conception, but he denies it indirectly by calling him the son of David according to the flesh, which clearly presupposes the natural paternity of Joseph the son of David. Besides, a supernatural conception of Jesus would possess no interest for him, because the higher nature of Christ did not depend in his estimation upon a miraculous birth, but was the result of his heavenly pre-existence, by which it was established on a much surer basis; for a person consisting essentially of heavenly spirit stands on a far higher level than an essentially earthly person only called into life by the causal act of God's creative spirit. The latter view did not appear among the Jew-

ish Christians until after the time of Paul, and no doubt as a
means of avoiding an application of Paul's doctrine concerning
Christ which at that time was thought to be dangerous. The
" being made man " therefore,.according to the view of Paul, is
the assumption of an earthly human body of flesh by the heavenly
human person of the pre-existing Son of God, Jesus Christ. And
here all those questions which have formed the subject of dogmatizing in a later age, regarding the way in which the " divine
and human nature" were united, lie quite out of the range of
vision ; nay, the question which lay nearest to hand, and which
as a matter of history really gave the impulse to the development of the Christological doctrine, namely, *whether Jesus Christ
had a human soul*, has no possible answer from the standpoint
of the Pauline Christology. We cannot escape from this *antinomy;* on the one hand, it is to the pre-existent spiritual essence,
the principle of life which constituted the ego, that the personality attaches, and a second principle of life which came into
being for the first time at the birth of Christ, an earthly human
soul, could not co-exist by the side of this without destroying the
unity of the personal life ;[1] on the other hand, the σάρξ which
Christ took upon him could not be dead matter, but must as
organized body have already been endowed with a soul.

Lastly, the question of the *sinlessness* of Christ is very closely
connected with the above. Here too we ultimately encounter
an insoluble antinomy. By means of the πνεῦμα ἁγιωσύνης, which
constituted his personality (Rom. i. 4), Christ was free from personal sin ; not merely from sinful actions, but from any personal
inward experience whatsoever of sin as his own ; he was ἁμαρτίαν
μὴ γνούς, 2 Cor. v. 21. Notwithstanding this, he partook, according to the flesh, or according to his ἔξω ἄνθρωπος, of the universal
human principle of sin, for he had as the material of his body *the
same σάρξ ἁμαρτίας as all other men.* This is still disputed, no
doubt, by most of the commentators, who explain the decisive
passage in Rom. viii. 3, ἐν ὁμοιώματι σαρκὸς ἁμαρτίας, as if it

---

[1] Compare *Zeller*, über Neutest. Christologie, in Theol. Jahrb. 1842, Pt. 1.

meant that Christ appeared only in a "likeness of sinful flesh," that is to say, in a body which resembled indeed the body of other men so far as it consisted of flesh, but was unlike them in this respect, that his flesh was *not* like that of all others, sinful flesh, the abode and principle of that ἐπιθυμεῖν which is sinful because contrary to the spirit. But this is evidently a misinterpretation of the passage, which involves two errors, a mistranslation of the word ὁμοίωμα, and an inadmissible separation of the two ideas, σάρξ and ἁμαρτίας. As regards the first, it is beyond question that if the words had merely been ἐν ὁμοιώματι σαρκός, no one would have hesitated to translate them simply "in fleshly shape," that is to say, in a shape or form of appearance which was the same as that of all human flesh, and in fact consisted of flesh. Similarly, ἐν ὁμοιώματι ἀνθρώπων in Phil. ii. 7 means that shape or form of appearance which belongs to all men, and does not indicate merely some kind of resemblance (which would be the doctrine of the Docetists pure and simple), but the complete identity of his appearance with that of other men. Moreover, ὁμοίωμα always,[1] when used abstractly, denotes sameness, or the relation of positive congruity, and precisely not the incongruity of the things compared; and where it is concrete, it denotes the appearance, shape, image, form, in which a being becomes apprehensible by the senses. How is it possible, then, that in this passage the word should suddenly come to mean precisely the *want* of identity between the σάρξ of Christ and the ordinary σάρξ ἁμαρτίας? Here as elsewhere it must necessarily mean either "sameness" (abstract), or, which seems to me simpler, "shape" (concrete); and in that case σαρκός ἁμαρτίας denotes the material of which the human form of Christ, like that of other men, consists. But that both these notions are inseparably connected, that the ἁμαρτία is not a mere accidental

---

[1] Compare my article in *Hilgenfeld's* Zeitschr., 1871, p. 523 f.; and *Overbeck* in the same periodical, 1869, p. 200 f.; and especially *Holsten*, who previously (in his treatise on the meaning of the word Σάρξ) gave with decisive reasons the right interpretation of the passage we are considering. *Hausrath* and *Lüdemann* have also adopted his explanation.

quality of the σάρξ, but an essential one, one therefore without
which it would no longer be actual but only apparent σάρξ, has
been already shown in treating of the Pauline anthropology
(Chap. i.).   Lastly, we must remember that, according to the
whole context of this passage, and of Rom. vi.—viii., the presence of ἁμαρτία in the σάρξ of Christ is so strictly a logical postulate, that the denial of it destroys the whole argument of this
portion of the Epistle, and cuts away the foundation of Paul's
peculiar doctrine of the doing away with the power of sin in the
flesh through the death of Christ (see the preceding Chapter).
Accordingly we may regard it as a well-established fact that,
according to Paul, the flesh of Christ, like that of other men, was
sinful flesh, the abode and the principle of that sinful ἐπιθυμία,
which consequently could in principle be destroyed in his death.
But the ἐπιθυμία of the σάρξ was not in the case of the Pauline
Christ, as in ordinary men, that of his personal ego ; for *his* ego
was, as we have seen, not merely ψυχὴ ζῶσα, which is subject to
the determination of the σάρξ, but it was πνεῦμα ἁγιωσύνης, to
which all fleshly ἐπιθυμεῖν is entirely alien.   Because Christ was
not ἄνθρωπος ψυχικὸς, but from the beginning ἄνθρωπος πνευματικός,
—not ἐκ γῆς χοϊκός, but ἐξ οὐρανοῦ,—therefore he continued, in
spite of his σάρξ ἁμαρτίας, to be personally one ἁμαρτίαν μὴ γνούς.

Only it must be admitted that to our minds the insoluble
question presents itself, What are we in that case to think of as
the subject of the ἁμαρτία of the flesh of Christ, if it was not his
ego, his soul, as that to which his indivisible personality attaches ?
Or how can the σάρξ pure and simple, entirely separated from
the personal principle of life, to which it serves as an organ,
have ἁμαρτία ?   Or how can a concrete ego exist in a fleshly life,
without feeling it as its own life, at least so far as to experience
its ἐπιθυμεῖν as its own ?   And this leads us further back to the
question, How is it possible at all that a personal spirit could, as
such, have a bodily birth, in such a way that the individual begotten and born as a man should be the same concrete subject
which subsisted before as pure spirit, and that the individual

body should thus be, not the basis of an individual spirit now in process of development, but the mere wrappage of a spirit which was already full-formed from the beginning, and is only infused into it from without?

It is easy to see that the inconceivability of these ideas to our modern psychology has tempted certain commentators to get rid of the difficulty by giving up the identity of the earthly and the pre-existent subject, making the latter an impersonal principle, and allowing the personality of the historical Jesus to begin with his birth in time. Although this, as we have seen, is not justifiable as an exposition, yet it is without doubt correct as a suggestion of what we have to regard as the *idea of the Pauline doctrine of Christ*; only when once we begin to separate the idea from the figurate conception in which it is presented, we should go through with it to the end, instead of halting half-way, as most of these commentators do. The difficulties of the Pauline Christology (in which the whole Christology of the Church of after ages was already contained, as it were, in a nut-shell) may certainly be traced back to the fact that it asserts an ideal timeless principle to be *immediately identical* with an empirical individual born in time. That Paul went altogether beyond the empirical individuality of the man Jesus, and made an absolute spiritual principle the main point of his Christology, constituted the peculiarity and the originality of his doctrine of Christ, by which, scarcely less than by his doctrine of the law and faith, he broke through the limits of the Judaistic conception of Christianity, and secured for it its absolute spiritual character. For this ideal principle of the personality of Christ was to him, as we have seen, nothing else than the spiritual man, the perfect image of God and the pattern of man, the picture of the Son of God, to the realization of which men, as potential children of God, were from eternity destined, and the realization of which in humanity began in principle in the historic Jesus Christ, as the "first-born among many brethren" (Rom. viii. 29). This is that Son of God, whom God revealed in him (Paul) that he should

preach him among the Gentiles (Gal. i. 16); whose glory as the
image of God is recognized when God allows the light of the
gospel to shed its enlightening rays on our hearts (2 Cor. iv.
4—6); into whose likeness we ourselves are changed, in that we
become spirit of his spirit (2 Cor. iii. 18); nay, who himself lives
in us, who are spiritual men, and is the life of our spirit (Rom.
viii. 10; Phil. i. 21; Gal. ii. 20); whom to know in ever fuller
practical knowledge, to lay hold of, and to be found in him, is
the Christian's highest desire (Phil. iii. 8 f.). In short, this *ideal
principle* of the Sonship of God, the *eternal* Son of God, the Lord,
who is the *spirit*, forms the absolute object of faith for Paul, with
which his subjective spiritual life (for the very reason that it is
an absolute spiritual object) could unite itself in complete mystical communion. Thus this higher Christology is essentially part
and parcel of the mystical depth and ideal power of the Pauline
faith. But this is only one side. The other side consists in the
fact that this ideal principle was so regarded by the Apostle that
in his eyes it is always immediately identical with the empirical
person of the historic Redeemer, Jesus of Nazareth. In him,
especially in his death, he saw the historical cause of his own
redemption, the source of his own spirit of adoption; on him,
therefore, were concentrated all his feelings of grateful love and
piety (Gal. ii. 20; 2 Cor. v. 14). By this means it happened,
and it was almost inevitable that it should happen, that the
historical instrument of salvation became himself the absolute
object of salvation; the intermediate cause of the consciousness
of adoption became the absolute principle (operative ideal) of the
adoption as children of God; and thus the absolute religious idea
was fused together with the individual appearance of him who
embodied and prepared the way for it, into the absolute and yet
at the same time individually determined and visible ideal. And
this combination was no less rich in results than it was unavoidable; the historical individual element, which culminated in the
act of love on the cross, gave to the image of Christ, as it presented itself to the community he founded, its living and pal-

pable features, its heart-moving warmth, its power to lay hold of
and to captivate the affections ; but that this heart-stirring picture should become the abstract of the absolute truth, the bodily
manifestation of the fulness of the Godhead, the unconditioned
source of all religious and moral satisfaction,—in a word, that it
should become the absolute object of salvation and ground of
belief of the community,—was only rendered possible by the
raising of the individual and temporal into the ideal and eternal,
by the identification of the historical person with the absolute
principle of the Sonship of God. As this identification sprang
necessarily from the religious spirit of Paul, so it will evermore
be indispensable to the religious life of the community; for this
life requires in an equal degree the presence of both these
moments or aspects in the object of faith, (1) unlimited spiritual
ideality, and (2) envisagement in a definite individual form that
appeals to the feelings. And in the immediate intuition or unreasoned perception of practical faith and public worship, these
two moments always harmonize perfectly well, and the more
easily, the less the immediacy of religious feeling and vision is
interfered with by reflection, whether of the orthodox, apologetic
kind, or of the rationalistic school which seeks to explain everything. For it is certain that as soon as thought begins to reflect
more precisely and accurately on the several features of this picture of Christ, which originated, as we have seen, by the fusion
of empirical individual elements with others that were ideal and
absolute, it cannot fail to perceive the heterogeneity of these
elements, and the impossibility of their co-existence in one and
the same subject. Then the understanding usually attempts to
repress either one side or the other, in order to avoid logical contradiction. But all these attempts to reason out the matter, made
from the standpoint of reflection, are foiled by the fundamental
presupposition on which the whole rests, and so urge thought
further and further on, until the solution of the riddle is found
in the *genesis* of the whole doctrine concerning Christ.

With this clue, all the several points of this Christology become easily intelligible. If the historical Redeemer be once identified with the idea of the man who is the very image of God and the representative of adoption as children of God, which realizes itself indeed in time, but is in itself timeless, then that concrete personality must partake of the eternal nature of this idea, must therefore have had a timeless existence in supramundane regions before it existed historically on the earth, or, in other words, must have been pre-existent, and have come down from heaven upon the earth. And as that idea could only realize itself in the historial life of humanity, but yet dwelt in human nature from the very beginning as a real potency, and as the operative ground of its humanity, so also must the concrete substantiation of that idea, namely Christ, have been not only the historical instrument of the new spiritual creation, but also the primordial instrument of the creation of the natural world. Further, if the historical Christ is only the appearing in time of that pre-existing ideal, then it is perfectly self-evident that absolute sinlessness belongs to him, for this plainly attaches to the notion of the ideal; accordingly the doctrine of the sinlessness of Christ is a simple consequence of Christological dogma, and for this very reason belongs to the domain of dogma, and not of history. But here it has already become apparent that the heterogeneous elements out of which the Christology has grown up, cannot coalesce to form the real unity of a person; absolute sinlessness belongs to Christ as the substantiated ideal of the spiritual man, and to Christ as the empirical man living in the flesh belongs the sinfulness which is inseparable from the essence of all flesh. These are simply two contradictory predicates which cannot be affirmed of one and the same subject.

There is yet another point on which the want of cohesion between the two elements of the Christology is strikingly displayed at the very outset of Paul's doctrinal system. So long as the historical Jesus was regarded as the point of departure, his resurrection appeared as the transition into his pure spiritual existence, consequently as the realization of the essence of a Son of God and pattern of manhood; and therefore Paul not only repeatedly connects the divine Sonship of Christ with his resurrection, but also in most instances holds up the risen one as the pattern for Christians (comp. Rom. vi. 4, 10 f.; 2 Cor. 4, 10 f.; Col. 3, 1 f.). On the other hand, so long as the historical Jesus is regarded as the appearing of the eternal pre-existent Christ, there is no longer any need that he should become, through the resurrection, that which he had already been before he appeared in the flesh; from this point of view therefore the resurrection could no longer be regarded (as is the case however in Rom. i. 4) as his *institution* into the full possession of the divine Sonship, but as a simple *return* to that δόξα of the Son of God which he had long possessed, and only temporarily laid aside. This is the necessary consequence of the doctrine of the pre-existence, a consequence which we see already distinctly drawn even in the Christology of John. In Paul, who has not yet drawn this consequence, we find the dogma concerning Christ in that stage of its evolution where the higher Christology is already, in the substantiation of an eternal Son of God, in process of developing itself out of the historical view, but does not yet react upon the latter. The historical and the ideal element are joined indeed for the first time in the Christology of Paul, but as yet so little wrought together that their want of cohesion is still everywhere apparent.

CHAPTER IV.

JUSTIFICATION BY FAITH.

SINCE Paul looks upon the object of salvation as indivisibly concentred in Christ, the appropriation of salvation also becomes for him a single act of faith, namely, the giving up of the heart to Christ, by which the salvation given in him is acquired complete in all its elements. Now in so far as Christ is above all things the Mediator of reconciliation, faith in him becomes, first of all, appropriation of the reconciling love of God; it justifies the sinner, and places him in the condition of a child of God, in which he is no longer an object of the anger of God (avenging justice), but of his love. But since Christ, as the Son of God, is at the same time the image of the holy God, and himself the holy πνεῦμα, faith in him places the believer at the same time in the communion of his holy πνεῦμα-life, and is thus consequently, in the man who was hitherto fleshly, the cause of a new life in the spirit, in which the pattern of the Son of God really exhibits itself, as in a copy, as a new moral personal life. Thus faith is the single root, as well of the change of the objective relation of man to God, in justification and adoption, as of the renewal of the subjective personal life of man, in sanctification; but faith, not as an abstract human act, or a subjective human disposition, but as a laying hold of Christ, as the act of uniting the human heart with the favourable will of God revealed in Christ.

FAITH.

Paul has nowhere expressly explained the notion of faith ; and without doubt for this reason, that the original sense in which he uses the words πιστεύειν, πίστις, was in no way peculiar, but the sense in which they were ordinarily understood. 1 Cor. xi. 18, καὶ μέρος τι πιστεύω : Rom. vi. 8, πιστεύομεν ὅτι καὶ συζή- σομεν : x. 9, ἐὰν πιστεύσῃς ἐν τῇ καρδίᾳ σου, ὅτι ὁ θεὸς αὐτὸν ἤγειρεν ἐκ νεκρῶν, σωθήσῃ : in these passages, πιστεύειν evidently means nothing more than believing, in the sense of *regarding as true, being persuaded of something,* and that on grounds which are not of a logically binding nature ; for if they were, the conviction would no longer be belief or faith, but simply knowledge. In this sense "faith" is used especially of such conviction as does not depend on sensuous perception, and is even the direct oppo- site of ocular demonstration, or ordinary experience by means of the senses. 2 Cor. v. 7, διὰ πίστεως γὰρ περιπατοῦμεν, οὐ διὰ εἴδους, which means that our life in the body is absence from the Lord, because he does not manifest his life in the realm of visible appearance and actuality, but only in the region of faith (not in the realm of the real, but in that of the ideal).[1] Similarly in Rom. iv. 18, it is related to the honour of Abraham, that he παρ' ἐλπίδα ἐπ' ἐλπίδι ἐπίστευσεν, that he doubted not the promise of God, in spite of all experience to the contrary, but gave glory to God, and was strong in faith, and had the firm assurance (πληροφορηθείς) that God was able to do that which He had pro- mised, however impossible it appeared in the light of previous experience. According to these passages, Paul's faith, like that of the Epistle to the Hebrews (xi. 1), is a being convinced of something beyond the senses, without or even against the evi-

---

[1] This interpretation is the only one which corresponds with the context, and gives throughout the true meaning of the words. Οὐ περιπατοῦμεν διὰ εἴδους indicates the very want that still affects our life in the body, and makes it an ἐκδημεῖν ἀπὸ τοῦ κυρίου, and is closely connected with the wish ἐκδημῆσαι ἐκ τοῦ σώματος. This is overlooked by those who would understand διὰ εἴδους to mean, under the principle of mere outward show, the deceitful world of appearances.

dence of sensuous experience. Only, the idea of Paul contains
something more than this general sense; the passage last quoted
shows that it has its true object in God, or more particularly in
his revelation of salvation, whether by way of promise or of
saving act. The faith of Abraham, according to Rom. iv. 3, consisted in this, that he ἐπίστευσε τῷ θεῷ, i. e. *put faith in God, had
confidence* that He could and would make good his word; and
thus far, as an act of confidence in God, it was a δοῦναι δόξαν θεῷ
(ver. 20). Whenever we "believe a man about anything," the
ground of our conviction lies in our confidence in our authority,
and this is an ethical act of personal respect and heartfelt trust
in the truthfulness of another. Just so, according to the authoritative passage, Rom. iv., religious faith is *holding for true without
logical ground, but on the ethical ground of trust in God and confidence in God's truth, power, and honour,* which implies the
due feeling of reverence towards God, the "giving Him the
glory," and therefore the key-note of religion. The expression,
πιστεύειν εἰς, or ἐπὶ θεόν, Rom. x. 14, iv. 5, 24, has essentially
the same sense as this πιστεύειν θεῷ; it means to have confidence
(i. e. take confidence) in reference to God, or, in other words, to
believe *in God.*

Now the specific Christian or justifying faith is identical with
this religious faith according to its psychological form, and analogous to it with regard to its object, as Paul unmistakably teaches
in Rom. iv. As the faith of Abraham was an undoubting assurance in the promise of God, which was contradictory to
appearances, so Christian faith is a "*trust in relation to God, who
raised Christ from the dead,*" and "*who justifies the ungodly,*"
Rom. iv. 24, v.; that is to say, in the first place, a trustful holding it to be true that God raised Christ from the dead, and thus
wrought a miraculous manifestation of his favourable will, analogous to that event the future happening of which was the
object of Abraham's assurance; secondly, a trustful acceptance
of the fact that the favourable will of God, evidenced by that
miraculous act, will henceforth be fulfilled in every sinner who

believes in the equally paradoxical act of justifying the ungodly.

These perfectly plain passages show beyond a possibility of doubt wherein, according to Paul, the πίστις Χριστοῦ, or πιστεύειν εἰς Χριστόν, consists. It is faith in Christ in the sense of *trusting in the favourable will of God revealed in Christ, in the righteousness that comes from God through the mediation of Christ* (Rom. iii. 22—26; Gal. ii. 16 f.). Christ is certainly not the object of faith in the same sense as God; it is not he in whom faith or trust is placed, to whose personality this trust attaches, for Paul nowhere speaks of a πιστεύειν Χριστῷ as he does of a πιστεύειν θεῷ. But he is the object of faith so far, that in him, especially in his death and resurrection, the favourable will of God, which is the real object of religious trust, has been revealed. He is the object of faith only so far as he (that is to say, his death and resurrection) supports and is instrumental in producing the specific Christian faith in God (namely, the trust in the historically revealed favourable will of God). Now, in so far as this faith in Christ refers, in the first instance, to matters of history (the death and resurrection of Christ), it is undeniably a *theoretical* act of holding for true, a being convinced of the reality of the resurrection of Christ, upon which depended, in the mind of Paul, the significance of the death of Jesus as a Messianic expiatory sacrifice, and consequently the truth of the favourable will of God. This is not only an obvious inference from the whole Pauline doctrine of redemption, but Paul himself says, with the greatest emphasis, that the belief in the miraculous resurrection as a historical fact, was for him an integral part of his notion of faith: "If Christ be not risen from the dead, your faith is vain; ye are yet in your sins," 1 Cor. xv. 17; "If thou believest in thine heart that God raised Jesus from the dead, thou shalt be saved," Rom. x. 9. In order rightly to understand the peculiar stress thus laid by Paul on the resurrection of Christ as the specific object of Christian faith, we must remember that Paul's own faith in Christ had no other starting-

M 2

point than the assurance by means of the vision that the crucified one was alive. This was not the case with the immediate
disciples of Jesus, whose faith had proceeded from trust in the
personality of their Master; nor, with the theological school of
John, in whose eyes the resurrection was only one of the numerous manifestations in which the existence of the Logos in Jesus
was outwardly attested; the faith of this school could not, therefore, be referred to that single fact, but to the divine sonship of
Jesus in general (John xx. 31). But the last-mentioned passage
(Rom. x. 9 f.) shows that with Paul also the faith of the Christian does not simply take the resurrection of Christ as a mere
external event of history, and therefore is not merely a theoretical act of holding something for true—καρδίᾳ πιστεύεται, ἐὰν
πιστεύσῃς ἐν τῇ καρδίᾳ σου. If it is the heart, the seat of the life
of feeling, in which and with which we must believe, then faith
itself is evidently also a matter of *feeling*, a specific state of the
emotional nature, as "*trusting*" is, in the sense developed above;
and if the confession that Christ is the "Lord" be the outward
counterpart of this faith of the heart (ibid. ἐὰν ὁμολογήσῃς ἐν τῷ
στόματί σου κύριον Ἰησοῦν), then faith must be the inward recognition of Christ as the Lord, therefore a subjection of the will to
the dominion of Christ. Consequently faith may be described
also as an *act of obedience*, ibid. v. 16, ὑπακούειν τῷ εὐαγγελίῳ, as
equivalent to πιστεύειν : and ver. 3, ὑποταγῆναι τῇ δικαιοσύνῃ τοῦ
θεοῦ, as the opposite of τὴν ἰδίαν δικαιοσύνην ζητεῖν : also 2 Cor.
x. 5, ὑπακοὴ Χριστοῦ, under which all human ratiocination that
contradicts the evangelical knowledge of God (here especially
the dialectic of the Judaizers) is to be brought into captivity.
The expression ὑπακοὴ πίστεως in Rom. i. 5, has precisely the
same meaning, where πίστεως is not the genitive of the subject,
but of the object, and denotes the principle of Christian faith, to
which the Gentiles were to become subject by the preaching of
Paul. But this "becoming subject to the principle of faith" is
plainly only another name for "becoming believers," and accordingly πιστεύειν here also denotes ὑπακοὴ, an act of obedience. But

in what sense is the Pauline faith called "obedience"? Not in some such sense as a morally good disposition, intention, and endeavour to perform the will of God, or the fulfilling of the law in principle. This would entirely pervert the Pauline notion of justifying faith, although not only modern theologians, but (as we shall presently see) even the earliest followers of Paul, have given this moral application to the notion. But the Pauline faith is an act of obedience exclusively in a religious sense, namely, as an act of self-determination, that consists in renouncing everything of our own, so far as it could stand in opposition to the favourable will of God towards us, or form a ground of self-glorification, whether in the shape of natural advantages, or moral acts or claims, or even inherited opinions and prejudices flattering to our self-love, and giving ourselves up wholly to the favourable will of God. Thus it constitutes the opposite to τὴν ἰδίαν δικαιοσύνην ζητεῖν (Rom. x. 3), or ἐν σαρκὶ πεποιθέναι (Phil. iii. 4), and is therefore identical with the truly humble spirit which wishes to have nothing and be nothing of itself, but, on the contrary, to receive everything from God, and which will rather consider all its own advantages as damage and loss, in order to obtain instead of them Christ, and consequently the righteousness which is of God (Phil. iii. 7 f.). In this absolute surrender of the whole man to God, faith is certainly the most complete fulfilment of the will of God, but, be it well understood, not (in the first instance) of that will which demands the fulfilment of the law, but of the will which bestows favour, of that will which has substituted for the old economy of law, with its demands and performances, the new economy of grace with its gift of favour, and now requires nothing from men with respect to this new religious principle but the behaviour which corresponds to it—a trustful acceptance of the gift of favour offered by God. This is something specifically different from a morally good disposition, from willing the good in principle in the moral life, for its aim is not doing at all, but receiving, not the moral perfection either of the person himself or of the world, but religious satisfaction—the setting of the human heart in the right relation to God, and the blessing to be expected therefrom; it is, in short, the key-note of all religious feeling, not that disposition which forms the basis of the moral will. This must be carefully borne in mind in order to the right understanding of Paul's idea of justification.

What Paul says about the *origin of faith* quite agrees with the above. Owing to the historical nature of the object of faith, faith can only come ἐξ ἀκοῆς, Rom. x. 17, from hearing the announcement of the gospel. It is so far dependent on being *handed down by men* (πῶς ἀκούσωσι χωρὶς κηρύσσοντος; ibid. ver. 14); just as the Apostle himself in preaching the gospel first of all delivered what he himself had received (from men)—the facts of the death, burial, resurrection and appearances of Christ (1 Cor. xv. 3 f.). Nay, regarded from this point of view, faith implies also a certain confidence in the truthfulness and trustworthiness of the men who handed down the gospel, as the "witnesses of God," who were set down as "false witnesses" through lack of faith in their testimony (ibid. ver. 15). Notwithstanding this, however, faith is by no means grounded on the word of men, any more than what is historical forms, as such, the chief part of its object; but as this is only the temporal form in which the favourable will of God to man attains its outward manifestation, so that which produces faith is not the human word of historical announcement, but the *word of God* finding expression through this means. The λόγος ἀκοῆς is to be accepted, not as the λόγος ἀνθρώπων, but καθώς ἐστιν ἀληθῶς, as λόγος θεοῦ, 1 Thess. ii. 13. In particular, the λόγος τοῦ σταυροῦ preached by Paul is to the Jews an offence, and to the Greeks foolishness, but to the called (who are destined to faith and salvation by the counsel of God, and actually called to this by the preaching of the gospel) it is θεοῦ δύναμις καὶ θεοῦ σοφία, 1 Cor. i. 18—24. The preaching of Paul does not consist in persuasive words of man's wisdom, but in demonstration of the spirit and of power. ·Therefore the faith of the Corinthians rests not ἐν σοφίᾳ ἀνθρώπων ἀλλ' ἐν δυνάμει θεοῦ (ii. 4 f.) And if we ask how far the word preached shows itself as the power of God, Rom. i. 16 f. leaves us in no doubt on this head;—it is because in it the righteousness which is of God is revealed as a consequence of faith for the purpose of faith (of awakening faith) ; that is to say, because it shows to man, who stands under the wrath of God, the only possible way of attaining to righteousness before God, and thereby to being made a partaker of salvation (σωτηρία, ver. 16). It is God himself who has committed to us the word of reconciliation, and who calls to men through the mouth of his ambassadors, "Be reconciled with God !" (2 Cor. v. 19 f.). It is as this message of assured reconciliation, of the offered righteousness of God, that the gospel of Christ the crucified is the power of God, on which that faith depends which awakens faith or human trust in the God who so reveals Himself. Thus it is once more made clear to us how justifying faith does not merely consist of a belief in the truth of miraculous events narrated by man, which could only be brought about by the convincing force of human testimony and by the art of human persuasion ; but whereas that forms only the external husk, the real kernel of faith is the trustful surrender of the heart to the favourable will of God, as it presents itself to us in the word of reconciliation.

Now if faith is, as above, trust awakened in the human heart by the offer of favour contained in the gospel, it immediately becomes a bond which connects God and man; in that trust there is directly involved a grateful love, which places man in a community of life with God and Christ. As the giving up of the heart to the love of God and Christ, it is not merely the acceptance of the message of salvation, but the *being incorporated with the object of salvation itself in a mystical unity of love and of life.* Pauline faith has in this attained to that *mystical depth,* by which, as a complete and central appropriation of the object of salvation, it was capable of becoming the complete and exclusive subjective means of salvation[1] (πίστει δικαιοῦσθαι χωρὶς ἔργων, which Luther rightly renders "by faith *alone*"). This mystical notion of faith is expressly contained in Gal. ii. 20, a passage no less clear than profound. Here ζῇ ἐν ἐμοὶ Χριστός is parallel to ἐν πίστει ζῶ τῇ τοῦ υἱοῦ τοῦ θεοῦ, τοῦ ἀγαπήσαντός με καὶ παραδόντος ἑαυτὸν ὑπὲρ ἐμοῦ, and both expressions denote the same real community of the Christian's life with the divine principle of salvation, the immanence of the latter in the human personal life. Ἐν πίστει ζῶ is not opposed to ζῇ ἐν ἐμοὶ Χριστός, as if the former were merely the condition of the latter and presupposed by it[2]— this is an abstract separation between man and the object of salvation, which is most decidedly excluded by the words ζῶ δὲ οὐκέτι ἐγώ and Χριστῷ συνεσταύρωμαι in this very passage. On the contrary, the only distinction between the two clauses is, that the one denotes the condition of the Christian with reference to its objective (immanent) principle, the other with reference to the subjective psychological means by which it is brought about. And this passage is especially instructive for this very reason, that it allows us to see the inner point of unity between faith in the sense of trustful acceptance, and the deep mystical notion of faith. This unity lies in the grateful love which is absolutely inseparable from entire trust; and we can now understand why Paul, above all others, arrived at this deep notion of faith. The reason was, that to him the object of salvation did not consist of a mere external good—for example, an object of hope like the coming of the Messiah's kingdom—but was directly presented to him in the person and in the loving act of the Mediator of reconciliation; consequently the faith that had *this*

---

[1] See the beautiful exposition of the Pauline notion of faith in *Biedermann*, Dogmatik, § 279.

[2] Contrary to the view of *Weiss*, p. 329. The misunderstanding of this mystical moment in the Pauline notion of faith is the cause of a defect which is painfully felt in Weiss's exposition of the doctrines of Paul, in spite of the appositeness of particular parts of it ; the truly organic interdependence of the various moments of the Apostle's religious speculation, and the living movement by which they are developed out of one another, is turned into a dead juxtaposition of scholastic doctrines.

for its object was able to attain to a depth that was quite beyond the reach of the Judaized faith of a James. Man attaches
himself in loving trust to Christ as his Lord, and thereby
becomes *one* spirit with him. (1 Cor. vi. 17, ὁ κολλώμενος τῷ
κυρίῳ ἓν πνεῦμά ἐστιν.) Christ, the personified revelation of the
Divine favour, then becomes the ruling principle of the personal
life of man, which is thus completely taken up into Christ's
saving work as into its own vital element. (Phil. i. 21, ἐμοὶ
γὰρ τὸ ζῆν Χριστός.) Since faith is the recognition of Christ
as the Lord, it introduces us into his family, and thereby at
once into mystical union with him; for "to be Christ's," and
"to have the spirit of Christ in one's self," are inseparable
(Rom. viii. 9, εἴ τις πνεῦμα Χριστοῦ οὐκ ἔχει, οὗτος οὐκ ἔστιν αὐτοῦ).
Nay, so little is true faith possible without the indwelling of
Christ in the believer, that the latter is expressly stated by
the Apostle to be the criterion of the former (2 Cor. xiii. 5,—
the certainty of being in the faith depends on the perception that Christ is in you; compare Rom. viii. 9). Here it
is made perfectly clear that faith is, as regards man, the form,
which if it is not to be empty form, i.e. unreal appearance,
must have the object of salvation, not outside of itself as a
mere object of knowledge, but in itself as a living principle.
This mystical notion of faith is also a remarkable characteristic
of the Epistle to the Philippians: becoming a believer is here
represented (iii. 12) as a "being laid hold of by Christ," as
striving "to win Christ;" being a believer as "being found
in Christ," as practical "knowledge of Christ," and more definitely knowledge of "both the power of his resurrection and the
fellowship of his sufferings by being made conformable to his
death" (ibid. vers. 9, 10). Faith is, according to this, a practical
acquaintance with Christ, which completes itself by personal
appropriation; a being made conscious of what the saving
power of the resurrection and the death of Christ really means,
which can only take place in the mystical communion with the
sufferings of Christ, and being made conformable to his death.

In short, justifying faith (compare ver. 9) is here the subjective taking into our inmost self of the principle of salvation in all its moments, as exhibited to us by way of example in (the historical) Christ.

But when Paul had once come to make faith a *laying hold of and appropriating the principle of salvation* for our own principle of life, he had come very near to the final step of apprehending it as the *development of this principle* in the whole course of the *life of salvation.* This is certainly an *enlargement* of the notion, and it must be distinguished from the original idea of justifying faith. For in this wider sense faith is no longer a merely passive attitude, but a *spontaneous active power.* Inasmuch as it has for its own contents the πνεῦμα ἅγιον, πνεῦμα Χριστοῦ, πνεῦμα ζωοποιοῦν, it must necessarily exhibit itself as a living impulse and power of good in every phase of personal life, in feeling, in moral conduct, and in the perception of truth, both religious and moral. It is by means of faith that God fills us with all manner of joy and peace (Rom. xv. 13). Faith it is which proves its active power by (brotherly) love (Gal. v. 6). Faith gives steadfastness to our convictions, at once religious and moral, as to what is morally permissible, and the conviction of Christian freedom in things indifferent, which is grounded in faith, may therefore itself be designated as πίστις, and the want of this inward freedom as ἀσθενεῖν τῇ πίστει (Rom. xiv. 1, 22 f.).

The fuller discussion of this subject belongs to the next Chapter, where the same states will present themselves to us as the effect of the spirit; which only shows that "faith," in this wider sense, denotes the same Christian principle of life as "spirit," only the former from a subjective, the latter from an objective, point of view.[1]

---

[1] *Baur*, N. Tle. Theol., p. 175, appositely remarks in connection with this subject, "πίστις is indeed the necessary presupposition of πνεῦμα,—inasmuch as πνεῦμα is obtained ἐξ ἀκοῆς πίστεως,—but is at bottom related to it only as form to matter, and in πνεῦμα alone comes to be the living actuality of the Christian consciousness filled with its positive content." And again, p. 176, "What is said of spirit, may also be said of faith."

It is consistent with this view, that faith according to Paul admits of *degrees*, and of *increase and decrease*. Christian self-esteem is to be measured, ἑκάστῳ ὡς ὁ θεὸς ἐμέρισε μέτρον πίστεως (Rom. xii. 3). As in the passage before quoted an ἀσθενεῖν τῇ πίστει (certainly in distinct relation to the perception of faith) was spoken of, so also there is an unusual strength of faith, a heroic degree of it, which is capable of the most extraordinary actions (this is what we are to understand by the χάρισμα of πίστις, 1 Cor. xii. 9, and by faith which can remove mountains, xiii. 2). Faith, being this Christian life which is susceptible of different degrees, can also grow (cf. 2 Cor. x. 15, αὐξανομένης τῆς πίστεως ὑμῶν). And because the possibility of its diminution is not excluded, there is an ever-recurring need of admonition to the faithful, στήκετε τῇ πίστει (1 Cor. xvi. 13), which with such expressions as ἀνδρίζεσθε, κραταιοῦσθε, evidently relates to the strengthening of the whole religious and moral life, and not merely to holding fast the assurance of justifying favour. All these applications of πίστις go beyond the original notion of justifying faith, though they are essentially connected with it, and naturally flow out of it. Their *one* root is the trustful surrender of the heart to Christ as the mediator of reconcilation, as the principle and the pattern of divine sonship. Hence proceed, on the one hand directly, the being placed in the condition of children of God by justification and adoption; and, on the other hand indirectly, the subjective quickening by the spirit of sonship, the "living in the Spirit." Since these are only two moments which are comprehended in their unity in the central mystery of faith, faith may be regarded equally well as the condition of justification and (from another point of view, of course) as living in the Spirit.

JUSTIFICATION.

For the meaning of the word δικαιοῦν, we must not refer to the classics, but only to its use in the Septuagint and in the New

Testament, especially in the Epistles of Paul themselves. In
the Septuagint, the word is applied to *judicial acquittal* and
declaration of innocence; e. g. Exod. xxxiii. 7, οὐ δικαιώσεις τὸν
ἀσεβῆ ἕνεκεν δώρων : Deut. xxv. 1, ἐὰν δικαιώσωσι τὸν δίκαιον καὶ
καταγνῶσι τοῦ ἀσεβοῦς : and also to judgment other than judicial,
in the sense of recognizing as just or righteous ; e. g. Ecclesiasticus xviii. 2, κύριος μόνος δικαιωθήσεται : Job xxxiii. 32, εἰ εἰσί
σοι λόγοι, ἀποκρίθητί μοι, θέλω γὰρ δικαιωθῆναί σε. Ἐδικαιώθη ἡ
σοφία, Matt. xi. 19, has the same meaning ; and δεδικαιωμένος,
Luke xviii. 14, is used in the Pauline sense. Now that Paul
uses the word, as it is used in all these passages, to mean a judgment of acquittal, is shown in the first place by the opposition
in which it stands to ἐγκαλεῖν = to accuse judicially, in Rom.
viii. 33, and to κατάκριμα = condemnation, in Rom v. 18. That
it denotes a *judicial act* is further shown unmistakably by Rom.
iii. 4, ὅπως δικαιωθῇς ἐν τοῖς λόγοις σου, καὶ νικήσῃς ἐν τῷ κρίνεσθαί
σε. It is evident that there can be no question here about any
kind of " making righteous," because God is the subject ; the
point of the quotation is the recognition of the righteousness of
God in a sort of judicial proceeding between Him and the sinner.
In Rom. ii. 13, οἱ ποιηταὶ τοῦ νόμου δικαιωθήσονται is opposed to
ὅσοι ἥμαρτον, διὰ νόμου κριθήσονται in ver. 12 ; as the latter is a
judicial condemnation, the former is a judicial acquittal, where
every idea of " making righteous " is excluded ; for the doers of
the law have no need at all to be made righteous, for they are so
already as doers ; the recognition of their righteousness is the
only thing that has any meaning here. The fact that in this
instance judgment of acquittal follows as the consequence of a
corresponding real character on the part of the person justified,
certainly establishes a difference in the circumstances of this
and the Christian δικαιοῦν, but not a difference in the meaning
of the word itself.

In addition to these indirect proofs, we have also a direct one,
in the explanation, both in positive and negative terms, which
Paul himself gives of his notion of δικαιοῦν. In Rom. iv. 2 f., he

explains δικαιοῦν by λογίζεσθαι δικαιοσύνην, or πίστιν εἰς δικαιοσύνην, negatively μὴ λογίζεσθαι ἁμαρτίαν. But λογίζεσθαι always denotes an ideal act of judging, considering, regarding, not a real act of making into something; and therefore λογ. δικαιοσύνην means to ascribe, or give credit for righteousness to some one in an act of judgment, negatively not to ascribe sin, to regard it as not there; λογίζεσθαι πίστιν εἰς δικαιοσύνην means to take count of faith, so as to attribute righteousness; or to ascribe righteousness on the ground of faith, because faith is there. Now whether this be an analytic judgment, which simply recognizes the righteousness which is there, or a synthetic judgment, which corresponds to a righteousness which is not yet in existence, is certainly not indicated by the word λογίζεσθαι, but the context clearly shows that the latter only is meant. In ver. 5, God is said to be δικαιῶν τὸν ἀσεβῆ—that is, one who declares him righteous who in himself is not so, but the opposite, namely, an ἀσεβής; consequently this δικαιοῦν or λογίζεσθαι δικαιοσύνην is not recognizing righteousness that is there, but ascribing righteousness that is not there to the man who is in fact godless. The same is very distinctly implied in the antithesis of λογίζεσθαι κατ᾽ ὀφείλημα, and λογ. κατὰ χάριν. To him who went about with works, sought his strength, his praise at the hand of God in works, wished to be regarded as righteous on account of his works, his wages (supposing that he were right, and that it were possible to make such a claim) would be due as a debt—that is, he would be treated according to his deserts, as that which he really is, and on which he could found claims of recognition; he would thus be declared righteous, and treated as such, on the ground of his being actually righteous. But the antithesis requires that the λογίζεσθαι κατὰ χάριν τῷ μὴ ἐργαζομένῳ πιστεύοντι δέ be a judgment which ascribes righteousness, not on the ground of the man's being correspondingly righteous, but on a presupposition of the opposite—namely, his being godless; a judgment, therefore, the ground of which is not in the man at all, not in his real character, or his moral worth and merit, but exclusively in the favour of God, which is

thus a δωρεὰ χάριτος. The whole point of Paul's doctrine of justification—its moral paradox and its religious idealism—lies precisely in this ideality of the judgment of justification; in its
being grounded, not on any real moral character of the man, but
only on God, on his favouring will and his ordinance of favour.
This imputed "righteousness" is the very opposite of that which
is the usual meaning of the term, and which to the Jew in particular was its sole meaning, namely, a subjective moral condition of conformity with the will of God expressed in his laws.
It denotes an objective religious principle—the right relation
between God and man, which, restored by God himself, presents
itself to the religious consciousness of man as something objectively given, as a new revelation of God, and which when it is
subjectively appropriated, but not before, proves itself to be also
a morally renovating principle. It is this objectivity of the
notion of righteousness that was the specifically new element in
the teaching of Paul, and his chief weapon against the Judaistic
party: to misunderstand this is to displace the foundation of the
whole gospel of Paul.

The Apostle has framed some peculiar expressions for the
righteousness imputed to man through justification, which
clearly indicate what the new idea is. He calls it the δικαιοσύνη
θεοῦ or ἐκ θεοῦ, and δικαιοσύνη διὰ πίστεως Χριστοῦ, Rom. i. 17,
iii. 22, x. 3; 2 Cor. v. 21; Phil. iii. 9. It is impossible to understand by this a *quality or power of God;* in that case it could
not also be called δικαιοσύνη ἐκ θεοῦ, nor would it be conditioned
and brought about by the πίστις Χριστοῦ; least of all could it be
said that we men arrive at δικαιοσύνη θεοῦ in Christ (2 Cor.
v. 21); this passage, taken together with ἐκ θεοῦ and διὰ πίστεως
in the texts quoted above, forces us to think of a gift which
comes from God, and which is to be received on the part of man
by faith; compare Rom. v. 17, δωρεὰ τῆς δικαιοσύνης. But neither
is it possible to understand by it a *quality of man,* a moral condition or moral power in him; for the expression, "righteousness of God," would be far too unusual and misleading a term to

apply to the human quality of being righteous; moreover, the predicate ἀποκαλύπτεται, i. 17, would be inapplicable; for a human quality may doubtless be caused by God, but certainly not "revealed;" and further, the revelation of δικαιοσύνη θεοῦ is here opposed to that of ὀργὴ θεοῦ (ver. 18), which in any case is an objective power exercised on man, that can indeed be subjectively felt by him, but has not its seat within him. The other expression, τῇ δικαιοσύνῃ τοῦ θεοῦ οὐχ ὑπετάγησαν, x. 3, also compels us to think of an objective power, and not a subjective quality in man, for a man may take up and form in himself a quality, but cannot "subject" himself to it. Now if by the δικαιοσύνη θεοῦ of Paul we can understand neither a quality of God nor a quality of man, because it appears at one time as something which comes to man, and at another time as something which stands over him, and is established by God for him, then there is nothing left for us but to understand it as *the true relation between God and man, which, being ordained by God, presents itself to the consciousness of man as a new religious principle, as a new regulator of his religious behaviour, and to which man has to submit himself, by allowing his attitude towards God to be determined by this divinely ordained principle.* Thus it is called δικαιοσύνη θεοῦ or ἐκ θεοῦ, because that true relation cannot be established by man, but only by the favour of God, by means of the institution of redemption (δικαιούμενοι δωρεὰν τῇ αὐτοῦ χάριτι διὰ τῆς ἀπολυτρώσεως τῆς ἐν Χριστῷ Ἰησοῦ, Rom. iii. 24); but the δικ. θεοῦ is received by man διὰ πίστεως Χριστοῦ, because faith alone, as ὑπακοὴ Χριστοῦ or εὐαγγελίου, submits itself to the favourable will of God, as it is revealed in Christ, and enters into the ordained relation of reconciliation, of peace with God. By this subjection of himself to the principle of favour ordained by God, the believer comes to stand in the true relation to God (δίκαιος κατασταθήσεται, v. 19); the favourable will accomplishes itself upon him, in declaring him to be righteous in consequence of his believing (δικαιοῦται ἐκ πίστεως or πίστις λογίζεται εἰς δικαιοσύνην); he counts henceforth in the judgment of God as a righteous man—that is, as a man who stands towards God as he ought (δικαιοῦται ἐνώπιον θεοῦ or παρὰ τῷ θεῷ, Rom. iii. 20; Gal. iii. 11); and this new relation to God, thus entered upon and ratified, then reflects itself upon the subjective consciousness in the feeling of peace, of unbroken harmony with God (δικαιω-θέντες οὖν εἰρήνην ἔχομεν, v. 1). The objectivity of the δικαιοσύνη θεοῦ is in no way disproved by 2 Cor. v. 21, but, on the contrary, receives fresh confirmation. For here the thought, that it is in Christ we attain to the δικαιοσύνη θεοῦ, is the correlative to Christ's having been made ἁμαρτία for us by God: now it is indisputable that the latter can only be meant in an ideal sense, that God has *regarded* Christ as a sinner, and treated him as such (made him the object of his avenging justice); therefore the former must be understood in a corresponding sense, that God *regards* us in Christ (by virtue of our belonging to Christ through faith in him) as righteous, and treats us accordingly, although we are as far from being so in reality, as Christ was from being a sinner. And this imputative notion of δικαιοσύνη θεοῦ is required by the connection with the preceding passage, for the expression is paraphrased in ver. 19 by μὴ λογιζόμενος αὐτοῖς τὰ παραπτώματα αὐτῶν. Accordingly, the "righteousness of God in Christ" is that condition of freedom from guilt which is brought about by not reckoning sin as condemning guilt, or by judicial justification. The objective nature of righteousness and sin, according to Paul, could not be more strikingly expressed than it is in this passage, where both appear as types of character, or parts which can be separated and transferred to other persons and exchanged one for the other.

This analogy of imputed righteousness with imputed sin brings us to a passage of great importance in its bearing upon this doctrine—a passage in which sin and righteousness are conceived as types characteristic of the race of natural and Christian humanity, represented, in connection with the history of the entire world, by Adam and Christ. Rom. v. 12—21 concludes that section of the Epistle which begins at i. 17, and which develops the δικαιοσύνη θεοῦ, which is there stated as the theme for discussion. The objectivity of this righteousness is finally corroborated here by the parallel that is drawn between it and the similarly objective sin of Adamitic humanity. We have already (in the first part of Chap. i.) discussed the introduction, and one member of the parallel (especially vers. 12—14). Here we have to do with the further carrying out of the comparison with regard to points of difference and of identity, vers. 15—19. First of all, vers. 15—17, the *difference* between the two members of the parallel (the relation of sinful humanity to Adam, and of justified humanity to Christ) is set forth in greater detail, in order to prepare the way for carrying out the positive analogy, which is the real object of the whole parallel. This difference is partly qualitative and partly quantitative. As to the *qualitative* —from Adam judgment went forth to condemnation, from Christ the gift of favour to justification (κρίμα εἰς κατάκριμα—χάρισμα εἰς δικαίωμα, ver. 16); in the former case, the παράπτωμα or the παρακοή of one issued in the death of many, the dominion of death over the race; in the latter case, the δικαίωμα or the ὑπακοή of one issued in the dominion of many in life (ver. 17); and as to the quantitative difference—in the former case, condemnation extended from one over all, simply without their personal co-operation (incurring guilt); but in the latter case, the gift of favour unto justification extended from one to all ("all," that is to say, according to the intention of God), not only without their personal co-operation (deserving it), but, on the contrary, under presupposition of ("in spite of") many transgressions (ἐκ πολλῶν παραπτωμάτων, ver. 16), on which account the gift appears as not only personally undeserved, but indeed, in consideration of the personal unworthiness of the recipients, as too great, so that there is an "excess" of favour beyond the justice that judges (ἡ δωρεὰ ἐν χάριτι ἐπερίσσευσε εἰς τοὺς πολλούς, ver. 15, and περισσεία τῆς χάριτος, ver. 17). But besides this qualitative and quantitative dissimilarity of the two members, the *positive analogy*, which forms the principal subject of discussion here, consists of the

similar relation of the respective races to their progenitor. In one
member of the parallel, as in the other, the fate of the whole
multitude—without regard to individual differences between the
several persons—is entirely determined by the act of the one
progenitor, which forms the ground of a divine judgment on the
whole multitude which depends on him, whereby they are
placed, in the one case, in a state of sin and of death, and in the
other, of righteousness and life. The religious status of these
two races is fixed *immediately* ἐξ ἑνὸς εἰς πάντας, consequently
without personal co-operation (of guilt or merit), in the one
case as that of sin, in the other of righteousness (ἁμαρτωλοὶ
κατεκρίθησαν—δίκαιοι κατασταθήσονται οἱ πολλοί, ver. 19). The
tertium comparationis, therefore, lies in the pure objectivity of
the religious status, both of natural (Adamitic) and of Christian
humanity. Neither sin and the dominion of death in the case of
the former, nor righteousness and life in the case of the latter, is
in any way caused by individuals; both, on the contrary, have
their origin in the Divine will, which displays itself as wrathful
will in a judicial sentence of condemnation, and as favourable
will in a judicial sentence of justification, passed upon the
whole; the occasion of which sentence is the act of the progenitor of the race, the misdoing of Adam, and the righteous
doing of Christ. But in this pure objectivity, neither sin nor
righteousness can be thought of as personal behaviour or a moral
quality, which would necessarily imply free action on the part of
the individuals; both indicate the general relation in which the
race (without individual freedom) finds itself placed towards
God, the *principle* ordained by God himself, which determines
the religious character of the race, and by which the religious
consciousness of the individual is conditioned à priori.

As, then, the sin of natural humanity and the dominion of
death, which is inseparable from it, do not depend on the free
act of the individuals, since they are, on the contrary, fixed as
the character of the race previously to any act of the individuals
(which character is seen in the act of the race performed by its

representative, Adam), so likewise righteousness and life do not depend on the free act of the individuals, but are given to the whole collectively, as a divine gift of favour in Christ, and are acquired as an actual possession by those who accept this gift of righteousness (τὴν περισσείαν τῆς χάριτος καὶ τῆς δωρεᾶς τῆς δικαιοσύνης λαμβάνοντες, ver. 17). The subjective effect of this, then, is a sovereign possession of life (βασιλεύσουσιν ἐν ζωῇ—as an evident contrast to the preceding ὁ θάνατος ἐβασίλευσε: instead of involuntary subjection to the sovereign dominion of death, we have here the sovereign possession of life). It is only with reference to this its subjective *effect in the possession and regal enjoyment of eternal life* (ζωὴ αἰώνιος, ver. 21), that justification is called in ver. 18 a δικαίωσις ζωῆς, and by no means in the sense of making the life righteous by a moral renovation, which would neither correspond with the immediate antithesis κατάκριμα, nor be consistent with the context and the line of thought of this entire section of the Epistle, in which, as we have said, the development of the idea of the δικαιοσύνη θεοῦ, propounded in i. 17 as the theme, is brought to its crowning point. The fundamental thought of this section is comprised in the dogmatic notions of the imputed sin of Adam and the imputed righteousness of Christ; although these words are not actually used by the Apostle, yet the sense of his expression, ἐξ ἑνὸς εἰς πάντας, certainly amounts to this.

What this idea of imputed (ideal, objective) righteousness is, may be shown indirectly by the consideration that Paul makes a very marked distinction between it and moral renovation or "sanctification" (ἁγιασμός). For instance, in 1 Cor. i. 30, Christ is made for us σοφία, δικαιοσύνη τε καὶ ἁγιασμὸς καὶ ἀπολύτρωσις. Here ἁγιασμός denotes the renovating and purifying influence of Christ upon our moral life, or the fact that the real condition of our life is in process of approximation to the moral goal of ἁγιωσύνη; consequently δικαιοσύνη cannot likewise denote this moral side, but must refer to what is presupposed as necessary to the moral process, the state of justification, the relation of a man to God as one who is reconciled, from which the process

of sanctification follows, and attains to its end in the final
ἀπολύτρωσις, which is the object of Christian hope. We find
precisely the same distinction in Rom. vi. 19: παραστήσατε τὰ
μέλη ὑμῶν δοῦλα τῇ δικαιοσύνῃ εἰς ἁγιασμόν. The members are to
be placed at the service of righteousness, as the present condition
of Christians—that is to say, so used as beseems the state of
favour in which the justified stand; but the end here aimed at
is moral perfection, to which Christians are gradually to attain
in the moral process of life, i. e. sanctification. And in ver 16,
εἰς δικαιοσύνην is not to be understood as equivalent to εἰς
ἁγιασμόν, for the moral character is expressed by δοῦλον εἶναι
ὑπακοῆς; but εἰς δικαιοσύνην is the counterpart to εἰς θάνατον in
the other clause, and refers therefore to the final result of the
moral process—justification at the final judgment; so it retains
here also its judicial sense, though with a different meaning from
that of the justification which constitutes the commencement of
the state of favour.   1 Cor. vi. 11 also agrees with this distinction of justification and sanctification: ταῦτά (gross sinners) τινες
ἦτε· ἀλλὰ ἀπελούσασθε, ἀλλὰ ἡγιάσθητε, ἀλλὰ ἐδικαιώθητε. The
order in which the ideas succeed each other here is certainly
different from that of 1 Cor. i. 30; but this does not justify a
different interpretation of their meaning, because this change in
the order is quite accounted for by the immediate occasion of
this passage: in contrast to the former grossly sinful life of the
Corinthians, it was very natural to present the sanctifying effect
of their becoming Christians both in negative terms, ἀπελούσασθε,
and positive, ἡγιάσθητε; the former denoting purification from
their former state of sin (in baptism), the latter the beginning
of a new direction of their life that was holy in principle (determined by the spirit of holiness); and ἐδικαιώθητε is added, not as
if it were the consequence of sanctification, which would be contrary to all analogy, but because it was a necessary part of the
full statement of the effects of God's favour.

From the judicial sense of the word δικαιοῦν, from the objectivity of the δικαιοσύνη θεοῦ, and from the decided distinction

between justification and sanctification, it follows that we must necessarily understand by Pauline justification, not a continuous process in man, but an *act of God*, performed once for all. And this logical conclusion is also confirmed by all the passages which refer to the subject, the bearing of Rom. v. and vi. upon this point being especially significant. It is upon the consciousness of being justified, as an established fact, that peace, hope, and the joyful certainty of salvation rest (δικαιωθέντες οὖν εἰρήνην ἔχομεν, ἐν χάριτι ἑστήκαμεν, καυχώμεθα ἐπ᾽ ἐλπίδι, vers. 1, 2; δικαιωθέντες νῦν—σωθησόμεθα ἀπὸ τῆς ὀργῆς, ver. 9; καταλλαγέντες σωθησόμεθα, ver. 10; καυχώμενοι ἐν θεῷ διὰ—Χριστοῦ, δι᾽ οὗ νῦν τὴν καταλλαγὴν ἐλάβομεν, ver. 11). The possession of favour, of which justification is the ground, is not the less an established fact because it still leaves room for the hope of future glory, as well as for the possibility of the favour of God being again lost; if justification itself is only a σωθῆναι τῇ ἐλπίδι (Rom. viii. 24), because the final σωθήσεσθε ἀπὸ τῆς ὀργῆς [1] is until the end an object of hope (v. 9 f.), yet it is nevertheless a being completely raised out of the state of sin under the law, and being placed in the state of righteousness under the favour of God (vi. 14 f.). And for the very reason that this being under favour is for the Christian presupposed as an established fact, the moral *warning* may be attached to it, to yield himself in his active life also to the service of righteousness and of God's favour, *to put into operation and to preserve the objective established relation of the righteousness of faith, in the subjective progressive righteousness of life.* The latter is a process, but the movement which constitutes it could never take place without the existence of the former. In the real moral condition of every one, relativity in each one of its moments is unavoidable; but a relative state of being justi-

---

[1] Δικαιοσύνη in Rom. vi. 16, εἰς δικαιοσύνην (opp. εἰς θάνατον), and Gal. v. 5, ἐλπίδα δικαιοσύνης ἀπεκδεχόμεθα, refers to this final σωθήσεσθαι, or the definitive sentence to be expected at the final judgment, unless perhaps in the latter passage ἐλπίδα denotes the hoped-for fruit of (present) δικαιοσύνη —that is to say, the eternal blessedness which follows from being justified.

fied, a standing partly under favour, which would consequently also be a standing partly under the curse of the law, is an impossibility. Consequently, the "process of justification" which presupposes this relativity of successive states of being justified is an utter absurdity.

If, notwithstanding its absurdity, many commentators have fallen into this error, the cause of this is to be found in the fact that they have considered justification to be dependent on the subjective operation of the Spirit in man, or on faith, as being already the real salvation life, or at least the active power of it, instead of only the passive act of appropriating salvation. The salvation life is of course a process, and therefore if justification in its Pauline sense were dependent upon it, then justification also could only be conceived as coming to be, as "the result at any moment of the stage of Christian development attained at that moment."[1]

But Pauline justification has its ground, as we have seen, not in man at all, in no corresponding righteousness or good moral character, and so forth, but it is groundless as far as man is concerned (δωρεὰν δικαιούμενοι), and has its ground in the favour of God, its intermediate cause in the redemption work of Christ (τῇ αὐτοῦ χάριτι διὰ τῆς ἀπολυτρώσεως τοῦ ἐν Χριστῷ Ἰησοῦ, Rom. iii. 24). Moreover, faith is, with regard to justification, nothing more than receptivity (ὄργανον ληπτικόν), by no means the efficient cause of it. This we have already recognized as the fundamental idea of the classical passage, Rom. v. 12—19, namely, that as sin came upon all men from Adam, so righteousness came from Christ on all, without their personal act or deed, only under the condition in the later case that they δωρεὰν

---

[1] *Lipsius*, Paulin. Rechtfertigungslehre, p. 47. The author has, however, long since given up the view he has there developed, of which fact I was ignorant when writing the article on Paulin. Rechtfertigung (Zeitschr. f. wis. Theol. 1872, II.). But the view which is here combated has many other defenders. Even *Baur* has shared it (cf. N. Tle. Theol. p. 175): "The whole process of justification is only completed in the πνεῦμα which fulfils πίστις; the highest expression for Paul's idea of justification is the νόμος τοῦ πνεύματος τῆς ζωῆς," &c.

τῆς χάριτος λαμβάνουσι, i.e. under the condition of faith. But faith does not make the δικαιοσύνην θεοῦ—in that case it would be again an ἰδία δικαιοσύνη, of which it is precisely the opposite —but it "subjects itself in obedience" to the righteousness instituted by God in Christ, and offered in the gospel. This is established from the time of the expiatory death of Christ, as an objective principle for mankind in general; so soon, therefore, as the individual accepts this new principle in faith, it becomes valid for him—he is justified. So far, then, is justification from being a process which advances gradually with the life of faith, that it would be much more in accordance with the Apostle's meaning to regard it as the act of God, concluded once for all in the expiatory death of Christ, and preceding the faith of each individual.[1] It must, however, be confessed that this view does not exactly correspond with Paul's way of representing it, for he makes justification an act which repeats itself in the case of each individual believer, as is very plainly shown by the expressions, οἷς μέλλει λογίζεσθαι τοῖς πιστεύουσιν (Rom. iv. 24), and δίκαιοι κατασταθήσονται οἱ πολλοί (v. 19), according to which justification is not already actually completed for all immediately in the death of Christ, but only the possibility of it is given for all, while its realization depends in each instance on the individual, and is therefore at the present time still future for the greater number.

This latter conception, however, certainly approaches very nearly to the truth, inasmuch as Paul's justification is nothing else than the individual application of the Christian principle of reconciling favour, the revelation of which has been made objec-

---

[1] So *Ritschl*, Altkath. Kirche, p. 93: "Justification is an act performed once for all, and is not capable of repetition; this judgment of God is completed in the death of Christ for the whole of the faithful collectively, and not in any other act, for each individual as such. But the new birth by the Holy Spirit, the consequence of justification, is essentially a predicate of the individual, and of all as individuals." P. 92: "The certainty of the individual believer regarding the new birth by the Holy Spirit is direct; the individual has not the certainty of justification directly, but only by arguing back from his new birth to his belonging to the multitude who are declared righteous in the obedience of Christ."

tively in the reconciling death of Christ, and the appropriation
of it subjectively in the act of faith. Now if this reconciling
death clothed itself, in the mind of the Apostle, in the form of a
vicarious punishment, it is quite in accordance with this view
that the individual appropriation of the reconciliation should
present itself to him again in the form of a *judicial act of God*—
an act of "acquittal, declaration of righteousness, and adoption."
This form, closely connected as it is with the Jewish mode of
thought, is precisely that *in which the Christian consciousness of
reconciliation assures itself of its being set free from its former condition under sin and the law.* It is true that the same idea had
already been more simply expressed in the discourses of Jesus,
especially in the parables showing the love of God to sinners,
but here the whole apparatus of dogmatic argument was wanting, by means of which, in the case of Paul, the Christian consciousness of adoption had to be accommodated to the standpoint
of the Jewish law. For Paul makes the reconciling favour of God
clothe itself in the categories of a judicial act which is really
the exact opposite of it ; and this makes the obvious paradox
of his doctrine, culminating in the conception of a God who δίκαιος
ὢν δικαιῶν ἐστι τὸν ἀσεβῆ.[1] But this paradoxical form was the
very best that could have been adopted, in order sharply to
mark out for the religious imagination the central Christian idea
of the free initiative of the Divine favour, and to guard it in its
undiminished ideality against the attempt, which is ever apt to
be made from the standpoint of moral reflection, to represent the
Divine favour as conditioned by human morality, and so to take
away the unconditional Divine initiative which belongs to its
essence. It is precisely this which found the most pregnant
expression in the conception of a transcendent and completed
act of pronouncing righteous prior to all moral renovation ; and
therefore this conception always presents itself to the Christian

---

[1] Cf. *Biedermann*, Dogm, § 290 : "Paul has retained this expression precisely in
order to indicate in the most striking manner that the standpoint of *the law* is raised
to the higher standpoint of favour."

consciousness, whenever it apprehends itself in its fundamental opposition to the standpoint of the law, as the palladium of the full assurance of salvation; the Christian wishes to possess reconciliation with God, not as something which is always coming into being, and which is relative, but as an already existing, accomplished fact; and can therefore only conceive it as grounded on something which is necessarily presupposed by the life of salvation which is always in process. And, in truth, the Christian principle of reconciliation, as proceeding historically from Christ, was something purely objective, preceding all moral life on the part of the subject à priori as its ground, and not dependent on it as a consequence, and also not in any way to be caused by faith, but merely to be appropriated, by being received into the heart. Consequently, justifying faith, in the eyes of Paul, is not a good moral disposition, but—apart from the consideration of any moral state—the religious act of acceptance of that Christian principle of reconciliation. And it is a quite unessential difference, affecting only the form in which the matter is represented, whether that principle appears as the saving truth announced in the gospel of Christ—in which case justifying faith is the trustful acceptance of this truth (assensus et fiducia); or whether it is identified with the person of the Mediator of reconciliation, and envisaged directly in him—in which case justifying faith is a laying hold of Christ, and being included in a mystical communion with him (unio mystica); though even then it is not to be regarded directly as a moral disposition, but as a willing acceptance of the object of salvation, for a personal possession, as an act of ὑπακοή in the religious sense.[1] On this latter

---

[1] Even the mystical notion of faith, then, does not directly contain, as *Weiss* declares (p. 329), "the moral moment of giving one's self up to the new direction of life represented in Christ;" faith is directly nothing more than the surrender of ourselves to Christ as the reconciler, or to the reconciling favour of God revealed in him, and only as this is faith justifying; but this certainly contains also the point of attachment for the development of the new life, because Christ is not only the reconciler, but also the πνεῦμα ζωοποιοῦν. The passages quoted above which speak of "justification *in* Christ," tell decisively against *Weiss's* view of justifying faith: compare what has

view of justifying faith are founded the expressions δικαιωθῆναι ἐν Χριστῷ (Gal. ii. 17), ἵνα εὑρεθῶ ἐν αὐτῷ—ἔχων—τὴν ἐκ θεοῦ δικαιοσύνην (Phil. iii. 9, cf. x. 12). These passages plainly forbid us so to separate justifying faith from the mystic faith which binds us to Christ, as to make the latter only the consequence of the justification which had preceded it; but faith is justifying precisely because it apprehends Christ as the reconciler—that is to say, apprehends the principle of reconciliation envisaged in Christ, by which means this latter is transformed into the subjective state of being reconciled, freed from the curse of the law —a transformation which presents itself to the imagination as a divine act of favour to the sinner who believes in Christ.

SONSHIP.

The new religious condition in which man sees himself placed by justification is the status of sonship. It also is still, in the first instance, an objective religious idea, and denotes the new relation of the justified man to God, not yet the new moral life. This is evident from the mere fact that it rests on the divine act of υἱοθεσία, i. e. adoption, taking into sonship, which, like that of δικαίωσις, with which it is in fact entirely identical, is a judicial act *in foro Dei.* The act of showing favour, in which God extends his favour to the sinner, is justification, inasmuch as the sinner is acquitted of the guilt of sin, and adoption, inasmuch as he is placed in the new relation to God, and is no longer an object of the divine anger, but of divine love. Now three moments go to make up this condition of sonship—two as immediate consequences of the υἱοθεσία, in which the new relation of man to

been said above, p. 169. It is quite in the Pauline spirit that *Al. Schweizer* repeatedly insists that it is merely a difference in the mode of expression whether salvation be described in the sense of a thing, as redeeming favour, or in that of a person, as Christ, since both mean nothing else than the religion of redemption offered in the gospel of Christ. Cf. Glaubenslehre, III. 183, 212, &c.

God at once displays itself, and one as the future right of a son. The former are, *being freed from the law*, and *being endowed with the spirit of sonship*, and the latter is the future *inheritance;* and we find them so mentioned together in the passage which is the chief authority on this subject, Gal. iv. 5—7. Because the νἱοθεσία is fully realized in the κληρονομία, but the latter consists essentially in the future συνδοξασθῆναι Χριστῷ, in the final glorification which is an object of hope, therefore the νἱοθεσία itself may be described as an object of hope and expectation: Rom. viii. 23, νἱοθεσίαν ἀπεκδεχόμενοι τὴν ἀπολύτρωσιν τοῦ σώματος—cf. ver. 17, εἰ τέκνα, καὶ κληρονόμοι μὲν θεοῦ, συγκληρονόμοι δὲ Χριστοῦ, εἴπερ συμπάσχομεν, ἵνα καὶ συνδοξασθῶμεν. This future hope is meanwhile guaranteed to us by the pledge of the *spirit of the son of God which belongs to the state of sonship*, and which is given to us at the present time, which we have received by virtue of our adoption, and which, in the subjective consciousness of sonship, attests to us the fact that we are sons (Gal. iv. 6, ὅτι δέ ἐστε νἱοί, ἐξαπέστειλεν ὁ θεὸς τὸ πνεῦμα τοῦ νἱοῦ αὐτοῦ εἰς τὰς καρδίας ὑμῶν, κρᾶζον Αββα ὁ πατήρ; Rom. viii. 15 f., ἐλάβετε πνεῦμα νἱοθεσίας ἐν ᾧ κράζομεν ’Αββα ὁ πατήρ· αὐτὸ τὸ πνεῦμα συμμαρτυρεῖ τῷ πνεύματι ἡμῶν, ὅτι ἐσμὲν τέκνα Θεοῦ). The spirit bestowed on Christians is here called πνεῦμα νἱοθεσίας, not as if it were the cause by which sonship is effected—this would contradict the declaration of Gal. iv. 6, ὅτι ἐστε νἱοί, ἐξαπέστειλεν, &c.—but because it belongs to those who through faith in the Son of God have become children of God (Gal. iii. 26), as the new principle of life which alone accords with their new status, and that so essentially and inalienably, that the existence of this spirit as the impelling force of the subjective life may be considered as the certain criterion of the objective truth of the state of sonship (ὅσοι πνεύματι θεοῦ ἄγονται, οὗτοί εἰσιν νἱοὶ θεοῦ, Rom. viii. 14). Of this spirit more will have to be said in the next Chapter; but here we have still to deal with the point, which occupies the first place in the notion of sonship, because it characterizes this state negatively by its opposition in principle to the former one, viz. *the freeing from the law.*

In Gal. iv. 5, the immediate purpose of the sending of the Son of God is thus indicated: ἵνα τοὺς ὑπὸ νόμον ἐξαγοράσῃ, ἵνα τὴν υἱοθεσίαν ἀπολάβωμεν, and the consequence of this, ὥστε οὐκέτι εἶ δοῦλος, ἀλλ᾽ υἱός. The coming in of sonship thus presupposes exemption from the law—that is to say, as is proved by the context, from the *demands* of the law, which by their external training had exercised a guardianship over humanity (that is, the people of Israel) while in its minority. The validity of these demands of the law was from the beginning established only for a certain period of time, namely, ἄχρι τῆς προθεσμίας τοῦ πατρός (ver. 2). Its abrogation, moreover, like that of the curse of the law (iii. 13), required a vicarious submission to it by the Son of God, who although he was really, as a son, free from the δουλεία τῶν στοιχείων τοῦ κόσμου, was nevertheless put under the law, in order that he might, by voluntarily satisfying its claims, redeem those who till then were under the law. Hereby alone was given the possibility of the coming in of the period of sonship or of faith. Inasmuch as we now, by faith in the Son of God, become likewise sons of God (iii. 26), we enter by this very means upon the enjoyment of the right of adult sons to freedom from governors, tutors, and guardians, under whom of course only minors are placed, who as such are in the position of servants. Having thus become sons through faith, we are no longer δοῦλοι, no longer δεδουλωμένοι ὑπὸ τὰ στοιχεῖα τοῦ κόσμου, under the law, so far as it has to do with externals, as with the course of the heavenly bodies which constitutes years, months, and days. And because in this epoch of full age and of freedom, ushered in by faith in the Son of God, both those who were formerly Jews are freed from their legal worship (iv. 3 and 5), and those who were formerly Gentiles are freed from their nature-worship (vers. 8 and 9), and thus the limit which hitherto separated these two sections is done away with in their common Christian freedom, therefore it is now said that within the Christian community οὐκ ἔνι Ἰουδαῖος οὐδὲ Ἕλλην, οὐκ ἔνι δοῦλος οὐδὲ ἐλεύθερος—πάντες γὰρ ὑμεῖς εἷς ἐστὲ ἐν Χριστῷ Ἰησοῦ, iii. 28. This equality and unity of all believers on Christ in the freedom from the law which belongs to them as sons, is a main point of the Apostle's teaching, which is in an incomprehensible manner overlooked by those who would limit Paul's cardinal dogma of Christian freedom from the law to Gentile converts. Those who had till then been Gentiles had not evidently to be redeemed from that law to which Christ became subject—that is to say, the Mosaic law; therefore verses 4, 5, like iii. 25, οὐκέτι ὑπὸ παιδαγωγόν ἐσμεν, can only refer to those who were formerly Jews. In v. 1, μὴ πάλιν ζυγῷ δουλείας ἐνέχεσθε, the word πάλιν most probably implies that among the persons addressed there were some who had been formerly Jews, although the contents of the next verse have reference immediately to Gentile Christians. In chapter iv. 21—31, the Apostle compares Christians as born after the spirit, with Isaac, who was born, in consequence of the miraculous promise, the free son of a free mother; and, on the other hand, those who are under the law, with the unfree son of the bondwoman Hagar, born in the ordinary course of nature, who is thrust out by the son of the free woman, because the son of a servant cannot inherit with the son of a free woman. "So then we are not children of the bondwoman, but of the free." "We" who are free from the law can only mean the whole body of Christians; for if it meant only the Gentile converts, then it is clear that the Jewish Christians, together with the Jews, would be among "the children of the servant," who had lost the inheritance! A similar allegorical proof of the abrogation of the law in Christianity is found in 2 Cor. iii. The evanescent brightness on the face of Moses indicated the merely temporary significance of the law; in order that the children of Israel might not perceive this, Moses veiled his face, and this veil still lies upon the Old Testament, so that its true sense, its destination, namely, to be done away with in Christ, remains concealed; but by turning to Christ, this veil is removed—"where the spirit of the Lord is, there is freedom." It is precisely for the Jew that this argument, like the foregoing one, would have significance; for it proceeds from his standpoint, and deduces the transient validity of the law from the law itself; it is the Jew, and no other, who by his conversion to Christ is to learn to recognize the fact which has hitherto been hidden from him, that the law is only a letter which kills, and therefore has an evanescent brightness, but the spirit of Christ is living and makes men free. In Rom. vii. 1—7, the abrogation of the law is deduced from the (certainly very lame) analogy of marriage, from the bonds of which, by the death of one party, the other becomes free. In the same way, those who were formerly bound to the law have become free from these bonds, by having themselves died to the law by their communion with Christ who was put to death, so that they can give themselves to a new lord and master, "in order that we may now serve in newness of the spirit, and not in the oldness of the letter." And the Apostle says this expressly to those "who know the law" (ver. 1)—that is, to Jewish Christians. To all this must be added what the Apostle says of himself, that he, through the law, was dead to the law, and crucified with Christ, by whose cross the world was crucified to him, and he to the world (all connection with the position and the opinions which he formerly held as a Jew was severed); that he no longer preached circumcision, and had to suffer persecution on that account; that he had become to those without the law as one without the law; and then again (on the very ground, observe, of being in principle outside the law), to those under the law as one under the law (compare Gal. ii. 19, vi. 14, v. 11; 1 Cor. ix. 21); and if all this be put together, there cannot remain the shadow of a doubt that the Apostle Paul absolutely and completely denies in principle that the Mosaic law has any validity or binding force whatsoever within the Christian community.

This *dogmatic principle* is all that we have to do with here; how far it was modified in practice by moral considerations of love and prudence will be discussed later on. In any case, the abrogation of the law was to him a main point of Christian knowledge (1 Cor. viii. 1—7; 2 Cor. iii. 4, 6), and to his adversaries the chief offence in his preaching of the crucified (Gal. v. 11).

CHAPTER V.

LIVING IN THE SPIRIT.

THE antinomianism of Paul's doctrine of faith has laid it open to misunderstanding and misinterpretation both by friends and foes, as if the believer in Christ were, according to Paul, relieved from all the demands of morality and could indulge in sin without any restraint, as his caprice might dictate. The necessity of refuting this false inference induces the Apostle to show how the principle of a real renovation of life, of cleansing from sin, is involved in that very union of the believer with Christ which makes him a free child of God; how the inward law of the spirit of Christ now takes the place of the outward law which has been done away—an inward law which no longer enslaves, but makes us for the first time really free, and brings to actual accomplishment that which the outward law could only demand.

THE BEGINNING OF THE NEW LIFE.

In Rom. vi. 1, the Apostle meets the objection—May the believer then remain in sin, that the favour of God may be all the more powerfully manifested?— by the emphatic denial, μὴ γένοιτο! and goes on to give the following grounds for the refutation of a fundamentally erroneous inference: "How shall we that are dead to sin wish to live in it? Or do you not know that all of us who have been baptized to Jesus Christ, have been baptized to his death? We have therefore been buried with him, through baptism to his death, in order that as Christ was raised from the dead by the glory of the Father, so we also should live a new life; for if we have grown one with him by copying his death, we shall also grow one with him by copying his resurrection; being assured of this, that our old man was crucified with him, in order that the body of sin might be done away, so that we might no more (be obliged to) be the slaves of sin; for one who is dead is lawfully freed from (the sovereignty of) sin. But if we have been crucified with Christ, then we believe that we shall also live with him; knowing that Christ having been raised from the dead, dies no more, death has no power over him. For in his death he died to sin once for all, but in his life he lives to God. So do you also consider yourselves to be dead to sin, but alive to God in Christ Jesus our Lord." The Apostle therefore regards baptism as an entering into communion with Christ as one who died and rose again, by which means his death and resurrection become ours also, that is to say, repeat themselves in us in a supersensuous, but none the less real way.

How this happens with regard to the *death* of Christ, cannot be doubtful. Inasmuch as participation in him by baptism is assumed to be an accomplished fact, this "dying with him" must consist in a spiritual process, namely, in that process by which a man becomes a Christian, one who belongs to Christ and his community. As Christ put himself out of all relation and connection with sinful flesh by the death of his body ($\tau \hat{\eta}$ $\dot{a}\mu a\rho\tau\acute{\iota}\dot{a}$ $\dot{a}\pi\acute{\epsilon}\theta a\nu\epsilon\nu$), so man, by entering through baptism into that state in which he belongs to the crucified one, withdraws from the connection of his life with flesh and the world, which had existed up to that time; the world is crucified to him, and he to it (Gal. vi. 14); that is to say, its life and being, its possessions and opinions, have no more power over him, and his life, wealth, and honour have nothing more to do with its domain, which is that of the vain and external. But besides this, the still closer

o

connection of the self with its own flesh is by this means done
away with in principle; "those who belong to Christ have (by
the very act of entering into this state, that is, in baptism)
crucified their flesh, with all its passions and desires" (Gal. v. 24),
i. e. they have taken away its free activity and sinful energy,
have reduced the principle which hitherto ruled them into a
state of powerlessness, like that of a person who is crucified, and
given it up to the process of gradual extinction. The intended
result of this crucifixion of the old man is the doing away with
the body of sin (i. e. the body in so far as it consists of the σὰρξ
ἁμαρτίας, and is therefore the abode of sin), in order that we
should no longer be the slaves of sin; in brief, therefore, the
real liberation from the dominating power of sin (Rom. vi. 6).
We must remember that this καταργεῖσθαι of the σῶμα ἁμαρτίας is
only connected with the συσταυρωθῆναι which occurs in baptism
as its intended consequence, and does not absolutely coincide
with it. This indicates that the dying of the old man is a
process that goes on continually, and which has in the act of
baptism only made a beginning in principle (though certainly a
decisive beginning), just as the death of the body is induced by
the act of crucifixion, but not in that instant accomplished. But
in principle certainly the old man is dead in him who is baptized;
he has experienced in his own person the accomplished fact of the
death of Christ, by surrendering himself in faith to Christ, and
becoming a member of Christ (baptism)—according to the canon,
"if one has died for all, then are you all dead;" that is to say,
the death of that one becomes a *common principle* for the whole
body of those who have the enjoyment of him by appropriating
him to themselves in faith, and their life is henceforth guided
by the determining influence of this principle, so that they now
only know and feel and will themselves as dead to their former
principle of life.

But it is a less simple matter to answer the other question,
how far the new *life* of the risen Christ repeats itself in that of
the Christian. According to the analogy of " dying with him,"

the idea of the spiritual or ethical living with Christ is so
obvious, that the greater number of commentators up to the
present day see nothing but this in the passage before us. But
this is decidedly incorrect. Since in ver. 5 ἀλλὰ καὶ τῆς
ἀναστάσεως ἐσόμεθα is opposed to σύμφυτοι γεγόναμεν τῷ ὁμοιώματι
τοῦ θανάτου, the change of tense clearly proves that this copying
of the resurrection of Christ does not simply correspond in time
with that of his death, i. e. with the moment of baptism as the
beginning to be a Christian; if we would give its due force to
the future as distinguished from the past tense which has gone
before, we must apply the words only to the resurrection after
this life, which is still future. But this is fully established
beyond the possibility of doubt by ver. 8, εἰ ἀπεθάνομεν σὺν
Χριστῷ πιστεύομεν ὅτι καὶ συζήσομεν αὐτῷ; here the communion
with the life of him who has risen again is presented to us not
merely as something future, but as also an object of our believing trustfulness, therefore of our hope and expectation, the
realizing of which will be by no means dependent on our own
action, but will be effected in us or presented to us by God;
this is the only sense of πιστεύομεν which accords with the use of
the word elsewhere. But in that case we must not understand
συζήσομεν to refer to our present new moral life; that would of
course depend on our own moral activity during the present
time, and therefore could in no way be an object of believing
trustfulness; it refers, on the contrary, to the communion of life
with their risen Lord which believers are to hope for on the
other side of the grave. Only, certain as this is, it is equally
undeniable, on the other hand, that in ver. 4, ἵνα καὶ ἡμεῖς ἐν
καινότητι ζωῆς περιπατήσωμεν, and in ver. 11, λογίζεσθε ἑαυτοὺς ζῶντας
τῷ θεῷ ἐν Χριστῷ Ἰησοῦ, can only be understood of the present
new moral life of Christians, of which the context of these
passages mainly treats. If we observe, however, that this new
moral life of the present is put forward as something intended
and required (ἵνα . . . περιπατήσωμεν, and λογίζεσθε), but the eschatological living with Christ as something to be believed, we may

o 2

find the key to the difficulty. The Apostle evidently understands the living with the risen Christ, which is the result of
communion with his death, first of all in the actual sense of the
eschatological life of the resurrection; it is an object of faith to
him as such; but this object of dogmatic hope forthwith changes
into a determining principle of the ethical life of the present,
which latter, by the very fact of its being dominated by that
principle, becomes itself a new life, and so in truth the present anticipated beginning of that future life. *The eschatological
living with Christ changes itself, therefore, in the mind of the
Apostle into the ethical new life of the Christian present;* the
καινότης ζωῆς remains no longer a mere object of hope, but
becomes the rule and the element of the spontaneous activity
of life. Given Paul's mystic faith, this could not be otherwise.
The Christian has already inwardly experienced in baptism the
death of his Master, and entered into communion, in the bonds
of faith, with him who died in order that he might be Lord over
all, and that they who live might no longer live to themselves,
but for him who died and rose again for them (Rom. xiv. 9;
2 Cor. v. 15). This "living no more to themselves, but living
to Christ and God," which is required by the death of Christ,
and implied in the communion with his death in baptism, is
therefore already in fact the beginning of a new life, which shares
with the resurrection-life of Christ the specific character of being
devoted to God, and therefore can no longer be specifically distinguished (as to its essential inward quality) from the real
future resurrection-life of the Christian. But we must remember, as having an important bearing on the Apostle's whole
tone of thought, including his ethical views, that the πιστεύομεν
ὅτι συζήσομεν, i. e. the certain faith in the eschatological living
with Christ, is still the foundation on which the ethical reflection
first rears itself; so that the latter is not something which merely
ought to be, but has from the commencement its ground in that
which is, to faith (if not also to sight), already established in
existence. The believer knows himself to be already one with

Christ, and therefore *in the ideal possession of eternal life* (the idea of Rom. v. 1—11), whence the duty of living a new life follows, for him, as a simple logical consequence. The *moral* "*newness of life*" is now no other than the self-evident external activity of that which is, to the religious mind, a good already existing by faith, the ideal possession of "life" in the absolute sense. The moral consciousness is here no longer entangled in the abstract standpoint of the law, but reposes on the consciousness of reconciliation, of absolute inward peace and satisfaction.

Baptism is therefore, according to the passage before us, the beginning of the new life, inasmuch as it places man in a mystical connection with Christ, by virtue of which he knows that his old life is dead with Christ, and that the new life of Christ is appropriated by himself, not only as an object of hope, but also as a present inward possession. On man's entering by baptism into that state in which he belongs to Christ, the bodily dying and rising again of Christ accomplishes itself in him, as a virtual act of his soul, as liberation from that sphere of life in the flesh and the world in which he has hitherto lived, and entrance into the sphere of Christ's life, which henceforth completely envelops him, as in a garment (Χριστὸν ἐνδύσασθε, Gal. iii. 27), which becomes the element in which he lives and moves, so that he is ἐν Χριστῷ. This formula is Paul's specific and most significant expression for being a Christian, and is applied to particular relations, states, and actions, so far as they are connected with Christianity, and denote something that belongs to the Christian life. Thus "churches in Christ" (Gal. i. 22) are simply equivalent to Christian churches; "dead, asleep in Christ" (1 Cor. xv. 18; 1 Thess. iv. 16) to dead Christians; "fathers, brothers, fellow-workers in Christ" (1 Cor. iv. 15; Col. i. 2; Rom. xvi. 3) indicate that these are not the natural and ordinary relations as usually understood, but that they belong to the sphere of Christian life; the Apostle's fetters at Rome "are manifest in Christ," that is, as fetters which he had to bear, not for an ordinary offence, but as a Christian and for

being a Christian (Phil. i. 13); "ways in Christ" (1 Cor. iv. 17)
are Christian modes of behaviour with special reference to lead-
ing the life of the Christian community; and in particular the
several spiritual conditions, gifts, and powers which are peculiar
to the Christian, are presented in their special Christian character by the expression ἐν Χριστῷ; for instance, life (Rom. viii. 2),
God's love or favour (Rom. viii. 39; 1 Cor. i. 4; 1 Cor. xvi. 24),
glory, comfort, and hope (Rom. xv. 17; Phil. ii. 1, 19, iii. 3),
freedom (Gal. ii. 4), holiness and perfection (1 Cor. i. 2; Phil.
i. 1—4, 21; Col. i. 28), wisdom, and also infancy, that is unripe-
ness of understanding (1 Cor. iii. 1, iv. 10).

But the gist of this formula ἐν Χριστῷ is nothing else than
Paul's mystic faith, in which the believer gives up himself, his
own life to Christ, and possesses the life of Christ in himself:
he in Christ, and Christ in him; he dead with Christ, and
Christ become his life,—these are inseparable and convertible
ideas, expressing one and the same relation of unity between
man and the divine object of salvation; and this relation of
unity is nothing else than faith itself. In fact, it is impossible
to point out any difference between Paul's mystical notion of
faith as collected above (p. 169 f.), and that which we find here
as the communion of life with Christ brought about by baptism.
And this view is supported by the connection between vers. 26
and 27 of Gal. iii.; that all who are baptized to Christ have put
on Christ, is made the ground of the assertion that all believers
in Christ, as such, by means of this faith of theirs, are sons of
God. According to this, to have put on Christ, and to have
become a son of God, are one and the same thing. Now as the
latter is simply brought about by means of faith (ver. 26), baptism, which is the means of bringing about the former (ver. 27),
cannot be anything specifically different from faith, and must
therefore be related to faith, as the phenomenal form to the
spiritual substance; and for the very reason that baptism is the
externally completed entrance into the connection with Christ
by faith, it may be considered as the *ground of recognition* of

that existing communion with Christ, the *real ground* of which is *faith*. If we add to this, that the sonship of God, which depends on the union with Christ by faith (διὰ πίστεως ἐν Χριστῷ, ver. 26), is, according to iv. 6, the condition of receiving the spirit of the Son, it follows plainly enough that receiving the spirit is not the ground of communion with Christ, but, on the contrary, communion with Christ, of which faith is the ground, is the logical *prius* of the receipt of the spirit of sonship. This is at all events in perfect accord with the remarkable fact (which has however remained generally unnoticed) that in Rom. vi., although the new life of the baptized in their communion with Christ is spoken of from the beginning to the end of the chapter, this is nowhere grounded on the reception of the spirit; nay, *not a single syllable is uttered about* πνεῦμα *at all!* How is it possible to explain this on the supposition of that which is ordinarily taken for granted, that the communion of life with Christ depends upon the reception of the spirit in baptism, and consequently this (and not faith) is the root of the mystical doctrine of Paul? We shall therefore be justified in considering this assumption, general as it is, to be incorrect, and in seeing in the remarkable fact just noticed a decisive confirmation of that which we have already found as the result of our analysis of Paul's notion of faith; namely, that the mystical element of Paulinism depends immediately and exclusively on his notion of faith. Because faith was actually to Paul that deep and full act of the devotion of the whole heart which he describes in Gal. ii. 20, therefore, and for that reason only, was he in this act conscious of mystical union with the absolute object of salvation. But when he wishes to remind his Christian readers of the fact of their communion with Christ (whether as the ground of their Christian freedom and equality, Gal. iii. 27 f., or as a motive for their Christian moral life, Rom. vi.), he naturally called to mind that external tangible and visible act in which the inmost heart's act of faith was concluded and sealed—the act of baptism.

In this mystically deepened notion of faith, the most special peculiarity of Paul, there was contained further the possibility and the incentive to deepen and modify a doctrine which was not originally peculiar to Paul, but was traditional in the primitive Church, the doctrine of the *Messianic* πνεῦμα which the Christian receives by virtue of his baptism (Acts ii. 38). The Christian community understood by this Messianic πνεῦμα nothing essentially different from the Old Testament prophetic spirit of revelation, the general communication of which had been already promised in Joel as a characteristic of the last time. This spirit is represented as a supersensuous substance of the higher divine world which comes upon man (by being poured out), and produces in him supernatural gifts and miraculous effects, such as seeing visions, speaking with tongues, and powers of healing (cf. Acts ii. 16—19, x. 46, xix. 6). Now Paul also starts from this same conception, as when he also alleges these miraculous gifts and powers as essential evidences and characteristics of the Christian πνεῦμα (1 Cor. 12; Gal. iii. 5). Only this is no longer, for him, the only nor the essential function of the Christian πνεῦμα; on the contrary, the principal thing appears to him to be this, that the divine πνεῦμα becomes in the Christian the constantly operating principle of his whole life of faith, which manifests itself not only in prophesying, but in all kinds of Christian knowledge; not only in working miracles, but in every Christian duty; above all, in that which is the foundation of all goodness, in love. In short, the πνεῦμα is changed, in the mind of Paul, from an abstract, supernatural, ecstatic, Apocalyptic principle, to an immanent, religious, moral principle of the life of renovated humanity, to the nature of the καινὴ κτίσις. By this means Christianity was established as a new historical principle in independence of the Jewish religion, and at the same time a bridge was constructed from the ecstatic phenomena of the enthusiasm of the primitive Church, to a constant historical development of the Christian community.

How then did Paul arrive at this view of πνεῦμα, which made an epoch for the whole course of Christian speculation? It might be supposed (and it appears to be the ordinary assumption) that Paul had from the beginning a peculiar notion, a deeper and more spiritual one, of πνεῦμα. But this is not the case. Even the Pauline πνεῦμα is *in itself* a transcendent physical essence, a supersensuous kind of matter, which is the opposite of the earthly sensuous materiality of the σάρξ. As the latter is the weak, perishable, impure, relatively sinful element of the world, of that existence which is not divine, and is therefore excluded from the kingdom of God, so the πνεῦμα is the strong, enduring, pure, and holy element of the divine existence, of heaven, and therefore has also the power to make alive, and to purify or make holy (comp. especially the contrast drawn in 1 Cor. xv. 42—50). It can therefore only relatively be called immaterial, in so far as it is not earthly and sensuous materiality, but heavenly, supersensuous matter; hence its close affinity to that which was considered by the ancient world as the most subtle earthly material, the air, of which the etymology of the word πνεῦμα itself reminds us, and light, the brightness of which (δόξα) is to be regarded as the permanent form of appearance of the πνεῦμα. It is a material notion that the πνεῦμα was poured out into the heart like water (Rom. v. 5), that it streamed in like a ray of light (2 Cor. iv. 6), even changed the bodies of those in whom it dwelt into brightness (2 Cor. iii. 18), nay, that it could itself, like σάρξ, become material for bodies (σώματα, equivalent to forms with limbs); for Paul represents the bodies of the risen as such σώματα πνευματικά, consisting of the heavenly light-substance of different degrees of brightness (1 Cor. xv. 40 f.). Now this supersensuous substance originally belongs to God, and then to Christ the Son of God, in such wise that it constitutes their divine essence (he was in the form of God), and is presented in a concrete form in them; but it does not form a separate personality in each of them. It is true that the spirit more often appears as an acting subject with consciousness and will; he dispenses his gifts as he will (1 Cor. xii. 7), searches the depths of the Godhead (ii. 10), intercedes for us with God

(Rom. viii. 26), and bears witness with our spirit (v. 16). But if it be granted that this personification is something more than a mere mode of speech, that it is an essential part of the Apostle's conception, yet this is still far from being a distinct idea of a separate personality of God and of Christ. In the personification of the spirit in 1 Cor. xii. 11, it is still God (see ver. 6) who does everything; and the spirit who searches the depths of the Godhead, in 1 Cor. ii. 10, is still only the ego of God, which distinguishes itself from itself, that is to say, is self-conscious; in Rom. viii. 16, 26, the indwelling spirit of God, or of Christ, is not distinguished from the indwelling Christ himself (comp. vers. 9 and 10); in 2 Cor. xiii. 13, it is true that the κοινωνία τοῦ ἁγίου πνεύματος is put by the side of χάρις Χριστοῦ and ἀγάπη θεοῦ, but not as if these were three independent, co-ordinate moments, of which each had an independent personal cause; but they are related to each other as cause (ἀγάπη θεοῦ), means (χάρις Χριστοῦ), and effect (κοινωνία τ. ἁγ. πνεύματος); for thus the manifestation of the favour of Christ, proceeding from the love of God, arrives at its subjective conclusion. If we add to this the expressions, the spirit is sent by God (Gal. iv. 6), is given (Rom. v. 5), administered (Gal. iii. 5), received by man from God (Gal. iii. 2; 1 Cor. ii. 12), and possessed as one's own (1 Cor. vi. 19; Rom. viii. 9), we cannot fail to see in the texts thus brought together a wavering between the notion of the spirit being a thing and being a person, which plainly shows that the latter notion is not fixed. The divine πνεῦμα exists as concrete substance (excepting in God himself) only in the exalted Christ, for ὁ κύριος τὸ πνεῦμά ἐστιν (2 Cor. iii. 17).

In all these terms, so far as they relate to the nature of the πνεῦμα itself, nothing is as yet implied which is peculiar to Paul. But the connecting link is already contained in the last-named point, according to which the πνεῦμα does not belong to the Messiah as a mere *donum superadditum*, as an endowment of his office (as it was still regarded in fact by the Jewish Christians), but substantially constitutes the person of the exalted

Christ (as it also does that of the earthly Christ, at least as regards its inner side; comp. p. 128). From this point, that fundamental view of Paul which regarded faith and baptism as a real union with the crucified and risen Christ, formed the transition to the peculiar Pauline doctrine of the πνεῦμα, as we have seen it expanded in Rom. vi. If the faith which completes itself in baptism is a giving up of the man to the dead and risen Christ, so that he belongs to him, and has inward communion of life with him, and if this risen Christ is in his substance heavenly πνεῦμα, then it is a plain inference, that the Christian consequently, by faith and baptism, becomes a partaker of that heavenly πνεῦμα; and as this πνεῦμα is now in Christ the principle of life which forms his person, so must it necessarily become also in the Christian, who κολλώμενος τῷ κυρίω ἓν πνεῦμά ἐστιν (1 Cor. vi. 17), a constantly immanent principle of the new personal life, of the καινὸς ἄνθρωπος. Accordingly we have to explain the peculiar Pauline doctrine of πνεῦμα by the flowing together of *two streams* of thought—*on the one hand the traditional doctrine* that we receive in *baptism* the (miracle-working) Messianic πνεῦμα, and *on the other hand the original Pauline doctrine of faith* as the heart's act of trusting, loving *union with Christ* the reconciler and the holy Son of God, κατὰ πνεῦμα ἀγιωσύνης; hence it was that the *dogmatic form*, the fixed idea, and also the deep *religious moral content*, were derived, which soon widened into a river of speculation; here also was the source of the innermost affections and most personal life of Paul. How much more congenial to the Apostle's mind the latter of these views was, and how much more essential he thought it than the first, may be inferred from the fact, that he places the reception of the spirit in direct connection with believing three times (Gal. iii. 2, 5, and 14), but with baptism only once, and that indirectly (1 Cor. xii. 13, ἐν ἑνὶ πνεύματι ἡμεῖς εἰς ἓν σῶμα ἐβαπτίσθημεν): on the ground of this fact we are quite justified in assuming that Paul for his part had accepted the traditional doctrine of the reception of the spirit at baptism; but we must be on our guard

204 LIVING IN THE SPIRIT.

against allowing to this point so central an importance in Paul's
doctrine of salvation as is generally given to it, by setting baptism as a communication of the spirit, by the side of justifying
faith as a second principle of salvation. If this had been the
Apostle's opinion he must have declared it, and therefore must
have distinctly made the reception of the spirit depend on
baptism, as justification and sonship were dependent on faith.
Instead of this, however, he connects on the one hand with
faith the reception of the spirit and sonship in an equal degree,
and on the other hand in an equal degree baptism and faith with
the mystic communion with Christ. What, then, really becomes
of that specific significance of baptism, which is generally attributed to it at the present day?

What has just been said will receive further confirmation if
we now turn our attention to the changes which are produced in
man by the divine πνεῦμα. The most general effect of the πνεῦμα
appears to be ζωή. As the attribute of living essentially belongs
to it, so its effect is essentially ζωοποιεῖν, in the most comprehensive absolute sense of the word, as comprising within itself different moments. Among these, however, the transcendent physical or eschatological idea of "life" occupies undoubtedly the
first place in the Apostle's mind. Thus in the important passage
where he is speaking of Christ himself, he is said to have become
(in the resurrection) a πνεῦμα ζωοποιοῦν, 1 Cor. xv. 45. This
ζωοποιεῖν, according to the context of the whole chapter, can only
refer to Christians being put in possession, through Christ, of
imperishable heavenly life, and being raised from the death
which they must die as children of Adam, to the new (eternal)
life, bearing the image of him who is risen (that is to say, his
glorified spiritual body). In this sense it is said in the same
passage "As in Adam (in unity of race with the originator of
natural humanity) all die, so in Christ (in the unity of faith
with the originator of a new humanity) all are made alive"
(ver. 22). Similarly, in an eschatological sense, yet so that
the ethical sense is already apparent in it, we understand the

instructive passage, 2 Cor. iv. 10—v. 5. The Apostle says of himself, that he always bears about with him in his body the dying of the Lord Jesus, ἵνα καὶ ἡ ζωὴ τοῦ ᾿Ιησοῦ ἐν τῷ σώματι ἡμῶν φανερωθῇ. Now, according to the context, we can understand by this νέκρωσις ᾿Ιησοῦ nothing else than the constant wearing out of his bodily life by external causes and bodily sickness (ver. 7, ὀστράκινα σκεύη, and ver. 16, ὁ ἔξω ἡμῶν ἄνθρωπος διαφθείρεται), which he both endures for the sake of Jesus, and as a repeated setting forth of the suffering of Jesus. But what is the φανερωθῆναι of the ζωὴ ᾿Ιησοῦ ἐν τῷ σώματι ἡμῶν? According to the context it appears to me that it must be one of two things; either, with reference to ver. 16, it must mean the renewal of the ἔσωθεν ἄνθρωπος, which is parallel to the wearing out of the ἔξω ἄνθρωπος, or, with reference to ver. 14, the rising from the dead with Jesus. By the latter, one cannot in any case, without an exercise of the most arbitrary caprice, understand anything but the eschatological resurrection, since the whole tenor of the passage from ver. 17 is purely eschatological. If we should take ver. 10 to refer to the renewal of the ἔσω ἄνθρωπος by the life-giving power of Christ, then we should have to understand φανερωθῆναι ἐν τῷ σώματι as being manifested, that is being operative in the bodily life, during the earthly existence of the Apostle; but as this application of the passage appears less natural than the other—to be manifested *upon* our body, so that this is itself the object to which the φανέρωσις of the ζωὴ ᾿Ιησοῦ refers—we must understand this latter to refer to ver. 14 in preference to ver. 16, and accordingly to signify the manifestation of the resurrection-life of Christ in the rising of the Apostle's own body from the dead. Nor need the substitution of σαρκί for σώματι in ver. 11 perplex us; for although the σάρξ itself certainly cannot rise again, yet the power of the resurrection can be so manifested upon the fleshly substance of the body, as to change it into the new substance of the resurrection body (cf. Phil. iii. 21, μετασχηματίσει). But although, according to this interpretation, we must refer the words primarily to the escha-

tological life, yet we shall find again in this very passage clear
indications that in the Apostle's mind this ζωή, although its
φανέρωσις still has the first place in his thought, has notwithstanding an inward reality at the present time, namely, in the
ἀνακαίνωσις of the ἔσωθεν ἄνθρωπος already effected by the spirit
of Christ, while the wearing out of the ἔξω ἄνθρωπος is going on,
and by means of it. To this end has God, in the spirit which
he has given us, imparted to us already a real *earnest* (ἀρραβών)
of the heavenly life, nay, a *preparatory* beginning of it (ὁ κατεργα-
σάμενος ἡμᾶς εἰς αὐτὸ τοῦτο, θεός, ὁ καὶ δοὺς ἡμῖν τὸν ἀρραβῶνα τοῦ
πνεύματος, v. 5). Here we look right into the laboratory of the
Apostle's religious thought: he knows that the life of Christ
will one day be manifested in him as that which it is, that is to
say, as absolute life whose perfection extends to the body; this
certainty he has by virtue of his possession of the spirit, which
inwardly guarantees it to him (by the witness of his sonship to
God, Rom. viii. 16); but in this inward certainty, guaranteed by
the spirit, of the life which he will one day possess, he already
at the present moment lives the preparatory commencement of
that life—in the constant renewal of his inner man, in the true
spiritual, religious, and moral process of his life of faith. From
this we shall be able to understand how, in other passages, the
two ideas of the ζωή, the eschatological and the ethical, interpenetrate one another. Thus in Rom. viii., when it is said of
Christ (ver. 10), τὸ μὲν σῶμα νεκρὸν δι' ἁμαρτίαν, τὸ δὲ πνεῦμα ζωὴ διὰ
δικαιοσύνην, the νεκρόν of the first clause must, on account of the
parallelism, τὰ θνητὰ σώματα ὑμῶν, ver. 11, be understood to refer
to bodily death, and that in the sense that the body is forfeited
to death on account of sin (as the wages of sin), and is so far as
good as dead already, in which case the ζωή predicated of the
spirit must also, in order to correspond with this physical notion
of death, be understood in a physical sense, of enduring, eternal
life. Moreover, if we understood this in an ethical sense, we'
should have a tautology in διὰ δικαιοσύνην, which does not mean
for the purpose of righteousness, but, corresponding with δι'

ἁμαρτίαν, on account of, or in consequence of, the righteousness which belongs to him. Finally, from the fact that the spirit of the Christian is life, the inference is drawn that his body also will be endowed with life (ver. 11); this physical ζωοποιήσει also presupposes, in ver. 10, the physical notion of the ζωή. Now it is not said in the verse before us that the spirit will at some future time be or have life, but that it is so now. This verse, therefore, directly presents to us the significant thought, that the ζωὴ αἰώνιος is already present in the life of Christians on this side of the grave, as an immediate inward possession of the spirit. But in what should this immanent ζωὴ αἰώνιος, regarded in a psychological sense, consist, if not in a new ethical quality of the personal life? Thus the physical or eschatological · notion of life, by taking its commencement as an attribute of the Christian spirit in the present time, immediately changes itself into the ethical notion of life, which latter is also to be found in the context of the passage before us, ver. 2, πνεῦμα τῆς ζωῆς ἐν Χριστῷ, and ver. 6, φρόνημα πνεύματος ζωὴ καὶ εἰρήνη. In the latter case, the connection with εἰρήνη points to the ethical notion of the life which is united with God and pleasing to Him; yet here also we may think of the eternal life as the final object (τέλος, cf. vi. 22) which is aimed at by the striving of the spirit. We have already found just the same interchange of eschatological and ethical life in Rom. vi. 4—11. Lastly, there are not wanting passages in which both these sides are held together in inseparable unity, and so the idea of ζωή has its absolute significance; this will be the case in every instance where ζωή simply indicates Christian salvation in general, as in the expressions, λόγος ζωῆς = the gospel of life = salvation in Christ (Phil. ii. 16), τὸ πνεῦμα ζωοποιεῖ (2 Cor. iii. 6), ζωὴ ἐκ νεκρῶν (Rom. xi. 15).

Having thus seen how a present ethical life arises in the Apostle's mind out of the notion of a future physical life, we have now to develop in its several moments the inward working of the πνεῦμα in the Christian. In general terms, it is a new

personal life, a καινὴ κτίσις, an ἄνθρωπος πνευματικός, who has the
πνεῦμα as his element, his guide, his moving principle, just as the
παλαιὸς ἄνθρωπος has the σάρξ (ἐν πνεύματι, κατὰ πνεῦμα εἶναι,
πνεύματι ἄγεσθαι). To go into further detail, there are different
moments of the personal life, which we can also distinguish in
the writings of Paul—the feeling heart, the thinking and willing
(acting) reason, which have their part in the new life of the πνεῦμα.
In the *heart*, the centre of the personal life, the immediate consciousness, the love of God is poured out by the holy spirit,
so that it becomes the object of the subjective inner being and
the personal experience of the reconciliation it has received,
consequently a ground of joyfully elated self-consciousness, of
"glorying." The favour of God is now no longer merely an
objective relation of God to man, but it becomes a subjective
possession of man, a condition of peace with God, in which
he feels himself placed (Rom. v. 1—5). Peace and joy in the
holy spirit are therefore the key-note in the kingdom of God
(Rom. xiv. 17). It is indeed a joy, the strength of which reposes
essentially on hope (Rom. v. 2, viii. 24, xv. 13), because its
object still belongs essentially to the future (the φανέρωσις τῆς
ζωῆς Ἰησοῦ) ; nay, it not only does not exclude θλίψεις, but it is
not raised beyond στενάζειν, the sighing expectation of final and
complete ἀπολύτρωσις. But notwithstanding all ἀσθένεια which
is still unavoidable, the divine πνεῦμα gives to ours the consoling
evidence that we are children of God, and its unexpressed sighing and longing, which is concealed in the heart and never
comes into the clear consciousness of man, comes before God
and intercedes with Him who is acquainted with the heart
(viii. 26 f.). In the category of these στεναγμοὶ ἀλάλητοι, or
workings of the πνεῦμα which belong only to the life of unconscious feeling, falls also that γλώσσῃ λαλεῖν which the Apostle,
1 Cor. xiv. 13 f., opposes as a προσεύχεσθαι τῷ πνεύματι to the
προσεύχεσθαι τῷ νοΐ, because in the former the νοῦς is ἄκαρπος ; it
is a mere activity of the divine πνεῦμα which dwells in the heart,

while the personal self-consciousness is at rest (according to our
psychology, an ecstatic state in which the life of feeling acts
independently, its excessive excitement dispensing with the
forms of conscious thought).

But the πνεῦμα proceeding from the heart, where its light first
went up (2 Cor. iv. 6), takes possession also of the νοῦς, the
thinking and willing activity of the reason, and effects here also
an ἀνακαίνωσις (Rom. xii. 2), to the end that we may learn
to prove what the will of God is. The higher *perception*, of
which the νοῦς is rendered capable by the πνεῦμα, is according to
this passage (and likewise Col. i. 9 f.) the moral power of
judging of good and evil, of distinguishing that which is pleasing to God from that which is to be avoided. But especially
the spirit causes the perception of the divinely purposed salvation, reveals that secret wisdom of God which the rulers of this
world have not perceived, and which the natural man cannot
possibly perceive, because he is without the divine πνεῦμα, which
alone knows divine things, because it searches the deep things
of God. It is this πνεῦμα, however, which Christians have
received, ἵνα εἰδῶμεν τὰ ὑπὸ τοῦ θεοῦ χαρισθέντα ἡμῖν : it therefore
produces a conscious insight into the blessings of salvation pro-
vided by God (1 Cor. ii. 7—12). The spiritual man has precisely the νοῦς of Christ, that is to say, he finds himself in possession of the perception of absolute truth, which perception is
no longer excluded by any limit from the deep things of God.
This is of course only true at first in principle ; in the concrete
the Christian also has γιγνώσκειν ἐκ μέρους only, so long as he
walks in faith and not by sight ; he only sees the truth at first,
δι' ἐσόπτρου ἐν αἰνίγματι, in the reflection of a mirror, and in many
ways veiled (1 Cor. xiii. 12); but in principle he has notwithstanding the entire truth, since the perception of the glory of
Christ, as the very image of God, is lighted up in him, and this
light is reflected upon him with " open face," so that he is
changed more and more into the same image (2 Cor. iii. 18—
iv. 6). This Christian perception is thus one which advances in

proportion as the assimilation with the object of perception advances; it is always conditioned by the practical religious experience.

For this reason the renewal of the *theoretical* and that of the *practical* activity of the reason are inseparably connected together. If previously the θέλειν of the good were the highest to which the νοῦς could attain, which good it could not bring to κατεργάζεσθαι, because the ego was sold as a slave under the dominion of sin, it has now become free from the determining power (νόμος) of sin and death, by the higher power (νόμος) of the spirit of life in Christ; sin will no more have the rule over him; he is no longer bound to the flesh as a debtor, to live according to its guidance (Rom. viii. 2, xii. 6, 14). Now the moral will of the spiritual man also enters, with this state of things, into a relation to the law directly opposed to that in which he stood before.   He was then under the law, but at the same time so little in accord with the law (with the holy will of God revealed in the law), that, on the contrary, it was precisely by means of the law that the παθήματα τῶν ἁμαρτιῶν became operative in his fleshly members, so as to produce fruit unto death (vii. 5); now he is no longer under the law, but under the favour of God, yet, for this very reason, in the possession of the spirit of sonship which corresponds with the state of favour, by means of which he is endued with the power and the will to bring to actual accomplishment the δικαίωμα τοῦ νόμου, that is, the moral contents of the law in love, which is the fulfilling of all law (Rom. vi. 14, viii. 4; Gal. v. 14).   On the one hand, we have in combination bondage to the law and sin; on the other hand, freedom from the law under the favour of God, and the fulfilment of the substance of the law through the spirit of love.   It is important to observe this, because the whole reasoning of the Apostle in Rom. vi. 14 f. rests upon the fact, that in his mind "to be under the favour of God" is the same thing [1]

---

[1] Not as if this implied that the idea of χάρις suddenly became entirely different; it is the same as in vi. 1, and this again with that of iii. 24—v. 21, and remains

as "to be led by the spirit," since both are in an equal degree
the exact opposite of "being under the law;" comp. Rom.
vi. 14 with Gal. v. 18. By this morally renovating πνεῦμα the
δικαιοσύνη which the law could never effect is really produced;
real righteousness, or the new moral character of life which
is brought about by the spirit, is added to ideal righteousness, or
the right harmonious relation to God, in which the faithful, by
virtue of his mere trust in the favourable will of God revealed
in the death of Christ, had already been enabled to stand. In
the former sense we should understand δικαιοσύνη in Rom.
viii. 10 with reference to the whole context, especially ver. 4;
and in Rom. vi. 16—20 we can hardly fail to see a wavering
between the ideal and real notion of δικαιοσύνη. At first, indeed,
we must take τῇ δικαιοσύνῃ δουλωθῆναι in the same sense as ὑπὸ
χάριν εἶναι, namely, as the state of the justified man, conformably
to which the conduct of his life is to shape itself; but as πνεύματι
ἄγεσθαι is included in the notion of ὑπὸ χάριν εἶναι, and thus
χάρις itself obtains, in addition to the significance of a religious
principle, that of a moral agent, so also the notion of δικαιοσύνη in
this chapter expands itself, until the moral sense of righteousness of life, which is the effect of the morally renovating favour
of God, is added as a further moment to the specific Pauline
sense of the righteousness by faith, which is the effect of God's
reconciling favour. But the former is only *added to* the latter,
it is *not put in its place*, not at least in such a way as to annul
the whole of the former doctrine of the righteousness of faith,
and to substitute for it an entirely new doctrine of moral righteousness.[1] The real righteousness of the πνεῦμα and the ideal
righteousness of faith are, on the contrary, connected with each
other as a new relation to God and a new moral vitality, of

dominant throughout; only the new religious relation is here completed on its moral
side, by being indicated as the necessary ground of new moral vitality, of καινότης ζωῆς
(ver. 4).

[1] I can only consider this opinion of *Lüdemann's* (ut supra, p. 165 f. and 208—215)
as an extraordinary mistake, the refutation of which may be found in the former
part of this work (Chap. ii. iv. v.).

which neither can take the place of the other, but which are
necessarily in need of each other to make up the whole, but in
such a way that the religious idea always remains as the foundation, and (both to the Apostle and to the religious view of all
time) the chief thing. However, the Apostle also makes much
less use of the idea of righteousness for the moral renovation of
life than he does of *holiness*.

But this idea also obtains in the writings of Paul a deepened
meaning, corresponding with that of πνεῦμα. The word ἅγιος, on
the ground of its usage in the Old Testament, denotes primarily
in the writings of Paul also the being devoted to God, belonging to God, standing in relation to Him. Everything is holy in
this sense which rests on divine revelation (γραφαὶ ἅγιαι, Rom.
i. 2; νόμος, ἐντολὴ ἁγ., vii. 12), or which is connected with divine
worship (ναὸς τοῦ θεοῦ ἅγιός ἐστι, 1 Cor. iii. 17; θυσία ἁγ., Rom.
xii. 1). So Israel also as a whole, as a theocratic community,
is compared to a holy root and to holy leaven; and the individual members of this people, inasmuch as they have grown as
branches from the root, have the predicates which belong to the
whole expressly applied to them. And as in Israel the individual members participate in the holiness of the community of
the Hebrew nation, so the same thing is true of the Christian
community, so that the natural connection with it which is
effected by the relation of man and wife, parent and child,
extends the holiness which belongs to the Christian part to the
other part which is not Christian; the non-Christian husband
or wife is made holy by the Christian wife or husband, the non-
Christian child by the Christian parents (1 Cor. vii. 14). In
this purely objective sense, which rests on the Old Testament
view, we must in the first instance take the standing predicate
of the Christians, ἅγιοι; they are this simply on the ground of
their being called to the fellowship of the Christian community
(cf. κλητοὶ ἅγιοι, Rom. i. 7; 1 Cor. i. 2). But in this union with
the body of Christ, the Christian, we must remember, also
receives the spirit of Christ, the πνεῦμα ἅγιον, which, as we have

seen, becomes in him the principle of a new personal life. In this respect the Christian is now holy, not only on account of his belonging to the chosen Messianic community, but essentially on account of his subjective possession of the principle of holiness, the holy spirit. Christians are ἅγιοι in the Apostle's eyes, not only as the κλητοὶ καὶ ἐπικαλούμενοι τὸ ὄνομα τοῦ Κυρίου (as belonging to the community which calls itself by the name of Christ), but essentially as the ἡγιασμένοι ἐν Χριστῷ Ἰησοῦ (1 Cor. i. 2), that is to say, as those whose life has become holy in principle by its communion with Christ. Thus the converted Gentiles are called a sacrifice, ἡγιασμένη ἐν πνεύματι ἁγίῳ (Rom. xv. 16), and the Corinthians are reminded, Ye were once gross sinners, but now ἀπελούσασθε, ἡγιάσθητε ἐν πνεύματι τοῦ θεοῦ ἡμῶν,— in which words the union of the two predicates, and the opposition in which they are placed to the previous life of sin, shows that this ἡγιάσθητε denotes not merely devotion of themselves as belonging to God, but moral purification and sanctification in principle, or, in short, the presence of the πνεῦμα in Christians as the principle of holiness.

Before we proceed to consider the development of this principle in the process of sanctification, or in the Christian moral life, which belongs to this part of our subject, we must answer the question, how this new Christian πνεῦμα is related to the natural πνεῦμα of man, which was described in Chap. i. as occupying the middle point of indifference between the opposing principles of πνεῦμα (in the higher sense) and σάρξ, and constituting the neutral substratum of the personal life. We have to consider, with reference to this point, statements of the Apostle which are of two different kinds; in the one, he implies that the Christian πνεῦμα and the natural human πνεῦμα co-exist and work upon one another; in the other, he makes no difference between them. Of the first kind, the most important are to be found in the following passages: Rom. viii. 16, αὐτὸ τὸ πνεῦμα συμμαρτυρεῖ τῷ πνεύματί μου, ὅτι ἐσμὲν τέκνα θεοῦ: and ver. 26, τί προσευξώμεθα οὐκ οἴδαμεν, ἀλλ᾽ αὐτὸ τὸ πνεῦμα ὑπερεντυγχάνει ὑπὲρ

ἡμῶν στεναγμοῖς ἀλαλήτοις : ix. 1, συμμαρτυρούσης μοι τῆς συνειδή-
σεώς μου ἐν πνεύματι ἁγίῳ. To this class belong also the passages
which speak of conditions of the πνεῦμα of the Christian which
cannot be said to be conditions of the indwelling spirit of God,
which is itself strength, and life, and holiness; such are comfort,
and peace of mind (2 Cor. ii. 12, vii. 13; 1 Cor. xvi. 18), or defilement (2 Cor. vii. 1), or sanctification, and keeping pure (1 Cor.
vii. 34; 1 Thess. v. 23), or, lastly, rescuing from destruction
(1 Cor. v. 5). These passages presuppose that even in the Christian who possesses the πνεῦμα ἅγιον, there is still a human πνεῦμα
different from it, which is capable of suffering, and of defilement,
and of perishing, and is in need of the inworking of the divine
πνεῦμα, in order to be freed or protected from all these, and
which is thus related to the divine πνεῦμα as the receiving
to the giving subject (see above, Chap. i. p. 65). But by
the side of these passages there are also others to be found
which do not assume or even admit of any distinction between
the divine and human πνεῦμα in the Christian. So in Rom.
viii. 10, τὸ πνεῦμα ζωὴ διὰ δικαιοσύνην, where we are compelled by
the antithesis τὸ σῶμα νεκρὸν δι᾽ ἁμαρτίαν to refer the words to
the individual πνεῦμα of the Christian, which, however, can only
be "life" by virtue of its unity with that of God, as is stated in
vers. 9 and 11, with regard to πνεῦμα θεοῦ and Χριστοῦ; further,
in 1 Cor. xiv. 14 f., τὸ πνεῦμά μου προσεύχεται, and προσεύξομαι τῷ
πνεύματι, it is the πνεῦμα of the Apostle himself which prays in
him, or with which he prays (in speaking with tongues); but
this πνεῦμα can nevertheless be only the supernatural principle
of the χαρίσματα bestowed by God, for speaking with tongues is
one of these. To this class, again, belong those passages in which
the πνεῦμα is connected with human virtues as their subject,
such as 2 Cor. iv. 13, τὸ αὐτὸ πνεῦμα τῆς πίστεως : 1 Cor. iv. 21,
and Gal. vi. 1, πνεῦμα πραότητος : Rom. xv. 30, ἀγάπη τοῦ πνεύματος :
1 Thess. i. 6, χαρὰ πνεύματος ἁγίου : and especially 2 Cor. vi. 6,
ἐν ἁγιότητι, ἐν γνώσει, ἐν μακροθυμίᾳ, ἐν χρηστότητι, ἐν πνεύματι ἁγίῳ,
ἐν ἀγάπῃ, &c. In all these passages it is certainly much easier

to understand the πνεῦμα simply as the subject of these virtues, than (according to the common interpretation) to separate it from the Christian subject, and make it the cause of the virtues named in connection with it. Especially in the passage last quoted, ἐν πνεύματι ἁγίῳ, in the midst of the other Christian virtues, must necessarily denote another spiritual condition of the Christian, namely, his being filled with the holy spirit of God (cf. ζέοντες τῷ πνεύματι, Rom. xii. 11). In all these and similar passages, the separation between πνεῦμα ἅγιον as being objective, and the subjective Christian spirit, is not exegetical exactness, but rather scholastic abstraction, which certainly perverts the meaning of the Apostle. This we shall find, on the contrary, to be, that the divine πνεῦμα and the natural human πνεῦμα coalesce in the Christian into the unity of *a new subject*, a καινὸς or πνευματικὸς ἄνθρωπος (they unite therefore in substance, comp. 1 Cor. vi. 17), but yet in such a way that this union is not absolutely complete from the beginning, but always progressing merely, and therefore always in part not existing; consequently both substances are always in another sense distinct, and related to each other as that which is active and giving, to that which is passive and receiving. It is this very process of the union of the divine and the human spirit, constantly advancing towards the unity of a personality in the image of God, which is ever becoming more complete, that we have now to consider further.

THE DEVELOPMENT OF THE NEW LIFE; SANCTIFICATION.

By virtue of man's having obtained for his own, in his union with Christ by faith, a new principle of life, the πνεῦμα ἅγιον, the possibility is given to him, and with it the moral necessity, of framing his own life so as to be pleasing to God and to resemble Him; in short, to be a holy life. There is, it is true, no physically compulsory necessity in this principle, but its realiza-

tion takes place only through the free self-determination of man
to allow himself to be directed by the spirit which dwells in
him.   Because, by virtue of his being a Christian, he *lives* in the
spirit, so he ought, and has the power, spontaneously *to walk* in
the spirit as his actual element, or according to the spirit as
his actual guide (Gal. v. 25, εἰ ζῶμεν πνεύματι, πνεύματι καὶ
στοιχῶμεν: Rom. viii. 4, ἵνα τὸ δικαίωμα τοῦ νόμου πληρωθῇ ἐν
ἡμῖν τοῖς μὴ κατὰ σάρκα περιπατοῦσιν ἀλλὰ κατὰ πνεῦμα).   Nevertheless, the Apostle regards the progress of the new life as by
no means the spontaneous action of man; but as its beginning
depended on a close union of man with Christ, in faith and
baptism, so also does its progress consist in the divine human
process of the ever more complete realizing of the Christian
principle of salvation, according to all its moments, in the
spiritual life of man; salvation is likewise continually said to
grounded in God (1 Thess. v. 23), wrought out by human freedom (2 Cor. vii. 1), and both together (Phil. ii. 12, 13).

Now, to pursue the matter further into detail, sanctification
consists in the carrying on of the same two-sided process, of
dying and rising again with Christ, which has already begun in
baptism.   The Christian *has* already, in giving himself up to
Christ as his own, crucified his flesh, with its passions and
desires; henceforth he *is to* mortify continually the πράξεις τοῦ
σώματος (Gal. v. 24, ἐσταύρωσαν; cf. Rom. viii. 13, εἰ— θανατοῦτε
ζήσεσθε); he *has* put on Christ in baptism, now he *is to* put him
on continually by walking honestly as in the day (Gal. iii. 27
with Rom. xiii. 14); he is already in Christ, apprehended by
Christ, now he *is to* lay hold of him more and more, to change
himself into his image, and let Christ be formed within him
(Phil. iii. 12; 2 Cor. iii. 18; Gal. iv. 19); the old *has* already
passed away in him, and all has become new, but now he *is to*
transform himself continually by the renewal of his mind, by
the daily renewal of the inward man (2 Cor. v. 17, compared with
Rom. xii. 2, and 2 Cor. iv. 16).   The latter passages may guard
us from misunderstanding the former; the θανατοῦν τὰς πράξεις

τοῦ σώματος does not mean a sensuous mortification of the body and its natural needs and functions, not an ascetic self-castigation; that would be far from according with the free spiritual apprehension of these externalities, which is repeatedly expressed in other passages by the Apostle (comp. especially Rom. xiv. 13—23, 1 Cor. vi. 12); but it points to such a restraint being put upon the fleshly externalizations of life (the ἐπιθυμίαι and παθήματα, which peculiarly belong to the flesh, as constituting the body), that they shall not be able to gain the mastery over the self-conscious spiritual ego; cf. 1 Cor. ix. 27, ὑπωπιάζω τὸ σῶμα καὶ δουλαγωγῶ, μήπως ἄλλοις κηρύξας αὐτὸς ἀδόκιμος γένωμαι, with which, however, the ἐλεύθερος ὢν ἐκ πάντων (ver. 19) is perfectly consistent. In the same way, in vi. 12, the consciousness of the most complete autonomy is closely united with the principle of the strongest self-control (πάντα μοι ἔξεστιν, ἀλλ᾽ οὐκ ἐγὼ ἐξουσιασθήσομαι ὑπό τινος). This warfare is not directed against the body as such, but only against the body as it consists of σάρξ, and allows the ἐπιθυμεῖν of the latter, which is contrary to the spirit, to prevail in it; the body itself, however, is, notwithstanding this, according to its true destination, a temple of the holy spirit (1 Cor. vi. 19 f.), and God can and ought to be glorified in it; it ought to be holy (vii. 34), and its members instruments of righteousness (Rom. vi. 13, 19). Thus Paul thoroughly recognizes a positive relation of the body to the holy spirit, as the aim of sanctification; but as sanctification (frequently in the case of the Gentiles with whom the Apostle has to deal in his Epistles) starts from a condition in which the body, as a matter of fact, behaves in just the contrary manner, and is only an organ of the anti-spiritual flesh, it is easy to understand why, in treating of sanctification, Paul gives, as he certainly does, so much more weight to the negative side of the question regarding the body.[1]

The Apostle accounts the συμπάσχειν (Rom. viii. 17), i. e.

---

[1] Compare with the above, the apposite remarks of *Biedermann*, Dogmatik, § 292. *Holsten*, ut supra, p. 443, takes a different view.

bearing the sufferings which the Christian encounters in his
calling as a Christian, therefore for the sake of Christ and in
imitation of him, or generally in his Christian life, as an essential part of the negative side of sanctification, or of dying with
Christ. He describes his being in constant danger of death for
the sake of Jesus (ἀεὶ παραδιδόμεθα εἰς θάνατον διὰ Ἰησοῦν, 2 Cor.
iv. 11) as a carrying about in his body of the putting to death of
Jesus (νέκρωσις Ἰησοῦ), the purpose of which was that the life of
Jesus also might be manifested in his body (ib. ver. 10, cf. ver. 14)
in the day of the resurrection. The Apostle thus regards his
sufferings as a copied repetition of the sufferings of Christ, which
is essential in order to the completion of the transformation into
the image of Christ. As in him suffering was a putting to death
of the outward part of man (Ἰησοῦ), and at the same time a condemnation of sin in the flesh (Rom. viii. 3), an ἀποθανεῖν τῇ
ἁμαρτίᾳ, in order to live henceforth to God (vi. 10), so the sufferings of the Christian serve to wear away the fleshly outward
man, in order that the inward man may be daily more renewed,
and made capable of reflecting in that day, in a corresponding
form of appearance, the exceeding δόξα of Christ (2 Cor. iv. 16 f.,
v. 1 f., iii. 18). In this certainty he says, "As the sufferings of
Christ abound in us, so our consolation also aboundeth by
Christ" (2 Cor. i. 5. In Phil. iii. 10, the end of faith is the
knowledge of the power of Christ's resurrection, but also—and
in fact as the condition of this knowledge—"the fellowship of
his sufferings, in being made conformable unto his death").

To this negative side of sanctification, which thus consists in
the mortification of the flesh, and in the patient endurance of
sufferings, is related the *positive* side, as in Christ the resurrection life is related to suffering and dying. As the risen one has
become a perfect spirit (2 Cor. iii. 17), so sanctification, in its
positive side, is a life ἐν καινότητι πνεύματος, or briefly ἐν πνεύματι,
where the πνεῦμα is imagined as the *element*, in which the subjective life essentially reposes, in which it has its fulness and
its power; or it is said to be περιπατεῖν πνεύματι, κατὰ πνεῦμα,

where the πνεῦμα is imagined as the *rule* by which the free self-determination guides itself, as the *law* (Rom. viii. 2, ὁ νόμος τοῦ πνεύματος τῆς ζωῆς ἐν Χριστῷ) by which the life is ruled in the individual. And further, as the life of the risen one is a ζῆν τῷ θεῷ (Rom. vi. 10), so also is sanctification a ζῆν τῷ θεῷ ἐν Χριστῷ Ἰησοῦ, a παριστάναι ἑαυτὸν τῷ θεῷ, and δουλωθῆναι τῷ θεῷ (ib. vers. 11, 13, 22). That Christ, who is bound up in a mystical union with the believer (the indwelling spirit of Christ), is the animating power, and that the will of God is the highest and final end of the life of sanctification, is expressed by the peculiar but significant figure, that the Christian, freed from his former wedded lord (the law), has become the spouse of the risen Christ, in order that he may, in this new marriage-bond, become fruitful for God (καρποφορῆσαι θεῷ, Rom. vii. 4).

What this fruit of the spirit in us should be is said in Gal. v. 22 f.; it is *Christian virtue,* displayed in its numerous manifestations, as love, joy, peace, long-suffering, righteousness, goodness, fidelity, gentleness, temperance. Whilst joy, and perhaps also peace (if it be not here equivalent to a peaceful disposition), express the religious key-note of the Christian, and temperance expresses the virtue of self-command with reference to his own sensuous nature, all the others relate to his right conduct towards his neighbour, and are modifications of the fundamental social virtue of the Christian, *love,* which is therefore placed before all the others. It is regarded by the Apostle as at once the highest gift of the spirit (1 Cor. xiii.), and the complete fulfilling of the law, that is to say, in its moral essence (δικαίωμα τοῦ νόμου, Rom. viii. 4), which—after the Mosaic law has been stripped of its worldly sensuous element—is materially identical with the law of Christ, so that love may be said to be the πλήρωμα νόμου, as well with regard to the Old Testament law (Rom. xiii. 8—10; Gal. v. 14), as with regard to the law of Christ (Gal. vi. 2). Because it is itself the fulfilling of the law, the law is no longer against it (Gal. v. 23), has neither to demand anything of it, nor to condemn it, has lost its significance *as a written law with respect to it*, and thus that freedom from the law which was already contained as an ideal right in the νἱοθεσία, and guaranteed objectively by the death of Christ (see above), has become real in love. At the same time, however, love is precisely that which — does not, indeed, outwardly fetter, but — inwardly constrains our freedom, and puts it at the service of our neighbour (Gal. v. 13), as it is itself a being bound by the love of Christ; 2 Cor. v. 14, ἡ ἀγάπη Χριστοῦ—towards us which he displayed in dying for us—συνέχει ἡμᾶς, i. e. keeps us within bounds, bridles and rules our conduct towards others, by means of gratitude to him, which admits no more of self-seeking. A practical example of this is seen in 1 Cor. viii. 11 and Rom. xiv. 15, viz., the loving regard for the weak brother for whom Christ died. Christian brotherly love is thus only the natural reflection and imitation of the love of Christ and of God which we have made our own by faith (2 Cor. viii. 9 ; Rom. xv. 2 f.). For this very reason, it cannot but happen that faith, saturated with such contents, should exercise its power outwardly by love; in faith itself, the love of God to us which we accept changes itself into active love for our neighbour; πίστις is δι᾽ ἀγάπης ἐνεργουμένη, Gal. v. 6. Love, therefore, is not added to faith from without to complete it, but it has in faith (which makes us of *one* mind with Christ, or has the spirit of Christ for its concrete contents) its organic germ, which, if only faith itself remain alive, necessarily expands into the moral energy of love. For faith, as the giving up of the heart to God, makes us free from the ungodlike will of the flesh and of our own selves, and therefore also from the law, which is only valid against the carnal mind; but this it does only by placing our own freedom in dependence on God; but in this free bondage to God is to be found the source of that power which binds man to man in freedom, namely, love; in faith the Christian is ἄνομος, ἐλεύθερος ὢν ἐκ πάντων, in love he is ἔννομος Χριστῷ, πᾶσιν ἑαυτὸν δουλώσας

(1 Cor. ix. 19 f.).[1] Moreover, as the inwardly binding law of freedom, love may, under certain circumstances, demand an *external limitation of the use of Christian freedom*, an abstinence from that which is in itself permissible; for instance, where it is required by *regard for weak brethren*, whose faith is not yet strong enough to be free from the letter of statutes, and whose consciences might therefore be shocked by the free practice of stronger brethren (Rom. xiv. 13 f.; 1 Cor. viii. 9). Yet, on the other hand, even this loving regard for those who are not free must not go so far as to injure the right of freedom and the truth of the gospel (Gal. v. 1—12, ii. 3—5, 11—21); it must, therefore, extend only to really indifferent matters, and the Apostle himself certainly seems to have held, concerning the limits of this extension, at one time a stricter, and at another time a more tolerant, opinion (cf. below, Chap. viii.); and it must be practised only with reference to those who are really weak, whose consciences, not being free, require loving consideration and tolerance on the part of the stronger, but who have no desire to acquire for themselves any right to rule in such matters (Rom. xv. 1); whilst against those who wish to rule, to set themselves up as masters over the faith of others, and to make their own narrowness a slavish yoke to limit the Christian freedom of the community, the exclusive right of Christ to sovereignty is to be energetically maintained, as he is the only Lord and Judge of the conscience, whose dominion is incompatible with any yoke whatever of bondage to men (Rom. xiv. 3—12; Gal. ii. v. 1; 1 Cor. vii. 23).

In this way, then, in his religious principle of faith, the Apostle has at the same time indicated the immanent principle of a Christian morality which is neither without law, nor has to seek its law outside of itself, beyond the Christian sphere, in that of Judaism, but which bears its law essentially within itself, namely, in the religious principle of Christianity, which lies at

---

[1] *Luther* gives the most beautiful and truly Pauline exposition of this thought in his treatise "Von der Freiheit eines Christenmenschen."

the root of it. If we are by faith in Christ set free from the
schoolmaster of the external law, which was a law of bondage,
then we have attained a *new law* in the love of Christ (i. e. love
for Christ), namely, "the law of the spirit of life in Christ,"
which no longer stands externally over against us, as an enslav-
ing and condemning letter, but which works in us real freedom,
strength to live the new life. This freedom from the external
(Mosaic) law, which had become to justifying faith an ideal
right belonging to sonship, now attains its completion in the
truly freeing and animating *power* of the spirit of life given by
Christ, which frees us from the law of sin and of death by working in us love, which is the fulfilling of the law, and the realization of the δικαίωμα τοῦ νόμου (Rom. viii. 2—4). And inasmuch
as the ideal relation of sonship first begins to work subjectively
in this real state of freedom, sonship is so inseparably connected
with the existence of the spirit, that from the fact of the spirit
working in a man it may be concluded that he is a child of God
(Rom. viii. 14).

In this way the Pauline opposition of faith to law and works
now attains its essential completion. Faith is not opposed to
every law, but only to that law which cannot give life, because,
being external, it has its insuperable limit in the fleshly nature
(ἐπιθυμεῖν) of man (comp. Gal. iii. 21 with Rom. viii. 3, 7), therefore to the Mosaic letter of the law (and to every law which, like
that of Moses, opposes to the will of man the rigid "thou shalt"
as a foreign will; and this is indeed the case with law in
general, if we look to the bottom of it, from the standpoint of
the natural man). But faith is not opposed to the *new Christian
law*, which consists in the impulse of the holy spirit, and which
accordingly no longer merely commands, but at the same time
gives life, i. e. pleasure in and strength for the accomplishment:
the Apostle calls this, according to its true nature, "a law of
the spirit of life in Christ," and, according to its origin, "the law
of Christ" (Rom. viii. 2 ; Gal. vi. 2). Now this law is certainly
valid also for the Christian; but the true moral essence of the

old (Mosaic) law, its δικαίωμα, is not only contained in it, but is
for the first time brought into full validity and effectiveness
(Rom. viii. 4, xiii. 8—10). So far it is certainly correct to say
that Paul in his doctrine of faith (that is to say, faith filled with
the πνεῦμα and working by love) does not overthrow the law, but
sets it up; only we must not introduce this thought into the
words of Rom. iii. 31, where it would very abruptly and unneces-
sarily interrupt the development of the doctrine of justification;
these words, on the contrary, form the transition to the Scripture proof of the doctrine of justification which follows, and
therefore ὁ νόμος in that passage can mean nothing else than the
Old Testament revelation in general, and especially that which
was made to Abraham. From this point of view we shall also
be able to understand the striking passage which appears to
form a contradiction to Gal. v. 6, namely, 1 Cor. vii. 19, "circumcision is nothing, and the foreskin is nothing," ἀλλὰ τήρησις τῶν
ἐντολῶν θεοῦ. Here also both Judaism and Heathenism are alike
said to be nothing, in comparison of the new religious moral life
of the Christian; but whilst in Gal. v. 6 the latter is apprehended in its ground and in its manifestation as πίστις δι᾽ ἀγάπης
ἐνεργουμένη, here the moral manifestation alone is brought forward, and that in a form which was certainly the usual mode
of expression for Jewish morality, or for righteousness in the
Jewish legal sense. Nevertheless, that this cannot be meant
here is clear, because circumcision above all things belonged to
the τήρησις ἐντολῶν in the Jewish sense; and as this integral
part of the Jewish keeping of the law is here said to be nothing,
it is self-evident that by ἐντολαί here is meant the law, not in its
Mosaic form, but only in its universal moral essence, abstracted
from the positive Jewish law, that is to say, the moral law as it
is comprehended in love. It is also self-evident that the
Apostle demands from the Christian moral fruit, not only in
virtues (Gal. v. 22), but also in the actual practice of them, that
is to say briefly, in works; it would certainly be a mistake to
suppose that the Apostle meant an abstract piety which should

not attain to moral action. He expressly demands of the Galatians ἐργαζώμεθα τὸ ἀγαθὸν πρὸς πάντας, μάλιστα δὲ πρὸς τοὺς οἰκείους
τῆς πίστεως: and not to be weary in doing good is, according to
him, the condition of the future harvest, is therefore virtually
that which he before called sowing to the spirit (Gal. vi. 8—10).
Again, he wishes for the Corinthians that the favour of God may
come abundantly upon them, in order that they themselves may
act abundantly in every good work (πᾶσαν χάριν περισσεῦσαι εἰς
ὑμᾶς ἵνα—περισσεύητε εἰς πᾶν ἔργον ἀγαθόν, 2 Cor. ix. 8), and the
proportion of the harvest will be conditioned by the sparing or
abundant proportions of this sowing (ver. 6). This leads us to a
further point connected with this subject.

The "walking in the spirit," according to the sense of the new
Christian morality which has just been developed, is not only
the necessary (i. e. infallible and obligatory) fruit of accepted
salvation, but it is also the indispensable means and condition
of the perfecting of salvation, the final σωτηρία. This is expressed by the Apostle by many different turns of thought,
which, however, are perfectly consistent with each other. He
says to the Philippians in plain words (ii. 12), μετὰ φόβου καὶ
τρόμου τὴν ἑαυτῶν σωτηρίαν κατεργάζεσθε, they are to work out
their final salvation by their moral action, and that with fear
and trembling, on account of the constant possibility of falling
back through moral slothfulness, and after all losing their salvation. But he immediately adds the ground on the presupposition of which alone that κατεργάζεσθαι is really possible, and
therefore also becomes a duty, ὁ θεὸς γάρ ἐστιν ὁ ἐνεργῶν ἐν ὑμῖν
καὶ τὸ θέλειν καὶ τὸ ἐνεργεῖν: it is the willingness and the power to
perform morally good works, effected by God, by imparting the
πνεῦμα ἅγιον, on the ground of which we are put in a position to
work out our salvation for ourselves, namely, by giving activity
to that principle in the particular acts of moral life. This
exactly agrees with what the Apostle acknowledges of himself
(iii. 12), οὐχ ὅτι ἤδη ἔλαβον ἢ ἤδη τετελείωμαι, διώκω δέ, εἰ καὶ
καταλάβω, ἐφ' ᾧ καὶ κατελήφθην ὑπὸ τοῦ Χριστοῦ Ἰησοῦ: certain

as he is of being apprehended by Christ, of having found in him
the righteousness of God (ver. 9), he is still so far from thinking
that he has already attained completely or finally to the purpose
for which he was destined by God, to which he is called, that, on
the contrary, the favour which he has obtained is only so much
the stronger motive never to be satisfied with the degree of
moral perfection that he has at any time attained, but to strive
and advance ever further forward after the still unattained end
of absolute perfection. Nay, he says in fine irony to the Philippians, those who are now perfect should likewise be of this mind
(ver. 15); that is to say, those who consider themselves perfect,
pattern Christians, should prove themselves to be so by striving
most zealously after that real perfection which was not yet
reached. The same thought is also to be found in the figure
of the race for the prize of victory in 1 Cor. ix. 24—27. If
deprivations were imposed, for the sake of a perishable crown,
upon those who contended in the Corinthian games, much more
should the Christian impose struggles and self-denial upon himself for the sake of the imperishable crown (everlasting σωτηρία),
as he himself, the Apostle, subdued his body by severe discipline, so that he might not, while preaching to others, be cast
away himself. This evidently presupposes, as being ever present
(at least *in abstract*), the possibility of losing the favour of God
in consequence of the flesh recovering its mastery. Accordingly,
the certainty of justification which is attached to salvation must
not be conceived so abstractly as to exclude the moment of subjective freedom, with its possible vacillations and backslidings.
The modest hypothetical expressions, therefore, in Phil. iii. 11,
εἴπως καταντήσω, and 12, εἰ καὶ καταλάβω, are by no means to be
regarded as affording any ground for doubting the genuineness
of this Epistle; on the contrary, they only prove (like the whole
of the passage in connection with them) that the most sober
consciousness of his distance from the moral ideal was perfectly
consistent with the most joyful faith in the favour of justification which he had experienced (ver. 8 f.); and this very insepa-

rable connection of the religious realism of a complete and
satisfied consciousness of salvation, with the idealism which
looks forward, and struggles, and is still only hoping for salvation, and ever striving after the goal of perfection, is most
characteristic of the evangelical ethics of Paul.   But for the
very reason that this moral struggle has as its presupposition
and its root the religious existence of man as justified and
endowed with the spirit, the consequence of that struggle, the
goal of Christian hope, appears not merely as an external recompence, or a purely supernatural fulfilling of a promise, as was the
case in the Jewish, and more or less also in the Jewish-Christian
view, but it appears as the natural fruit, in which the development of the Christian spirit attains to maturity.   Accordingly,
the moral action of the Christian is called a sowing to the spirit,
which will produce the harvest of eternal life from the spirit
(Gal. vi. 8); the existence of the (holy) spirit in man is therefore
the presupposition for both, for the sowing and for the harvest,
for the moral action, and for the eternal blessedness; but between this fruit and the seed-plot in which it is potentially
contained, must intervene the moral action of man, by which
the forces latent in the spirit are let loose and put in operation,
made powerful to impel and to produce fruit—that is to say, if
this action is ἐν πνεύματι and κατὰ πνεῦμα, has spirit for its element
and its rule.   But because action of an opposite kind, sowing to
the flesh, which reaps the harvest of destruction, is also a possibility for the Christian, he has need of the earnest warning, μὴ
πλανᾶσθε, θεὸς οὐ μυκτηρίζεται, ὃ γὰρ ἐὰν σπείρῃ ἄνθρωπος, τοῦτο
θερίσει (ver. 7).   It is only the unconditioned dominion of sin
in the flesh which has ceased in the Christian by virtue of his
having received the spirit (ἁμαρτία οὐ κυριεύσει, Rom. vi. 14), but
the impossibility of allowing himself to be led by the flesh is not
thereby established (the *non posse non peccare* has ceased, but he
has not arrived at the *non posse peccare*, but only at the *posse non
peccare*).   Christians are no longer debtors to the flesh, so that
they *must* live according to it, but yet the *two-fold possibility*

still remains, εἰ κατὰ σάρκα ζῆτε, μέλλετε ἀποθνήσκειν, εἰ δὲ πνεύματι τὰς πράξεις τοῦ σώματος θανατοῦτε, ζήσεσθε (Rom. viii. 12 f.).

If we are thus to understand the Christian life as a process of organic growth, which has the life of the spirit proceeding from God as its *principle*, and again as its *end*, then we have already an answer to the question, how far Christian salvation is to the Apostle a *future object of hope*, and how far it is a present possession of faith. For we find this two-fold way of regarding it in all the different ideas which represent Christian salvation to the mind of the Apostle; above all, in that most general idea of σωτηρία, σώζεσθαι, which comprises the others within itself. The Apostle says, νῦν ἡμέρα σωτηρίας (2 Cor. vi. 2), from the fall of the Jews σωτηρία has sprung up for the Gentiles (Rom. xi. 11, comp. 15, καταλλαγὴ κόσμου); Christians are the σωζόμενοι (1 Cor. i. 18), for ἐσώθημεν τῇ ἐλπίδι (Rom. viii. 24); but the other way of looking at it still preponderates, according to which the salvation already anticipated as a fact by the hoping consciousness is nevertheless only realized in the future—σωθησόμεθα ἀπὸ τῆς ὀργῆς (Rom. v. 9, &c.), σωτηρίαν κατεργάζεσθε, εἰς περιποίησιν σωτηρίας (Phil. ii. 12 ; 1 Thess. v. 9), ἐγγύτερον ἡμῶν ἡ σωτηρία (Rom. xiii. 11). Similarly, we are already indeed children of God by faith, and, on the ground of our being so, have received the spirit of sonship (Gal. iii. 26, iv. 6); but yet we are still in this temporal life υἱοθεσίαν ἀπεκδεχόμενοι, τὴν ἀπολύτρωσιν τοῦ σώματος ἡμῶν (Rom. viii. 23). As children we are also heirs, κληρονόμοι (Rom. viii. 17 ; Gal. iii. 29), and that of all the promises which from the beginning belonged to the people of God as the seed of Abraham—first of all, therefore, of the promise of the holy spirit (Gal. iii. 14); but, on the other hand, our κληρονομεῖν is also a future one, consisting in future συνδοξασθῆναι, conditioned by present συμπιτάσχειν, or in the future possession of the βασιλεία θεοῦ (1 Cor. vi. 9 f., xv. 50; Gal. v. 21). If, in the passage last named, the kingdom of God appears as the Messiah's kingdom, which began with his coming, it is again, on the other hand, a present and inward one, and consists in righteousness, peace, and joy in the holy spirit (Rom. xiv. 17; comp. 1 Cor. iv. 20). We have seen that the same two sides were contained in the idea of ζωή (above, p. 205 f.). What is peculiar to Paul is not this two-fold view of Christian salvation, but the fact that the two sides are fused together again by him into a higher unity, namely, in the πνεῦμα, which, for all its transcendence, is nevertheless also present and immanent, and, for all its immanence, is yet at the same time transcendent and future. As salvation is already set forth ideally as present in justification, so also it is set forth really in the possession of the ἀπαρχὴ πνεύματος, in which we have a pledge and seal of our future redemption on which our hope may support itself (2 Cor. i. 22, v. 5, ἀρραβὼν τοῦ πνεύματος). In this way Paul's doctrine stands half-way between the transcendent idea of salvation which preponderates in Jewish Christianity, and the immanent idea of it which preponderates in the theology of John, and forms the transition from one to the other.

CHAPTER VI.

THE CHRISTIAN COMMUNITY.

THE first form of Christendom as the association of believers is the separate communities which were formed here and there in different towns. These separate communities, according to the analogy of the political assemblies of the people of the Greek towns, were called ἐκκλησίαι, Gal. i. 2, 22 ; 1 Cor. xvi. 1, 19, and many other passages. But this name was further extended to the collective body of Christians, and these, although they never appeared as an external community or assembly, were called the ἐκκλησία τοῦ θεοῦ, that is, the commonwealth of God (1 Cor. x. 32 ; Gal. i. 13).

The nature of this community is only indicated by figurative comparisons, as Jesus only described the nature of the kingdom of heaven in parables. It is called in 1 Cor. iii. 9, a *field of God*, in which the Apostle plants, another waters, God grants the increase ; or a building of God, of which the Apostle lays the foundation, another continues the building (ibid. vers. 10 f.). And indeed this foundation is Jesus Christ ; it is laid once for all, for the whole Church, by God, and in each individual case is laid anew by the preaching of the Apostle, in founding every community. The advancement of the Christian life of the individual community, like that of the individual Christian, is therefore, in connection with this figure, naturally called edification or building up (1 Cor. xiv. 4, 12, 26, &c.). More particularly, this building is called a *temple of God*, because it is the abode of his holy spirit, which, as we have seen in the last chapter, dwells in the Christian. And this predicate is affirmed both of the whole community as such and also of the individuals in it; which indeed forms the specific difference between the Christian and the Old Testament community (cf. 1 Cor. iii. 16 f. and vi. 19). If the figure of a building, the foundation of which is Christ, shows the stability of the community in its entire dependence on the historical Redeemer, its own immanent vitality, in consequence of the possession of Christ's spirit of life, is more prominently displayed by the figure of the "*body of Christ.*" As oneness and manifoldness are inseparably connected and interpenetrate each other in the body, so Christians are one with each other through their communion of life with Christ in the holy spirit, or through the one spirit which fills them and the one Lord to whom they belong (1 Cor. xii. 4 f.); but this unity is no uniformity, but a unity of manifold hearts, each of which, through its special peculiarity, serves the whole in a special way.

We shall have first to consider this manifoldness of gifts and offices in the community; then to fix our attention on its oneness, as it exhibits itself externally in the love-feast of the community; and lastly, to see how this comes into existence by a selection from Gentiles and Jews, the difference between whom is merged in the higher union of the Christian community.

THE GIFTS AND OFFICES IN THE COMMUNITY.

The one spirit reveals itself in different powers or capacities, which, inasmuch as they are always bestowed by the favour of God on the individual as a special distinguishing possession, are called gifts of favour, χαρίσματα, but inasmuch as they are at the same time for the use of the whole, qualify and call to a *performance of service* to the community (διακονία). Every individual endowment within the community includes also within itself an individual task in the service of the community, therefore a call to office; but every office depends solely on the special qualification of the individual by extraordinary endowment of the holy spirit. The distinction between official and unofficial gifts is therefore evidently a false one; for all gifts are in the first place individual, depend only on the disposal of the free will of God, but all at the same time form the ground of a capacity, and therefore of an obligation, to perform a public service, to take some office in the community. There were as yet, in the primitive community, no other offices than these which depended on individual endowments of the spirit, the rights and duties of which were simply consequences of personal power and capacity.

Among the gifts which are often enumerated by the Apostle (especially 1 Cor. xii. 8—10, 28, 29, xiv. 6, 26; Rom. xii. 6—8), but never in systematic order and completeness, we may most suitably distinguish those which relate to the advancement of the life of the community in general, and those which relate especially to the edification of the community by the worship of God. The former again divide themselves into those which belong to the *service* of the community (in the narrower sense of the word διακονία), and those which belong to the *guidance* of it.

The διακονία, in general, consisted in taking a careful and helpful interest in the members of the community (ἀντιλήψεις, 1 Cor. xii. 28) in all their spiritual and bodily anxieties and necessities, and particularly in giving spiritual comfort (παρακαλῶν, Rom. xii. 8) to those who were troubled in mind, imparting to the poor the necessary gifts (ὁ μεταδιδούς, ibid.), sympathizing with the unhappy (ἐλεῶν, ibid.), especially tending the sick, and finally in healing diseases by the miraculous power of faith. With the last named are connected the πίστις, the χάρισμα ἰαμάτων, and the ἐνεργήματα δυνάμεων of 1 Cor. xii. 9 f. By this πίστις we are not, of course, to understand simply believing, which is clearly not an individual gift of favour serviceable to the community, but the root of the very existence of the community. We must therefore understand by it, faith under a special form of activity; and if we take into account its connection with what follows, χαρίσματα ἰαμάτων and ἐνεργήματα δυνάμεων, we cannot conceive of it otherwise than as a special power of *trusting faith* in God, an *enthusiasm* or *heroism of faith.* Such faith may be able to accomplish extraordinary acts for the welfare of the community, such especially as *healing the sick.* Such miraculous cures were effected at that time, as at all times,[1] by means of the psychological fact, that strong faith inspires strong faith, and this has a reviving and strengthening effect on the physical organism of the sick (at least in certain diseases). It is harder to say what we are to understand by the somewhat vague expression, ἐνεργήματα δυνάμεων. Perhaps we must take it to refer chiefly to the driving out of devils.

We have next to consider in connection with the διακονία, *the guidance of the community,* κυβέρνησις (1 Cor. xii. 28), to which προϊστάμενος in Rom. xii. 8, although it may more generally be understood of every office of authority, mainly refers; also in Phil. i. 1, ἐπίσκοποι καὶ διάκονοι is precisely the same juxtaposition of leaders (overseers) and servants, excepting that we have here to think in anticipation of offices which were only established at a later period. This is clearly proved by the *plural* ἐπίσκοποι, which can denote nothing but what is meant in 1 Thess. v. 12 by προϊστά-μενοι, and in other passages by πρεσβύτεροι, namely, those who, by virtue of a special endowment qualifying them for it, took upon themselves the task of ἐπισκοπεῖν and κυβερνᾶν in all the affairs of the community. As, according to the nature of things, both these forms of activity, the service and the guidance of the community, are nearly related to each other, so we may see from 1 Cor. xvi. 15 f.

---

[1] It is undeniable that cures by means of prayer, wrought by persons who have special powers of inspiring confidence, occur not unfrequently even at the present day (a notable instance is that of the Suabian pastor *Blumhardt* in *Boll*). We are by no means justified in thinking that there is anything in such phenomena different from the δυνάμεις ἰαμάτων in the Bible, unless we proceed on the extraordinary assumption of Protestant dogmatism, that the privilege of miracles was confined to the ancient period of the Biblical records, and that these were something supernatural in the strongest sense of the word. But these suppositions are dogmatic postulates which both history and experience entirely contradict.

how both of them did actually often, or perhaps always, in the communities established by Paul, fall into the same hands. The Apostle here exhorts the Christian community to submit themselves to the family of Stephanas, whose relatives had devoted themselves to the service of the saints (Christians), as well as to every one who co-operated with them, and worked (for the community). We here get a view of the first beginning of church government as it is coming into existence. The right to claim submission from the other members of the community rests simply and solely on the fact that one or more persons have devoted themselves to the service of the community, and have carefully and laboriously attended to the needs of their fellow-christians. Not only do we find no mention in the Epistles with which we are here dealing of a regular office of leadership, with which an individual had in any way been formally entrusted by the Apostle, but this passage in the Corinthians unmistakably contradicts this supposition by the words ἔταξαν ἑαυτούς, which could not have been used if they had been appointed by the Apostle; besides, in this case the duty of the community to submit themselves to the household of Stephanas would have been made to rest simply on the authority of the Apostle, by virtue of which they had been appointed to their post of dignity; whereas here, on the contrary, it is evidently looked upon as a grateful return for their having voluntarily devoted themselves to the service of the saints (observe the expression, καὶ ὑμεῖς, you also—corresponding with that which they do for you). Moreover, it would be very extraordinary and incomprehensible, if the Apostle had really appointed leaders in his communities, that he should never make them responsible for the disorders which occurred in the communities of Corinth and Galatia; and still more so, that in the excommunicating and receiving again of the sinner at Corinth, he very emphatically speaks of the community acting with him, the Apostle, but never mentions a leader of the community, whom he would certainly in this case have had primarily to deal with as the official representative of the community;

on the contrary, he represents the matter as if the exclusion and
interruption of communion with the brotherhood had been left
entirely in the hands of its individual members.   For when it is
said in 2 Cor. ii. 6, "this punishment which has come upon the
sinner from the greater number is enough," it is clear that this
refers not to a presbytery of the community as an official court,
but only to the greater number of the members of the community, which (probably as belonging to the party of Paul) had
obeyed the command of the Apostle (1 Cor. v.), and had broken
off their intercourse with the incestuous person, while others
(probably the anti-Pauline party) had opposed the formal ex-
communication. Nothing could show more clearly than this how
entirely a fixed organization was wanting to the Pauline communities, and accordingly how everything was completely dependent on the personal influence of a man who impressed others
by his capacity, and who had distinguished himself by serving
the community.   Thus also in the Epistle to the Philippians the
community is exhorted indeed to concord and unselfish humility
towards each other (ii. 2—5), but not to submission under the
ἐπίσκοποι, which would certainly have been the case if the later
conception of office had been already current (compare the
pseudo-Ignatian letters).   And in 1 Thess. v. 12 f., grateful
recognition is demanded for those who work as overseers of the
community, but expressly only in the sense that they should
"be esteemed so much the higher in love" for the sake of their
work of love. The relation of the community to their leaders is
thus still entirely that of free, moral, high esteem and respect,
and not that of official, hierarchical subjection. This is also
shown by the exhortation to the correction of the disorderly,
being addressed in the same passage (ver. 14) simply to all the
members of the community (ἀδελφοί, ver. 12), according to which
the discipline of the church is here also, as in the Corinthian
community, the business of the whole community, and not that
of a privileged office or class.

Let us turn now to the χαρίσματα, which relate to the edification of the community by the worship of God, including λόγος σοφίας, and λόγος γνώσεως, or διδαχή, ἀποκάλυψις or προφητεία, γένη γλωσσῶν and ἑρμηνεία γλωσσῶν or διάκρισις πνευμάτων. At the head of these stand the "speech of wisdom" and the "speech of knowledge," both of which are comprised in the more general notion of διδαχή (this word is therefore wanting in 1 Cor. viii. 12, λ. σοφ. and λ. γνώσ. being substituted for it, as conversely it is substituted for these two in xiv. 26; on the other hand, in xiv. 6, ἐν γνώσει and ἐν διδαχῇ correspond with each other, and are synonymous, as do also ἐν ἀποκαλύψει and ἐν προφητείᾳ). Both σοφία and γνῶσις refer to the knowledge of Christian salvation, but with this difference, that σοφία denotes the elementary consciousness of faith, the knowledge of elementary Christian truths in the simplest and most direct form of actual fact, without any insight into the How and the Why. Preaching of this kind, therefore, does not possess the convincing power of proofs derived from human wisdom, but that of the direct proof of the spirit, the divine power of which manifests itself to the heart (1 Cor. ii. 1—50). On the other hand, γνῶσις is the deeper knowledge which is not directly given with faith, and which therefore cannot come to all in an equal degree (cf. 1 Cor. viii. 7, οὐκ ἐν πᾶσιν ἡ γνῶσις). Its objects are the μυστήρια (xiii. 2), which consist partly of questions regarding the eschatology (xv. 51), partly of those important questions about the right of Christian freedom, of which 1 Cor. viii. expressly treats. But these are connected with the more general question of the relation of the Christian to the Jewish law, and this again with the significance which attaches to the crucifixion of Christ, with reference to the law, and in general with the apprehension of the person and the work of Christ in the divine scheme of salvation. It is therefore mainly in relation to these points that we shall have to consider the Pauline gnosis. The ability to not merely understand these deeper and more difficult questions, but also to impart this knowledge to the community in learned discourses for their edification, is a gracious gift of the spirit in a much higher degree than the plain "speech of wisdom," which only discourses in an edifying way about the elementary truths of the gospel, without giving any explanation of the deeper secrets of faith.

Further, ἀποκάλυψις is to be taken with προφητεία, wherefore the latter only is mentioned in 1 Cor. xii. 10, and only the former in xiv. 26, but in xiv. 6 the two correspond with each other as cause and manifestation.   They consist in revelations regarding the future of the community, on which the consciousness of believers was intensely occupied, as we know, in the primitive church.   Between the historical facts proclaimed by the Apostle and the prophetic picture of the completion of salvation, the remaining doctrines revolved as round a fixed centre, for they only represented, as it were, the series of connecting links between the beginning and the conclusion; hence we have in juxtaposition in 1 Cor. xii. 28 and 29, "first apostles, secondly prophets, thirdly teachers."   But as practical exhortation, comfort, and encouragement for the present Christian life, would most naturally have been connected with the prophetic hopes of the future, so we shall have to understand by προφητεύειν, in its wider sense, all those addresses to the community, the purpose of which was not so much to instruct them on questions of faith, as, by pointing to what ought to happen and would happen, to awaken an enthusiasm of faith, and animate them with the life of faith.   This practical character of the προφητεύειν, by which it comes most directly home to the hearts of the hearers, whether in smiting them down or raising them up, we may see most plainly in 1 Cor. xiv. 24.   And it is quite in accordance with this view, that it is just this practical, edifying προφητεύειν which stands in the closest connection with that χάρισμα which belongs to the sphere of the excited emotional life, the speaking with tongues.

The γλώσσῃ or γλώσσαις λαλεῖν, a highly valued and very frequent χάρισμα in the primitive church, but which so early as the second century had ceased to be any longer known by experience, was, according to the description in 1 Cor. xiv., a mono-

logue uttered by a person in an ecstatic state, unintelligible to
ordinary hearers, and therefore requiring interpretation before it
could edify the community, for whom it was wholly unfruitful
without this interpretation, but edifying for the speaker himself—
edifying, as we may suppose, in that sense in which the expression of a lively emotion is always a necessity and an enjoyment
to him who feels it. The ecstatic character of this mode of
speaking is indicated by its taking place, according to ver. 14 f.,
only in the spirit, without the intervention of the νοῦς, i. e.
(cf. above, Chap. i.) of the understanding consciousness, therefore in the living energy of immediate feeling, in consequence
of which the speaker probably produced the impression of his
being unconscious, not master of himself, possessed by a power
that was not his own, and only acting with his tongue as the
instrument of the unconscious spirit, not with the self-conscious
ego. That which was uttered in this manner appears to have
been of different kinds, for the Apostle speaks of γένη γλωσσῶν:
perhaps at one time mere inarticulate sounds (cf. ver. 9, μὴ
εὔσημον λόγον), at another time unconnected exclamations of a
hymn-like character, which might have a certain resemblance to
a psalm (hymnus), but without yielding any determinate sense,
so that the community, although it might perceive that what
the speaker with tongues expressed was the praise of God, was
not enabled to join in it, or to say the responsory amen to it
(ver. 16). It is easy to understand that such a thing was so far
from being able to act in an edifying way upon those present,
that it produced, on the contrary, an uneasy impression of confusion of mind, or of madness, and at all events disturbed the
order of the meeting assembled for the purpose of worship, and
gave to bystanders occasion for mockery and blasphemy, rather
than for conversion (ver. 23 f.). The Apostle therefore, without
undervaluing this gift, in the possession of which, on the contrary, he gloried, while giving thanks to God for it, yet, in
in the interest of the community, desires that they should only
speak with tongues in the assembly when the speaker himself

or some other person was in a position to translate that which was uttered in this ecstatic state into intelligible language, for the edification of all (vers. 27, 28). This *interpretation*, again, is also reckoned as a special gift, consisting probably in the power of transporting oneself into the half-expressed feelings of another, and clothing them in suitable language. By this interpretation of what is spoken in tongues, the outpouring of the feeling of the individual is turned into the utterance of the feeling of the assembled community, so that the ecstatic monologue becomes a responsory dialogue between the speaker and the community (ver. 16), in which the beginning of a church liturgy may perhaps be found.

Thus we see how these gifts embrace the entire community as an organic whole, with all the activities which mutually work on each other within it; the diversity of these operations, which are necessary for the whole, corresponds with the different individual gifts, as they again, as operations of the one spirit of Christ, are serviceable to the one community for the one purpose of its edification. But the oneness of this manifoldness does not remain a merely inward unity in the one spirit, but also comes forth in outward manifestation, in the first place by the *rite of baptism, which establishes communion*, by which the individuals are united to one body in one spirit; and secondly, by the *rite of the love-feast, or the Lord's Supper, which preserves that communion, and renders it perceptible to the senses by a figure*, which two things are declared, in the classical passage on the subject of the community, to be, together with the body of Christ, the means of holding it together, and the visible manifestations of its organic unity (comp. 1 Cor. xii. 13). Of baptism we have already (Chap. v.) spoken; we have now, therefore, to treat of

THE LORD'S SUPPER.

When the Apostle, in 1 Cor. x. 16, calls the cup of blessing a " communion (κοινωνία) of the blood of Christ," the bread which

we break a " communion of the body of Christ," we must take
this as an abbreviation for a *means of communion, means of binding together, bond;* his words do not directly inform us what the
nature of this union is, but we may learn it from the context.
This union with the blood and the body of Christ, by drinking
and eating at the Supper, is represented by the context of the
passage as a contrast to that union into which those who eat of
the sacrifice enter with the altar of sacrifice, and him to whom
it is devoted; Israel with God's altar and with God, the Gentiles
with the altar of demons and with the demons themselves (vers.
18, 20 f.). Now it is clear that this union with the altar and
the being to whom it is devoted, can be no other than that
which is implied in belonging to him, being personally united
and bound by the recognition, in an act (by means of a symbol),
of his supremacy.[1] The idea in this its general form is neither
Christian nor Jewish, but has formed part of the popular belief
in *all* nations, religions, and times;[2] and for the very reason that
it was an idea generally acknowledged and recognized, the Apostle
was able merely to indicate it in this pregnant manner, without
any fear of being misunderstood by his immediate hearers. Accordingly, it is no actual partaking (whether material or spiritual)
of the body and blood of Christ, and of course no mere representation of the absent Christ, that is here intended; but the real
meaning of the Apostle surely is, that partaking of the Lord's
Supper puts us into *mystical union and real connection of life*
with the Lord himself, just as the partakers of the flesh of
heathen sacrifices were put into such a connection with the
demons, whereby they were subjected to their dominion and
their influence. It is all the more necessary to acknowledge the

[1] *Meyer,* in his commentary on this passage, calls it a "theokratischer Konnex;"
for the rest, his explanation of the meaning of the word κοινωνία is correct, though
not exhaustive; nor does he say why it is connected with blood and body.

[2] I may remind the reader of the Greek legend, that by eating a fruit of the nether
world a man is given over to it; also of the German popular sayings about leagues
with the devil being sealed by the acquisition, use, or enjoyment of things which
belong to demons.

existence of this mystical element in Paul's conception of the
Lord's Supper, because it does in fact lie at the very root of the
ancient idea of worship; the symbol is here never mere symbol,
but always mystical representation, medium of a real connection
with the actual and operative object of worship. (The explanation of this phenomenon, which constantly recurs in the history
of religion, is a psychological question, which belongs to the
philosophy of religion rather than to an exegetical inquiry like
the present.) But how is it that a union, not simply with Christ,
but with the body and blood of Christ, takes place by eating and
drinking at the Lord's Supper? We shall find an answer to this
question also by the analogy of the communion of the altar, ver.
18. Of course, the mystical union that is established by the act
of worship can in reality only relate to a person, but to the
person according to the definition and characteristics indicated
by the things which belong to him. Thus the communion with
the altar is a communion with the God who has his place of
worship and of revelation *there;* so also the communion of the
body and blood of Christ is a communion with Christ, not in a
general sense, but very specially, according to those characteristics which are indicated by his (broken) body, and his (shed)
blood; therefore, in short, a *union with Christ as the crucified
Redeemer*—therefore essentially the same as that which is
effected by faith and baptism (see Chaps. iv. and v.). But
that this thought should be expressed precisely in this and
in no other way, was suggested by the use of bread and wine
as symbols, and required by the words of Jesus himself at the
institution of the rite. The view[1] that by $\sigma\hat{\omega}\mu\alpha$ $\tau o\hat{v}$ $X\rho\iota\sigma\tau o\hat{v}$, in
ver. 16, we are not to understand the real body of Christ at all,
but his ethical body—that is, the community—is incorrect, as
the parallelism of the blood contradicts it, as well as the addition
of the words, δv $\kappa\lambda\hat{\omega}\mu\epsilon v$ to $\check{\alpha}\rho\tau o s$, which would in that case have
no meaning. $\Sigma\hat{\omega}\mu\alpha$ has this figurative sense for the first time in
ver. 17; but even if we allow that the word $\sigma\hat{\omega}\mu\alpha$ in ver. 16 may

---

[1] Put forth as a conjecture by *Baur*, N. T. Theol. p. 201.

by an association of ideas have suggested the thought contained in ver. 17, yet this thought is in any case a new thought, and different from that of ver. 16. It connects the communion that exists between Christians and Christ with *that of Christians with each other*, and makes the latter, which, in the form of a meal eaten in common by the members of the community, is a fact directly apparent to the senses, the ground of recognition and proof of the former, which cannot be an object of outward observation. The truth that all belong in common to the one Lord, the crucified Jesus, becomes a visible fact in the oneness of the community finding expression in their partaking of the Supper together. It is not implied by ver. 17 (as is often said) that the bread of the Lord's Supper is separate from other bread; but what it means is, that eating the bread of this Supper is an act of uniting with Christ, because it is an act that openly proclaims the uniting of Christians with each other, which union can evidently have its real ground only "in Christ," in the spirit of Christ that makes them one. Thus this passage comes into the most exact accordance with xii. 13, where the two moments which are separated in vers. 16 and 17 are comprehended in the pregnant expression, πάντες εἰς ἕν πνεῦμα ἐποτίσθημεν, for this πνεῦμα is the spirit of Christ, and at the same time that of the community as the body of Christ.

The other classical passage, 1 Cor. xi. 23 f., contains nothing inconsistent with the interpretation which we have given to 1 Cor. x. 16, and which completely harmonizes with the fundamental ideas of Paul as expressed elsewhere. Here the Apostle, after giving an account of the institution of the Lord's Supper as he had received it from Christ, without any intervention whatsoever (of man), adds as a further explanation from himself of the words εἰς τὴν ἐμὴν ἀνάμνησιν, that the celebration of this Supper, as often as it occurred, was an act which proclaimed the death of the Lord (καταγγέλλετε indicative, not imperative); which we must certainly understand not in the bare sense of a proclaiming of that historical fact, but in the religious sense of

R

a confession of that fact, and a recognition of its significance for faith. The significance of the celebration therefore turns out to be the same here as in the previous passage, namely, to give again and again an actual expression, a fresh confirmation by a mystical symbolic act, to the fact of belonging to the crucified Redeemer. But not a single word is said in the whole passage of any partaking of the present body and blood of Christ: if that were the meaning of the Apostle, why has he not once in the whole passage said the decisive word, but always spoken of eating the bread and drinking the cup ? But when the unworthy partaker of this bread and this wine loads himself with guilt against the body and blood of Christ, because he does not distinguish (think of or take into consideration) the body of Christ, we must not exactly suppose that this body is partaken of, or is in any way present; the guilt, on the contrary, consists in the fact that the thoughtless partaker does not actually in earnest devotion realize to himself that to which his external act refers— the putting to death of the body of Christ; this irreverent celebration is itself a profanation of that which is holy, of that to which the celebration refers. Moreover, the offence of the Corinthians which the Apostle is here rebuking, consisted not only in want of due reverence for the Redeemer, whose death the solemn act of remembrance and confession represented, but also in the want of due love towards the community, so that this meal, instead of being a love-feast which showed the unity and equality of the community in the Lord, gave occasion, on the contrary, to a separation of the rich, which showed pride and absence of love, and to a shaming of the poor, and thus to a dividing of the community, ver. 20 f. This also reminds us again that the idea of the Lord's Supper is two things at once, an expression of communion with Christ by faith, and of the communion of Christians with each other by love.

The union of the community exhibited in baptism and the Lord's Supper is in 1 Cor. xii. 13 expressly *described as a union of those who had been Jews and Gentiles.* Although this does not appear at present to concern us nearly, we must consider that the main practical question for early Christianity, and especially for Paulinism, regarding the life of the community, was precisely this—were Jews and Gentiles to exist in the future as two separate parts that could not be bound together, or were they to be fused into the complete union of a new religious community? We have already seen the position that Paulinism took up theoretically with regard to this question, in the doctrine of the law and its abrogation by Christian sonship. And the practical carrying out of Paul's idea was rendered possible mainly by the fact, that far the greater part of the Christian community consisted of those who had been Gentiles, against whom the Jewish minority were *unable* to maintain for any length of time the particularism which was the essence of their law. But this very course of events, which was brought about by the mission of Paul to the Gentiles, and which supplied the most brilliant confirmation of the truth of the Pauline gospel, as it were by an actual judgment of God, was to a Jewish mind the almost insuperable stone of stumbling. That the children of Abraham should form only a dwindling minority in the Messianic community, compared with the Gentiles who had hitherto been kept at a distance from the Divine promises, while all the prophets had conceived of the future period of salvation as essentially within the limits of the theocracy, so that Israel was the main stem and the overpowering majority, the Gentiles being only admitted on sufferance as guests and not as principal actors—all this was a perversion of what they had held on the authority of the Scriptures to be the Divine plan of salvation, to which the Jewish Christians could not reconcile themselves, and was hardly a less bitter vexation to them than the Pauline doctrine of the cross of Christ as the end of the law.

In support of his view the Apostle had to show that, as the favour of God was the sole cause of the provision of salvation, so it was the sole and sovereign dispenser of the call to salva-

R 2

tion, and that consequently the composition of the community by the calling of its members from among Gentiles and Jews was a matter of the *free election of God's favour.* This doctrine is, as it were, the *key-stone* by which the peculiar system of Paul is a second time bound together, and so is the exact counterpart of that other specific Pauline doctrine, which we may call the foundation or corner-stone of his system, the redemption from the law by the death of Christ. But while the truth of the latter doctrine rests only upon consequences deduced from theory, the key-stone of the system derives its high significance from its theory being supported by actual facts.

THE CALLING OF THE COMMUNITY BY THE ELECTION OF FAVOUR.

The actual course of events in the preponderating conversion of the Gentiles in comparison with the Jews, was, as we have remarked, the more offensive to the latter (even to those who had become Christians), as it appeared to stand in direct contradiction to the Divine promises. This objection, that the word of God with its promises to Israel had been done away by means of the mission of Paul to the Gentiles, with its blessed consequences, he endeavours in Rom. ix.—xi. to encounter. And this he does by a double line of argument. First, by a sharp polemical attack directed against Jewish arrogance, which presumed that the Jew had a privileged claim to the Divine favour : he has no more right to it than any other man, for the Divine favour is unconditioned by anything human, and is absolutely free in its bestowal and refusal (chap. ix.). But, secondly, he endeavours to secure peace, by inspiring the hope of a conciliatory termination of the present discord, according to which the blindness which had fallen upon the greater part of Israel was to be only a temporary one, which should not prevent the final fulfilment of the promise of favour to Israel as a nation (chaps. x. and xi.).

In the first place, the Apostle proves from the Old Testament history that the Divine promises were not from the beginning attached to the natural offspring of Abraham, consequently not to the fact of externally belonging to the nation, but were quite independent of this, and purely a matter of free choice. Accordingly, of the several children of Abraham's body, it was only the child of promise, Isaac, who was to be the receiver of the promises which were given to the seed of Abraham, and the progenitor of those who were to be sons of God, i. e. belonging to God, members of the theocracy. It was the same, again, with the twin sons born to Isaac—only one of these, Jacob, who was inferior to his brother, born after him (whereby the Divine purpose was to be exhibited *as electing freely*, without regard to human conditions, κατ᾽ ἐκλογὴν πρόθεσις), was chosen to receive the promises, and that before he was born, therefore before there could be a question of any personal merit; the cause lay in no relation in which he stood to his brother, but wholly in God, who simply loved the one and hated the other (ix. 6—13). But that God has the full right to do this, He himself testifies with regard to both,—as to the freedom of ἀγαπᾶν, in the words which He says to Moses, "To whomsoever I am gracious, to him I am gracious; and on whomsoever I have compassion, on him I have compassion;" and as to the freedom of μισεῖν, by his speech to Pharaoh, "Even for this cause have I raised thee up in order to show my power on thee, that is, by thy destruction." Hence it follows, that whether a man obtains compassion from God or not, does not depend upon his own will and independent striving ("running"), but solely upon the will of God, which in both cases is equally an unconstrained will, whether He shows compassion on any one, or places any one in such a spiritual state that he is not an object of his love, but of his anger ("hardens," σκληρύνει). This is certainly exposed to the objection, that if the determination of the Divine will is thus free from limitation, the freedom of man, and consequently his responsibility, is done away. And what says the Apostle on this subject? Far from meeting this objection, which he himself makes, with μὴ γένοιτο, as he is wont in such cases, he silently admits it, and simply puts down all further questions and claims by the boldest inference from a religious mode of viewing the matter, which is magnificent in its one-sidedness. He silences all human claims by referring to the unconditional dependence of man upon God, which he could not have expressed in more stringent terms than by the figure of the potter and his vessel. As the shape has become what it is solely by the will of Him who shaped it, and who has free power out of the same material to make some vessels for honourable uses, and others for uses that are not honourable, —so man also is what he is, morally and religiously, only through God, and must not complain if he has become something bad, because God is unconditionally free, as we know, out of the same material of human nature, to stamp some as recipients of his compassion, with the final purpose of their being glorified, and others as recipients of his anger, with the final purpose of their perdition. But there is a further objection, which is not indeed expressed, but which is clearly in the Apostle's mind, and suggests to him what follows, viz., What possible ground can God have for making men recipients of his anger, destined to destruction? One would think that the most obvious answer to this would be, that He desired to display his anger, and to make known his power; the ground of such action on the part of God would thus be his purpose of revealing his holiness, which makes no exceptions, but absolutely annihilates that which is evil (whatever its origin may be), and his absolute power, which can do what it will, without asking any one else. Only it appears that the Apostle, while wishing to say this, felt himself that this purpose was no sufficient ground for action so gravely contradictory to the manifestation of the Divine compassion. But what if this apparent contradiction of his compassion should turn out to be, on the contrary, the most brilliant proof of it? And in fact it is in this bold carrying out of the doctrine of predestination that the Apostle's argument (ver. 22 f.) culminates: *But what if God, wishing to show his anger, and make known his power,* (not only made, ver. 21, but also) *endured with much patience vessels of anger, made for destruction, purposing at the same time to make known the riches of his majesty* (abounding in favour) *on the vessels of mercy whom He has prepared for glory?* We have here—and this makes the construction involved, although the thought is clear—two different motives for the predestinating action of God entwined together. First, the more general one, which refers to the vessels of anger merely as such, and to their existence, i. e. their having been made so by God (θέλων ἐνδείξασθαι .... δυνατὸν αὐτοῦ)—viz., revelation of the holiness and unlimited power of God; secondly, a more special motive, which refers to the vessels of anger in their relation to the vessels of mercy, and therefore not merely to their coming into being, but at the same time to their existing together with these, and which thus manifests itself also in the merciful preservation (ἤνεγκεν ἐν πολλῇ μακροθυμίᾳ) of the vessels of anger, καὶ ἵνα δόξαν—viz., revelation of his mercy, to which even evil must minister as means to good.

The harshness of this view has often given offence, and has led to all kinds of attempts to soften it down. In the first place, it has been thought that the passive κατηρτισμένα might be turned into a reflective verb, "who have fitted themselves" for destruction—in contradiction both to the true meaning of the word and that of the context. The word κατηρτισμένα corresponds too exactly to ἃ προητοίμασεν in the following, and to ποιῆσαι—εἰς ἀτιμίαν in the preceding verse, not to have God likewise for its active cause; and besides, is it not precisely the purpose of the whole section, xiv.—xxiii., to prove that μισεῖν as well as ἀγαπᾶν, σκληρύνειν as well as ἐλεεῖν, are matters of the free determination of the will of God? Any admixture of subjective human causality in connection with these is a distortion of the sense, which, as clearly as possible, by the consistently worked out figure of the potter and his vessel, excludes all human causality. But again, the convincing force of this analogy has been completely destroyed by understanding ver. 22 f. to express the opposite of ver. 20 f., as if the Apostle wished to say, that in the abstract God has indeed an absolute right over man, as the potter has over his vessel, but (δέ, ver. 22) in the concrete He has never made any use at all of this right; on the contrary, He has with great patience endured vessels of wrath, who, through their own fault (of unbelief), had fallen under the anger of God, and were ripe for destruction, in order to bring them to repentance.[1] But how thoroughly forced is all this! Κατηρτισμένα εἰς ἀπ., as we have seen, does not mean " ripe for destruction through their own fault," but fitted for destruction, that is to say, by God; and ver. 23 says with the utmost conceivable distinctness, that the purpose of ἤνεγκεν ἐν πολλῇ μακροθυμίᾳ is not the showing of favour on the vessels of wrath (by their conversion), but exactly the contrary, namely, the showing of favour on the others, the vessels chosen and prepared beforehand for mercy.

So far then is the Apostle from retracting in ver. 22 f. what he has said before, that he here, on the contrary, carries on his argument to its conclusion. Yet in this very conclusion his powerful dialectic turns aside again its sharpest point. The harshness of the thought that God has made vessels of wrath only to display his anger and his power, is evidently palliated, when it is shown that this is not the sole nor the final purpose, but is nothing more than a means to the end of compassion. According to this view, it is not abstract power (which as such is merely physical), nor abstract holiness (which as such is merely negative and condemnatory), the former being the characteristic of the Gentile, the latter preponderating in the Jewish notion of God, but it is compassionate love which is exalted above all else in the Christian idea of God; and the revelation of this is set forth as the only absolute final end in itself, to which the revelation of power and of holiness are subordinated as merely relative or intermediate purposes. But when once

---

[1] So *Tholuk*, Comm., and *Weiss*, N. Tle. Theol. p. 354; also in his article in Jahrb. f. d. Th. 1857.

the revelation of the holiness that judges, or of anger, as attributes of God, are recognized as relative and subordinate in comparison with the absolute end of the revelation of love, then it
is a very obvious and logically necessary conclusion, that this
relation of the Divine attributes to each other should also be
reflected in the present temporal state of mankind, in such wise
that the realization of the relative moment (anger) should also
be relative in respect to time, i. e. only a temporary means
towards the final goal of the absolute purpose, the revelation of
love; i. e. that the hardening of some should be, even for these
themselves, only a temporary state which should eventually end
in the universal bestowal of favour. This thought, which is
involved in the argument of ver. 22 f., is now indeed laid aside,
wholly untouched by the Apostle; for his main object here is to
establish in its full force, which smites down all human pride, the
unconditioned right of God to exercise his sovereign power both
in hardening and in showing mercy, and to assert this against
the arrogated right of the Jews. But what he here in grand
one-sidedness leaves out of view, he does not on that account
entirely forget, but brings it forward again in chap. ii., where
his attention is fixed on the final end of God's dealings with the
Jews in respect of the Gentiles. The Apostle then has certainly
not solved in chap. ix. the enigma of the present, which so
greatly shocked the religious consciousness of the Jews, but has
thrust it back into a predestination before all time, allowing it
to remain there in all the harshness of an opposing dualism, viz.
a loving God, who, with a freedom that acts without any grounds,
shows compassion on those whom He chooses, and prepares them
for glory, and a hating God who hardens those whom He chooses,
and fits these for destruction. The struggling of the reason,
which ever seeks for unity, against this dualism in God, is put
down by the authoritative words, Μενοῦνγε ὦ ἄνθρωπε, σὺ τίς εἶ ὁ
ἀνταποκρινόμενος τῷ θεῷ; nevertheless, it is this very dogmatical
hardness which, by its inward dialectic force, urges us on to the
perception that the love of God is wider than his anger, and

thus this duality resolves itself into the unity of the will to
love; a perception from the height of which a view of the philosophy of history opens out to us, which promises such a solution
of the religious enigma of the present as will satisfy our religious aspirations.

But before the Apostle enters upon this path in chap. xi., he
takes up (from ix. 30 to x. 21) the non-conversion of the Jews
from another point of view, viz. the anthropological and moral,
which serves to complete the theological and religious view. If
the hardening of Israel is, from the latter point of view, a
divinely-appointed *destiny*, against which it does not become
weak man to murmur, it is, on the other hand, from the former,
his own *fault*, because he did not submit himself obediently to
the word of faith, the gospel of righteousness, which was offered
as a gift by God, but, on the contrary, persisted in his proud
attempt to set up his own righteousness, to be won by works of
the law, and therefore came to fall against the gospel as a stone
of stumbling.   Israel, by struggling against the way of salvation
newly ordained by God, proved itself again—in spite of present
zeal on behalf of the law—to be a disobedient and stubborn
nation, just as it had before in the time of the prophets, who so
often had reason to complain of their stiffneckedness (the
Apostle quotes examples from the Pentateuch and Isaiah in
x. 16—21). It is true that so far as this want of faith in
the gospel on the part of Israel depends essentially on ignorance
and want of perception, which accompanied what was after all
a zealous striving after the good (x. 2, 18), the main element of
moral guilt disappears again; for it is plain that we are not
morally accountable for failing to understand a higher stage of
religion, in the same way as we are for offending against better
knowledge and conscience.   It is plainly to be seen, however,
throughout this exposition, that the Apostle has no intention to
restrict the view of predestination contained in chap. ix., which
would be in part to retract it; but the objective theological and
the subjective anthropological modes of viewing the matter

proceed here parallel to one another, and unreconciled, as if each were complete and separately valid, a peculiarity which we have already often noticed in Paul. And as before in a similar case (sin, according to 1 Cor. xv. f. and Rom. v. 12), we were obliged to reject the combination of the one with the other, as an introduction of ideas alien to Paul's mode of thought, so here also it would be a decided forcing of the train of thought to explain, i. e. to weaken, chap. ix. by chap. x., according to the well-known method of rationalizing exegesis, in the sense that, after all, the Divine ἐλεεῖν and σκληρύνειν, προσετοιμάζειν εἰς δόξαν and καταρτίζειν εἰς ἀπώλειαν, had their ultimate ground, not in the free will of God (ὃν θέλει), but in the free will of man, who believes, or by his own fault does not believe.

An attempt has been made to support this interpretation, which directly contradicts the sense of the words of chap. ix., by the help, among other things, of the idea of προγιγνώσκειν in Rom. viii. 29. In that passage, it is said, the predestining of God is dependent on his foreknowledge, the object of which is of course free human belief or unbelief; the unconditioned will of God acts therefore only to the extent of showing compassion on believers in general, and rejecting the unbelievers; but what individuals are included in one or the other category is also indeed predetermined by God, not however by an unconditioned determination of will, but by an application of will dependent on foreseen belief or unbelief, and therefore conditioned by man. Whether this separation of favour and freedom has any value or not, it is not Pauline. For, in the first place, it does an outrageous violence to the ὃν θέλει, which distinctly connects the Divine act of will, and that as an unconditioned sovereign act, with each single individual; and, moreover, it mistakes the real sense of Rom. viii. 29 f., especially that of προγιγνώσκειν. That this does not mean a merely theoretical foreknowledge of behaviour on the part of man (free belief or unbelief), independent of God's willing and acting, is proved by xi. 2, where προέγνω, applied to the people of Israel, cannot possibly mean anything

but the free election of God, by which that people became peculiarly his own.[1] Accordingly, προέγνω in Rom. viii. 29, may also
mean appointing beforehand, or electing some individuals in
preference to others.   And that it must mean this is proved by
the context.   The object of the passage is plainly to show that
the κατὰ πρόθεσιν κλητοί reach without fail the final goal which
is destined for them.   This πρόθεσις is now separated into the
two verbs προέγνω and προώρισε, of which the first denotes the
appointing = selecting of the *persons*, the second the destination
to which they are appointed ; both together are the ἐκλογὴ
χάριτος (Rom. xi. 5), i. e. the election which has the favourable
will of God for its ground, and the δόξα (viii. 30 and ix. 23) for
its final goal.   The acts of καλεῖν and δικαιοῦν, the calling through
the preaching of the gospel that is the cause of believing (x.
14, 17), and the justification that is its consequence, which occur
in time, form the *intermediate connection* between the act of predestination and that of glorification in the eternal life, both of
which transcend time.[2]   We should observe how, in this chain
of firmly closed links (προέγνω, προώρισε, ἐκάλεσε, ἐδικαίωσε, ἐδόξασε),
the Divine acts depend on one another in such a way that one
does not merely follow upon another, but is its necessary consequence.   For it is the very purpose of this passage to show that,
when one of these Divine acts has once occurred, the others will
likewise infallibly occur; or more particularly, whoever has once
known himself to be called and justified as a believer, may be

---

[1] Also in 1 Peter i. 20, Christ is said to be προεγνωσμένος πρὸ καταβολῆς κόσμου,
evidently not because God knew from the beginning concerning him that he would
come, but because God had from the beginning appointed him to come, as the Messiah
who should take away sin, and therefore should be a partaker of his glory, in which
character he has now revealed himself.

[2] This follows from the idea of δόξα which is found in all the writings of Paul, and
especially from the exact parallel in ix. 23, where δόξα, opposed to ἀπώλεια, must
mean eternal life ; comp. also 2 Cor. iv. 17.   We must not be perplexed by the aorist
ἐδόξασε in the passage before us; it represents the δόξα, which is to be hereafter
entered upon, as something which is already secured to him who is justified, as an
inheritance which the Son already as good as possesses, although he will only enter
into the enjoyment of it at a future time (cf. viii. 17).

sure that he has already been long before chosen by God in the ἐκλογὴ χάριτος, and predestined to the final goal of δόξα, which for that very reason will also surely be realized in him; so surely, that it is as good as realized already. This securely linked chain of Divine acts, which develope themselves infallibly from one another, nowhere, therefore, leaves an opening for any human self-determination taking part against or for Christ; yet faith is so far from being thereby excluded, that it is, on the contrary, the necessary means, but only the means, by which the Divine πρόθεσις which has been manifested by the καλεῖν first realizes itself inwardly in the man, in order finally to realize itself outwardly also in the δόξα. The question obviously arises here, how it is to be explained that the Divine καλεῖν through the preaching of the gospel, which manifests the πρόθεσις, has as its certain consequence the faith of him who is elected, which is presupposed as necessary for the further acts of δικαιοῦν and δοξάζειν. This question is put aside here by the Apostle, since he is only dealing with those in whom faith was already an actual fact, and he has therefore no inducement to reflect on the abstract possibility that they might not have become believers. On the other hand, we may find in ix. 23, προητοίμασεν, an inti- mation which bears upon this question; for this word appears to indicate, not merely, like προώρισε, an ideal predestination in the Divine counsel, but a real predisposition, i. e. a moral dispo- sition prepared by God, in consequence of which those who are affected by it are receptive of the Divine καλεῖν, and thus by the same cause infallibly allow themselves to be induced to believe. The reverse side of this is, that those in whose case the preach- ing by which they are called has not had this result, have not obtained the receptive disposition to it, or, to express it posi- tively, have been made unreceptive by God, hardened from the first, and thus fitted for destruction—κατηρτισμένα εἰς ἀπώλειαν. Thus Rom. viii. 28—30 completely agrees with chap. ix. in the sense of a decided doctrine of predestination, which is distinctly opposed to any introduction of free decision of the human will.

And how could it be otherwise in the view of an Apostle, whose most special peculiarity consists throughout in reflecting the actual world, with all its contradictions and all its harshness, into the other world of the Divine will, and apprehending it, not as a thing that is merely in some way permitted, but as expressly willed and wrought out by God?

If, however, this doctrine of predestination is left untouched and unsoftened in its harshness as regards the individuals affected by it, we must also remember that the Apostle nowhere specially reflects on these. In Rom. viii. 29 f., he speaks only of the elect, for whom the doctrine of predestination, precisely by reason of its determinateness, being independent of anything finite, serves as a most comforting support of their certainty of salvation; and therefore the harshness of the reverse side simply remains unnoticed. In Rom. ix. 14 f., both sides, it is true, are dealt with, election and rejection, vessels of wrath and vessels of mercy; but to whatever extent the abstract theory connects the two-fold counsel of God with individuals, yet the whole of this exposition refers in the concrete to the people of Israel as having —the majority of them at least—remained unbelieving compared with the Gentiles, who had been more inclined to Christianity. And the prospect of the future course of the Divine guidance of events offers a satisfactory explanation of this conduct, inasmuch as *the hardening of the one is recognized as a merely temporary means to a final universal bestowal of favour.* True it is that Israel as a people have stumbled (ἔπταισε, xi. 11), but not so that it should irretrievably fall. This is absolutely impossible; God cannot for ever repudiate his chosen people, whose root and progenitors, the patriarchs, were holy and devoted to God, because He cannot repent of his gifts and his calling (xi. 1, 16, 28, 29). And that He has not in fact done so is proved by there being a remnant chosen from the mass (λεῖμμα κατ᾽ ἐκλογήν), which now again, as a similar remnant did before in the time of Elias, maintains the continuity of the chosen nation, and constitutes a pledge that the Divine favour is still reserved for the chosen nation as a whole, in spite of the hardening of the present majority of those who belong to it. In virtue of this chosen remnant, the nation, which in regard to the gospel is at enmity with God, is still an object of his love, for the sake of the fathers (ver. 28). But why then has God allowed this nation to stumble at all? why hardened the greater part of it? From their false step, salvation is to come to the heathen; the natural branches are broken off, and the Gentiles, as wild twigs, have been grafted in. This actual course of events, which Paul had before his eyes as the result of his missionary labours, he recognizes as a Divine dispensation—the unbelief of the Jews is to be historically the means of applying the Divine compassion to the Gentiles (vers. 11, 17, 30). But if this were the only and the final purpose of God in this transaction, then would the chosen nation be sacrificed in favour of the Gentiles who were not chosen, and thus God's gift of favour and his calling would be revoked, which, from what has been said above, cannot be and is not the case. Therefore Israel cannot be finally sacrificed for the sake of the heathen, but his partial hardening is, according to the counsel of God, only to last for a time, namely, until the purpose of it is attained—"*until the time when the full number of the Gentiles shall have entered into the kingdom of God.*" Thus, as soon as this object is attained, the whole of Israel will also be made blessed (ver. 25 f.). And, in truth, the realization of this latter object in favour of Israel will be brought about again by the attainment of the previous object by the heathen, as the counsel of favour to be conferred on the Gentiles had before been brought about by the counsel of hardening which was to befal the Jews. And it will be brought about in this way— the fact of the Gentiles entering first into the kingdom of God, the more it advances to completion, and the greater the number of the converted Gentiles becomes, will so much the more incite Israel to emulation, so that they also, who at first were unbelieving with regard to the gospel, will at last themselves obtain mercy (vers. 11, 14, παραζηλῶσαι, ver. 31) by means of the mercy that the Gentiles have experienced (by being shamed and drawn on by this event). And further, if the Gentiles shall thus have helped the Jews to salvation by taking precedence of them, then again will those who have been the first derive the greatest advantage from it; for if the fall of the Jews was the riches of the Gentiles, how much more will abundant salvation accrue to the Gentiles from the completion of the number of the (converted) Jews! If the rejection of the Jews served as a means of reconciliation for the (Gentile) world, then must the final acceptance of the Jews serve no meaner end than the completion of the time of salvation for the whole world, the commencement of the final redemption that is to be ushered in by the resurrection from the dead (vers. 12, 15).

Thus in the Apostle's splendid philosophy of history, one moment ever becomes the means of attaining to the next higher moment of the Divine counsel, until at last the whole culminates in the *final end of the will of God to bestow universal favour—* "*for God has concluded the whole under disobedience, to the end that He might show compassion upon the whole.*" It is true that this text is not to be understood in the sense of the strictly dogmatic ἀποκατάστασις, because conversion in the world beyond the grave does not come under consideration here; on the contrary, the mode of treatment is essentially historical, reflecting on a final conversion of the whole of mankind who shall then still be on the earth. But even so, it advances in its speculative grandeur far beyond the narrow pale of the thoughts of ecclesiastical dogmatism regarding the future, whether it be that of Calvinistic predestination or of Lutheran indeterminism. In opposition to the latter, this passage yields conclusive evidence that Paul held the religious doctrine of predestination; for we are by no means justified in limiting the τοὺς πάντας, which denotes "all the individuals," to mere classes of persons, nor in adding mentally the condition that they actually believe, by which the whole point of the passage would manifestly be destroyed; for the object contemplated by the Divine counsel, the ultimate realization of which the Apostle declares to be certain, is precisely that *all*, including those who had before been disobedient, should finally be so no more, but should be converted and rescued. But this predestination is not that of a two-fold definitive decree, like that of Calvin. If the Apostle has in chap. ix. referred the contradictions which the reality exhibits to a two-fold will of God, yet here, in the prospect of the future, this duality resolves itself into the higher unity of a counsel of favour, which embraces all, and which no longer has its opposite beside it as a limit, but under it, as a means which serves the single final end. The rejected no longer stand over against the chosen, but those who appear to be such are in truth only those who have provisionally been passed over, and put back, whose turn to be taken up into salvation has not yet come, but who, on the contrary, are still for the present held fast by the will of God in the bondage of sin and disobedience, but this, nevertheless, only in order that by means of the others, who have entered before them into favour, they also may yet become partakers of the same salvation, and that so salvation may come upon all equally, as a free gift of the favour of God. But as this speculation on the philosophy of religion embraces the whole world's history, as the realization in successive moments of the Divine idea of the world, which is in itself one, though of many parts, so from this height, not merely the unbelief of the Jews, but at last the sin of man in general, is seen to be a moment in the process towards the absolute end of salvation. If the Divine counsel includes all under sin, for the purpose of realizing itself upon all as redeeming favour, then in fact sin also is included in that Divine counsel, i. e. not merely permitted, but ordained as a means to the revelation of favour. If we have already seen in the doctrine of the law, that it was given by God, according to Paul, not to guard against sin, but to increase it, for the sake of the redemption which is brought about through it, then it is but a small and logically necessary step which the speculation of the Apostle makes in gaining this crowning eminence of his dogmatic exposition, when he recognizes the fact of being in bondage under sin (the state of the natural man, Rom. vii.) as the means appointed by God for the realization of his favour—a height truly to which ecclesiastical dogmatism has been unable to follow him.

This universal realization of the favourable will of God forms, according to the Apostle, the concluding epoch of the development of the plan of salvation, and the commencement of the completion of salvation (xi. 15), to the consideration of which therefore we have now finally to pass.

CHAPTER VII.

THE COMPLETION OF SALVATION.

In this portion of his teaching, the Apostle Paul stands indeed, for the most part, on the common ground held by the primitive Church, although some specifically Pauline features will be found here also. Paul has made no attempt to accommodate these to the traditional eschatological views, nor to modify the latter in the spirit of his gospel. The consequence is, that it is here least of all possible to obtain a coherent representation of his views; on the contrary, we meet everywhere either with actual contradictions or at least with inconsistencies, which it is the business of our exegesis simply to note as such, and to explain genetically, instead of reconciling them according to our own arbitrary judgment.

The coming of Christ is with Paul also the central point of the eschatology; but the position of this event, both with reference to the intermediate state of individuals, looking to the past, and, looking to the future, with reference to the end of the world, presents many unsolved antinomies.

THE COMING OF CHRIST.

Paul, together with the entire primitive Church, expects the speedy return of Christ to the earth, in a visible form, to undertake the management of his kingdom; he calls it παρουσία, 1 Cor.

s 2

xv. 23; ἀποκάλυψις, or ἡμέρα τοῦ κυρίου, i. 7, 8, and v. Simultaneously with this event, the whole body of Christians will pass over into that state which is conformable to the kingdom of God, a spiritual corporeality, which not being fleshly is no more subject to decay, and is analogous to the heavenly body of the risen Christ, which consists, as before explained, of heavenly lightsubstance (δόξα). This transition will take place in those who are at that moment living by a *change* of their earthly bodies into heavenly bodies, and in those who are dead by the resurrection.

As regards the resurrection body, it is not, at all events, any longer the old fleshly body, for flesh and blood are, according to 1 Cor. xv. 50, precisely that which cannot enter into the kingdom of God; moreover, if it were so, the body of those who survived till then would require no change. It is not equally clear whether the resurrection body is to be a completely new one, having no relation to the old, or only a new and higher form of the old body, stripped of earthly and fleshly materiality. The latter view appears to be supported by the analogy of the resurrection body of Christ, which Paul conceived[1] not as an entirely new one, having no relation to the old (which would then have remained in the grave), but as identical, at least in its form, if not also in its material, with the body which was put to death, inasmuch as it came into being from that body, by being re-ani-

---

[1] *Holsten,* ut supra, p. 132 f. and note, maintains this very decidedly, and declares the contrary view to be a misconception of the main idea of Paulinism. Only he happens here again (as in many other instances) to be wrong in drawing a too strictly logical inference from the weak point of the conception. His argument is inconclusive, because it rests upon a dilemma to which Paul was indifferent, that either the resurrection body was an entirely new one, which had nothing in common with the body that was put to death, or it was the old *"fleshly body"* which had necessarily to be done away with, in order to the accomplishment of redemption. The above exposition, on the contrary, gives the tertium of the Pauline (and general primitive Christian) conception. (Moreover, Holsten's assertion (ut supra) that the doing away with the σάρξ in the death on the cross is the fundamental idea on which the Pauline gospel rests, is incorrect.) Holsten himself has elsewhere well demonstrated that this is rather the idea of the means of reconciliation, which belongs to quite a different range of thought. For further details on this subject see Chap. ii.

mated, and at the same time changed; for on no other supposition could such terms as "resurrection" and "rising from the dead" have been appropriately used. The analogy of the grain of seed, which comes into new life by dying, also supports this view, for the point of this analogy lies precisely in the *changing*, the passing over of the old out of decomposition into a new structure, where the substratum of the process still remains the same, and an entirely new thing does not take the place of the old. But in 2 Cor. v. 1 f., the resurrection body is spoken of as a "building of God" which we *have in heaven*, in the case of the dissolution of our earthly tent, which is the present body (as a substitute kept ready for us), which we therefore, even whilst we are here, *long for* in order that we may be clothed upon *from heaven*. According to this text it appears as if the resurrection body did not come into existence from the old one, which rested in the grave, by means of a change of its substance, but was related to it as a new garment, which previously existed in heaven, in order that it might be put on us from thence— whether as a substitute for the old, or put on over the old (ἐπενδύσασθαι). In this case, then, it would certainly not be easy to see why this new house or garment should not be given to us immediately after death, instead of waiting till the resurrection; especially as it appears from ver. 8 that the dwelling with the Lord begins immediately after the departure from the body. Is, then, the soul of the departed Christian which is dwelling with the Lord, to be nevertheless obliged to wait to be worthily housed until the general resurrection? Nothing in the passage before us points to such a conclusion; on the contrary, it may be inferred from ver. 3,[1] that we shall never be left in a condi-

---

[1] Of the different explanations of this passage, which is rendered doubly difficult by the various readings (an enumeration of which is given by the commentators), the simplest appears to me to be the following : "*Although* (εἴπερ) *should we even be unclothed* (ἐκδυσάμενοι, i. e. even though we may not depart without laying aside our old garment, without dying), *we yet shall not* (need to fear that we shall ever) *be found without a body*." Thus the Apostle wishes to limit the desire to be clothed upon, which he had before expressed, by reminding himself, as it were, for comfort in case of its non-fulfilment, that even in the less happy event of having actually to die,

tion of nakedness, i. e. existence without a body. Many commentators, therefore, clearly perceiving this difficulty, have supposed the heavenly house or garment to be merely a provisional body for the intermediate state. But not only is there no intimation of any kind in the passage before us that would justify this hypothesis, but it is one which is quite alien to the whole tenor both of Paul's teaching and that of the Bible; and it must, therefore, be regarded only as a desperate resource, adopted by an arbitrarily harmonizing exegesis, determined to reconcile at any cost the discordance which here manifests itself.

If the Christians rise from the dead together at the coming of Christ, then they are, until that time, in a merely provisional *intermediate state*, which can the less be regarded as a state of vitality and happiness in proportion as these qualities are more decidedly connected with regaining possession of the body.[1] The Apostle describes it as sleep, κοιμᾶσθαι (1 Cor. xi. 30, xv. 6, xx. 51), to which common expression he doubtless attached only the common meaning of a dim shadowy existence, from which the feeling of life and its activity are absent. As to the how and the where of this state, he had the less occasion to go into details, as he hoped, for himself and most of the Christians of his time, to survive till the coming of Christ, and so to pass directly, by being changed, from the earthly life to the higher life of the Messiah's kingdom, without passing through that intermediate state (1 Cor. xv. 52, ἡμεῖς ἀλλαγησόμεθα, opposed to νεκροὶ ἐγερθήσονται: and 1 Thess. iv. 15 and 17, ἡμεῖς οἱ ζῶντες οἱ

the soul will not be in a state of nakedness (without a body), but, on the contrary, will immediately (this is implied in ἔχομεν, ver. 1) obtain its new body from heaven (and be in heaven, ver. 8). In this sense the whole passage is entirely consistent with itself, though certainly at variance with the idea of the resurrection at the coming of Christ.

[1] The whole of the argument for the necessity of a resurrection in 1 Cor. xv. would be superfluous, without the supposition that the condition of the dead, previously to the resurrection, was an unhappy one. If it already consisted in communion of soul with the glorified Jesus in heaven (*Weiss*, p. 393), what necessity would there be in that case for the resurrection? And how could this communion with Christ be described as a κοιμᾶσθαι, whereas it is, on the contrary, according to Rom. viii. 17, a συνδοξασθῆναι?

περιλειπόμενοι εἰς τὴν παρουσίαν τοῦ κυρίου οὐ μὴ φθάσωμεν τοὺς κοιμηθέντας). But intelligible as it is that, assuming the nearness of the coming of Christ, the intermediate state might appear to be of little importance, and the unsatisfactory nature of it, according to the traditional Jewish view, might escape notice, it is yet equally certain that the matter would assume quite another aspect, so soon as the preponderating sense of the nearness of death brought the state that was to follow death, as being the object of immediate expectation, into the foreground of consciousness and of interest, and threw the prospect of the coming of Christ and of the general resurrection into the background. Consequently the object of *Christian* hope—the communion with Christ in the kingdom of glory—advanced a step nearer, as it immediately succeeded to the moment of death. If death is the laying aside of that fleshly body which has hitherto been the hindrance to full communion with the Lord, and to the realization of the freedom of sonship (Rom. viii. 21, 23), and whose fault it is that we are relatively at a distance from the Lord (ἐκδημῆσαι ἀπὸ τοῦ κυρίου, 2 Cor. v. 6), why should not that state, which is guaranteed as to its certainty, and prepared with respect to its real possibility, by the spirit of sonship which already dwells in us, commence at the moment when this hindrance ceases, at the death therefore of the fleshly body ? Comp. Phil. iii. 10, 11; 2 Cor. v. 5; Rom. viii. 11. In thus founding the resurrection on the communion of life with Christ which already exists, or on the spirit of Christ which dwells in us (wherefore this spirit is distinctly called "life," in opposition to the body which is forfeited to death, Rom. viii. 10), the ground of the Jewish eschatology, which depended on particular Messianic miracles, is implicitly abandoned, and the Christian idea substituted for it, according to which the completion of salvation depends on an essentially immanent development of the higher life, which is already inwardly present, as is brought out more distinctly in the theology of John. In fact, the acceptance of the intermediate state, which is connected with the waiting for

the coming of Christ, is inconsistent with the way in which
Paul joins Christian hope to the present possession of salvation
by the Christian. Is the object of Christian hope, according to
Paul, only the completion of that salvation which is not merely
promised by God (the Jewish Christian notion), but already
really present as life in Christ or in the spirit, and only hindered from external manifestation by the opposing reality of the
fleshly body ? If so, it is impossible to see why the realization
of that hope, the completion of the life of the spirit, which is
now already inwardly actual, by the external manifestation of
the δόξα, should not begin immediately after death, but be post-
poned till the coming of Christ, while the operative power of the
spirit remains as it were latent or suspended, in spite of the
removal of its hindrance (the flesh), from the time of death until
the coming of Christ.   From this standpoint of the already
present life in the spirit, the hope of passing immediately after
death into the state of completed salvation, of dwelling with
Christ, and being " clothed upon " with a body of a higher kind
corresponding with the spirit, is most obvious and most reasonable ; and the Apostle has undeniably (2 Cor. v. 1 f. and Phil.
i. 23) expressed this hope without the slightest reference to the
coming of Christ or an intermediate state.   Only it is in the
highest degree characteristic of the teaching of Paul, and a
repetition of the frequently remarked peculiarity of it, that this
specifically Christian turn of thought by no means sets aside
that conception which is derived from entirely different presuppositions, and belongs to the specifically Jewish sphere of
thought (the coming of Christ simultaneously with the resurrection) ; on the contrary, both views stand quite harmlessly side
by side, without any thought of their essential inconsistency,
much less any attempt to reconcile them.

The same thing happens with regard to the second point connected with the coming of Christ, the *judgment.* Agreeably to
the general Jewish and Jewish-Christian expectation, Paul
makes the Messianic reign begin with a great day of judgment,

and that catastrophe is called mainly in this sense "the day of the Lord" (1 Cor. i. 8; cf. 7, v. 5, iii. 13; 2 Cor. i. 14; Rom. ii. 16). On this day all *Christians* must appear at the judgment-seat of *Christ* to give an account of their deeds; and especially it will be made known whether their work done in the service of Christ was good or not (Rom. xiv. 10; 2 Cor. v. 10; 1 Cor. iii. 13). But, according to Rom. ii. 3—16, judgment will be passed on *all men* (not only on Christians) by *God* (not by Christ), when every man will be rewarded according to his works. Not only is no intimation of a second day of judgment given by the Apostle, which might justify us in regarding this judgment as distinct from the judgment of Christians by Christ at his coming, as just described, but, on the contrary, the identity of the two is proved by Rom. ii. 16, inasmuch as at the great day of judgment *God* will judge *through Christ*, or (according to 1 Cor. iv. 5) will dispense to every one his reward (and punishment?). Now a difficulty certainly arises out of the above statement, namely, that if the general judgment takes place at the coming of Christ, there would afterwards remain no enemy to be overcome during the reign of Christ, in the interval between his coming and the end of the world, as it is plainly supposed there will be, in 1 Cor. xv. 24, 25. This is connected with the question of the millennium, of which we shall shortly have to speak.

There is a further difficulty touching the principle on which the judgment will proceed. The Apostle, without any limitation and in general terms, states the rule to be recompence according to works (Rom. ii. 6—10), and also applies this specially to the Christians, who were to receive at the judgment-seat of Christ what they had done in (by means of) the life of the body, whether good or evil, i. e. the exact equivalent of their entire moral action, in the shape of a corresponding recompence of reward or punishment (2 Cor. v. 10). How does this agree with the Apostle's doctrine of favour, which (Rom. iv. 4) excludes all reward which might pertain to action as such, because this

would be a recompence κατ' ὀφείλημα, and therefore not κατὰ
χάριν? How does it agree with the Apostle's doctrine of predestination, according to which the Divine purpose is asserted to
be a purpose grounded on the free choice of favour, by the fact
of its not being directed according to human action (Rom.
ix. 11 f., xi. 6)? How does it agree, finally, with the Christian
hope of the immediate union of departed Christians with their
glorified Lord, expressed in 2 Cor. v. 1 f., Phil. i. 23, and therefore of a blessedness that should begin directly after the laying
aside of this body of death? This must necessarily have been
disturbed, if not taken away, by the prospect of a judgment yet
to come, by which morally defective conduct—and such must
that of the best Christian ever remain—had to expect punishment. We can hardly help perceiving that there appears here
again in the retention of the expectation of a Messianic judgment, the opposition which constantly pervades the dogmatic
teaching of Paul, between the Christian mode of thought, which
apprehends the relation of man to God from the standpoint of
favour and sonship, and Jewish presuppositions, which have
their root in the judicial relation of performance and reward.
It may certainly be pointed out that, after all, from the standpoint of Paul's doctrine of salvation, reward is not in every
sense excluded; that, on the contrary, it may find a place on
the ground of Pauline anthropology (the doctrine of flesh and
spirit), under the form of the natural congruence of the harvest
with the sowing (cf. Gal. vi. 7, 8. Comp. what is stated above,
Chap. v. p. 224 f.). Only, certain as it is that the true *moral core*
of the Jewish doctrine of recompence is contained in this ethical
teleology, it is equally certain that it is not to be identified with
the *judicial form* of this Jewish doctrine, as distinctly embodied
in the conception of a "day of judgment." For a recompence in
exact equivalent to the sum of the actions, dependent on the
sentence of a judge, is the precise judicial form of the doctrine
of recompence, and is in simple and plain opposition to the
Pauline gospel. The ethical system, which apprehends moral

life as an organic development, in which every force must attain
to a corresponding effect, every germ and every propensity to its
corresponding fruit, is based on quite a different point of view.
There, in the doctrine of judicial recompence, performance and
reward stand externally and mechanically over against each
other, and a balance is struck between them by an external
valuation (a thing impossible in the realm of morals); here, on
the contrary, performance and reward stand in the inwardly
organic relation, in which the one produces the other out of
itself, like force and its effect, and the reward itself becomes
again an operative force, which produces from itself new performances. But the idea of a recompensing judicial sentence
which shall on a single "day of judgment" assign to every one,
at the same time and for ever, his reward or punishment, cannot
possibly form part of such an organic and ethical apprehension
of the relation of moral cause and effect; for this organic moral
development is rather a constant process that varies in each
individual. It is accordingly not to be denied that the judgment which Paul allows to be connected with the coming of
Christ is as far from having anything in common with his fundamental anthropological views, as it is from agreeing with his
doctrine of the favour of God. Nothing therefore remains but
to see in it a remnant of Jewish dogmatism unassimilated with
the rest of Paul's teaching.

The resurrection of Christians and the judgment are the events
immediately connected with the παρουσία, but they by no means
constitute the end. On the contrary, the epoch of the Messianic
reign of Christ on the earth begins at the παρουσία, that epoch
to which the author of the Apocalypse assigns a duration of a
thousand years, and which is therefore technically called the
" Millennium," even when its duration is undetermined, as it is
with Paul. That Paul, as well as the writer of the Apocalypse,
assumes that there will be an interval (of undetermined length)
between the coming of Christ and the end of the world, during
which Christ will rule the earth in visible Messianic glory, and

after which he will resign this sovereignty to God, is unmistakably implied in 1 Cor. xv. 23 f.   In ver. 23, the order (τάγμα) of the resurrection is discussed : *first of all* is Christ " the firstfruits ;" *then* at his παρουσία follow those who are Christ's ; εἶτα τὸ τέλος, i. e. then is the end of the resurrection, namely, the resurrection of all ; which moment will be at the same time the end of all things, the end of this present world-period, because it coincides in time with the giving over of the sovereignty to God (ὅταν παραδιδῷ τὴν βασιλείαν τῷ θεῷ sc. ὁ Χριστός—note the present tense παραδιδῶ, which indicates that this giving over is simultaneous with the end of the resurrection).   We therefore have here a series (τάγμα) of moments of the resurrection, in which each is separated in time from the preceding one ; this is expressed by ἀπαρχή—ἔπειτα—εἶτα.   This distinct idea of a τάγμα, which consists of different parts, and comprises different periods of time, would be altogether destroyed by supposing that εἶτα τὸ τέλος is simultaneous with the preceding ἔπειτα—παρουσίᾳ αὐτοῦ : for in that case there would be, at the coming of Christ, only *one thing*, namely, the resurrection of the Christians, to be expected, besides that of Christ which had preceded it, which evidently would give no ground for speaking of a "series ;" and, moreover, the fate of the entire non-christian world would have been passed over in silence in an inconceivable manner.   But apart from this negative argument, the Apostle also positively says that the τέλος will occur at a point of time different from that of the coming of Christ, nay, at an opposite point of time.   That is to say, the point of time of the τέλος is that at which Christ *gives up* the βασιλεία to God, after he shall have conquered all hostile powers, for until that has happened he must βασιλεύειν. Now, according to the universal showing of the New Testament, the παρουσία is undeniably the point of time at which Christ *enters upon* the βασιλεία ; and to what end should he appear on the earth in visible glory, if not for the very purpose of entering upon his sovereign dignity, and administering his regal office in the place of God ?   A visible appearance on earth, not in order to enter visibly upon the sovereignty he had until that time exercised invisibly through the spirit, but in order to give it up immediately to God, would surely be a contradiction to common sense. Hence it follows undeniably that we must conceive the τέλος when Christ *gives up* the βασιλεία, as essentially different from the παρουσία when he *enters upon* it, and in fact separated from it by the period during which he reigns (βασιλεύει), i. e. by the period of the *millennium* (as it is called in the Apocalypse).

Thus, then, we find Paul agreeing with the author of the Apocalypse in the supposition of a period of the visible government of the world by Christ, between the παρουσία and the end of the world. He differs from him, however, not merely in the secondary matter of not assigning any definite duration to this period, but in the more important respect, that he makes out that the whole of this period is filled up with incessant warfare against hostile powers, and conquest of them; while the writer of the Apocalypse, on the other hand, imagines this period to be a time of blessed, unopposed, priestly dominion of Christ and the believers; while Satan is bound and unable to carry on his work of perversion until the end of the thousand years, when he will once more be let loose, and will be conquered in a short and decisive battle (Rev. xx. 2—6 and 7—10). But what gives to this difference its great importance is that, according to the *Apocalyptic* view, the millennium is the anticipation of heavenly sovereignty and blessedness on the theatre of the world, which is precisely the *Jewish idea of the Messiah's kingdom* painted in *Christian colours;* while according to the *Pauline* view, on the contrary, the millennium is merely the continuation of the present spiritual conquest of the world by the power of Christ, only in such wise that it will at the same time be visibly present, which we may describe as *the Christian idea of the kingdom of God in a Jewish form.* It certainly follows from this, that no really clear line can be fixed between the period preceding and that following the παρουσία, and that what is to be placed before, and what after it, remains in the greatest obscurity. As to the

conversion of the Gentiles and the Jews, for instance, we have
already seen, from Rom. xi. 15, that Paul looked forward to the
latter as the signal for the resurrection of the dead; but which
resurrection? The first, which is confined to the Christians and
connected with the coming of Christ? Or the second general
resurrection, which is connected with the end? The former
might appear the more obvious and natural in itself; only we
are met by the consideration that, after the complete conversion
of both Gentiles and Jews, no enemies would remain to be conquered in the Messianic reign of Christ during the millennium.
This question can hardly be determined with certainty from the
tone of thought or the statements of Paul. And the same is the
case with regard to the judgment. Paul everywhere speaks, as
we have shown, of *one* judgment, and .connects it apparently
with the coming of Christ. But if the final judgment shall have
been pronounced on that occasion upon all who are alive, where,
after that event, will the enemies be who have still to be conquered? And what becomes of the judgment to be passed on
the entire body of non-christians, who are not to rise until the
end of the period of the millennial kingdom? Simply to supply
this as " necessarily involved in the resurrection, although not
expressly mentioned by Paul in the context of this passage,"[1] is
no more justifiable than it would be to introduce any other of
the numberless hypotheses and combinations that might be made
on this subject, but could not be shown to be Pauline in character. Instead of such fanciful criticism, a scientific exegesis
has simply to note the inconsistency, and to point out how it
originated. The fact is, as we have already repeatedly shown,
that the whole of this circle of ideas which revolved round the
παρουσία, had got beyond the range of possible reconciliation
with the advanced Christian γνῶσις of the Apostle, and from the
very nature of the case must have done so. For this remnant of
the Jewish doctrine of the Messiah agreed neither with the theology of Paul, with its doctrine of favour and predestination, nor

[1] *Meyer*, Comm.

with his anthropology, which involved the immanence of the spirit of Christ in individuals and in the community. According to this, the realization of salvation in the individual and in the world is a constant process, a historical development; but the παρουσία originates in a circle of ideas, according to which salvation was something merely transcendental in its subject-matter, something to be expected from heaven, and whose realization was in its form a purely isolated miraculous act of God, without any inward connection with that which preceded or that which followed it. It is therefore natural that two elements so foreign to each other should not have been able to coalesce into unity. But here also we have again, in conclusion, the same thing which occurs in all the main points of Paul's teaching, namely, that the logical inference not yet drawn by Paul himself from his Christian γνῶσις, according to which the Judaizing elements would be completely set aside, is drawn in the *theology of John.* In this theology, the conception of the παρουσία is so far set aside, that it is resolved into or made potential in the coming of Christ in the spirit ; and in the same way the judgment is changed from being on the other side of the grave and accompanying the πάρουσία, into a process of separation in this world, introduced by the word and spirit of Christ, and constantly advancing towards completion (John xiv. 12, 31, 47 f., xvi. 8 f.). We now proceed from the παρουσία to consider the second focus, as it were, of the eschatology,

THE END OF THE WORLD.

As the millennium, or the Messianic regency of Christ in a visible form, is ushered in by the resurrection of Christians, so the end of the world is ushered in by the resurrection of all, as the last term in the series (τάγμα) of resurrections (vers. 23 and 24, εἶτα τὸ τέλος). This is the last act of Christ's government, because by it the last enemy, death, is definitely conquered (26). By it all powers hostile to God as such, as actually operative

forces, are done away, and thus all creatures are subjected to
Christ, and therefore to God.   Whether this is to be understood
in the sense that all have voluntarily subjected themselves, i. e.
have been converted, or that the effectual opposition of all has
been broken, and the opponents of Christ laid at his feet, bound
and powerless, cannot be decided by the words used; the words
which follow, however, θεὸς τὰ πάντα ἐν πᾶσιν, appear to support
the former view, of which more hereafter.   The grand universality, moreover, with which the eschatological perspective of
the Apostle truly embraces the whole universe, is notably
attested by his intimation (Rom. viii. 19—23) of a final redemption of πᾶσα ἡ κτίσις from the δουλεία τῆς φθορᾶς to the ἐλευθερία
τῆς δόξης τῶν τέκνων τοῦ θεοῦ.   Even nature, the irrational world
(for κτίσις, according to the context, can have no other meaning),
is in a state which does not correspond with its true destination,
namely, the reflecting of the Divine δόξα, for it is subject to the
bondage of corruptibility, and an instinctive feeling of this exists
in nature, and shows itself in groaning after redemption.   This
will also be granted to it, for it has been subjected by God to
this bondage, in hope, for the sake of Him who has subjected it,
that is to say, in order that He may manifest upon it the more
gloriously his power and his favour, by freeing it—precisely the
same fundamental idea of Paul's teaching to which he has given
utterance in xi. 32.   What Paul thought of the way in which
this freeing of the groaning creation was to be effected, we
cannot tell; but we may be certain that it was not by completely destroying and newly creating it in its substance, but by
changing its form, for he only speaks of the form (σχῆμα) of the
world in 1 Cor. vii. 31 as passing away.   It is worthy of observation how Paul has here given an application full of deep
meaning to the traditional expectation of a golden age in a
renovated world, for which authority is to be found even in the
prophets,[1] by placing it in direct relation to the specifically
Christian fundamental doctrines of favour and redemption.

[1] Comp. Is. xi. 6 f., lxv. 17—25; also Ps. cii. 27.

Now when Christ shall have thus accomplished the task of his Messianic regency, and made all things subject to himself, the whole created world, rational and irrational, then, *finally, he will make himself subject to Him who has made all things subject to him,* that God may be all in all (1 Cor. xv. 28). The thought expressed in this verse, taken with ver. 24, is very plain: when God's counsel of redemption has been fully carried out to its end, then the instrument of it, the historical Redeemer, retires from his exalted post; he has completed his task as the Redeemer and the ruler of the redeemed (which was part of the carrying out of redemption to its definitive and victorious realization), and now resigns his office of leader to God, in order to return into the ranks of the perfect created beings who are under God's immediate rule; just as a victorious general, after the close of the war, resigns his command into the hands of his king, and returns into the ranks of the ordinary citizens. This thought of the Apostle's is so simple, that regarded by itself its meaning could never have been mistaken, had it not given so severe a shock to the dogmatic consciousness of ecclesiastical interpreters. For there is no doubt that it can by no means be reconciled with the ecclesiastical doctrine of the Trinity. That the majesty and leadership of Christ is only a dignity conferred upon him by God for a time, certainly gives a deadly blow to the "homoousia" of the Church. But, moreover (and this it is which alone concerns us here), this doctrine, when viewed from the presuppositions of Paul's own Christology, certainly appears very extraordinary. For we have already seen that Paul makes the person of Christ, before his work on earth, in his pre-existence, take part in the creation of the world as the organ of God, and consequently does not date his more exalted position in the Divine plan of revelation from his historical work on earth as the Messiah; and now, notwithstanding that, is this Lord who existed before the world and before time, by whose means the creation was effected, all at once at the end of the period of the world's duration, to be stripped of his sovereignty, and to enter

T

into the ranks of the created beings as a subject like any other ?
It is hardly to be denied that there is a certain amount of contradiction here; and this would be quite unaccountable, if that
position of pre-existence, that cosmical significance and dignity
of Christ,. were the starting-point or the central idea of Paul's
Christology.   But this, as we have seen, is plainly not the case;
on the contrary, the complete sonship of Christ ἐν δυνάμει, dates
from no earlier time than his resurrection (Rom. i. 4), just as the
whole of the Christology is built up on the γνῶσις of the historical work of redemption (the death on the cross), and it is only
by means of the reflection into the past of the picture thus
obtained that the pre-existence comes to be added to it.   It is
perfectly consistent with Paul's Christology, starting *from this
point,* which was ever foremost even in the dogmatic consciousness of the Apostle, that the sovereignty of Christ, as it had its
beginning in time, should also have a limited duration in time;
but of course the pre-existence is in this case left out of view;
as soon as this is taken as the standpoint whence the matter is
regarded, the dignity and power of Christ, which he had before
all time, must also be conceived as unlimited by time, as endless,
which is the case in the writings of John.   Thus we have in
this peculiar Pauline doctrine of the subjection of Christ at the
end of the world-period, another conclusive argument in favour
of our view of the Christology of Paul,—the view, namely, that it
has indeed advanced in free speculation regarding the historical
person of Jesus to the dogmatic personification of the religious
principle developed in redemption, but that it has not yet gained
a firm footing on this standpoint of dogmatic speculation, has
not yet made the height of the absolute principle the dominating
point of view for the whole system, and therefore stands half-
way between the Jewish-Christian Christology and that of John.

    After Christ shall have subjected himself and his kingdom to
the Father, the grand final end of the world will have been
attained—*God will be all in all.*   This sentence, looked at by
itself with unprejudiced eyes, certainly supports the notion of a

conclusion of the world in unity, where no existing thing will be excluded from the kingdom of God, and therefore from the fulfilment of its destination—from blessedness; where no hell goes on by the side of the kingdom of heaven. For the supposition of the continued existence of the damned, outside of the blessed kingdom of God, would either limit unwarrantably the ἐν πᾶσιν to the half of the πάντες, which appears quite inadmissible in the case of a final comprehensive survey of the whole result, such as we have here; or it would make the expression ἵνα ᾖ—τὰ πάντα mean, contrary to the sense of the words, that God is only Lord *over* all—over the one part (the blessed) with their will, over the other (the damned) against their will, though without any limitation and without opposition. But ἵνα ᾖ—τὰ πάντα ἐν πᾶσι does not mean that He is completely Lord over all, but that He is the whole, the only and the all-determining inward principle in all, which is just the opposite to being Lord over subjugated enemies whose will is opposed to his. The termination of the world in unity, as above explained, might be brought about either by unbelievers being completely annihilated, or by their being all finally converted. In support of the former view it may be observed that no mention is made of a resurrection of the godless, therefore these might possibly be conceived as remaining for ever in death, and consequently (according to the Jewish view, which regards actual existence as essentially connected with the body) as no longer existing; but 1 Cor. xv. 22 appears to support the latter view: *"As in Adam all die, so in Christ shall all be made alive."* For in this passage πάντες can hardly be taken in a more limited sense in one clause than in the other, and as it applies in the first clause to all men without distinction, it must also be taken in an equally general sense in the second; and if the resurrection of all will be ἐν Χριστῷ, then it must be a resurrection to life and blessedness. And this is strikingly confirmed by Rom. xi. 32, where the universality of man's disobedience is contrasted with the universality of God's mercy in Christ, just as in the former passage the fact of all being made alive in Christ is contrasted with that of all dying in Adam. These two passages, together with the final "God all in all," would seem to show that Paul, when he speaks out of the fulness and the depth of his Christian view of the universe, is inclined to the idea of a termination of the world in unity, in the sense of the ἀποκατάστασις.[1] Nevertheless, those passages again are opposed to this view, which speak of a judgment with a two-fold termination—eternal life for some and perdition for others (Rom. ii. 5—12)—as well as the often-repeated mention of the ἀπολλύμενοι (1 Cor. xviii.; 2 Cor. ii. 15, xvi. 4, 3).   And thus even when we reach the end of the dogmatic teaching of Paul, we are still confronted by the unsolved *antinomy* between the termination of the world in unity, which was more in harmony with the Apostle's religious speculation on the doctrine of God's favour, and the two-fold end which is more conformable with the legal standpoint, not only of the Jews, but of moral reflection in general.   We have here once more, therefore, essentially the same antinomy which we have met with, in one form or another, in all the chief points of the Apostle's dogmatic teaching, and which, moreover, is nowhere more intelligible than in the case of the man who, from a Pharisee and a zealous upholder of the law, was called to be a chosen instrument of the gospel of the favour of God in Christ.

---

[1] "That an ἀποκατάστασις is entirely irreconcilable with the presuppositions of Paul's doctrine of election, which assumes throughout a two-fold termination of man's destiny" (*Weiss*, p. 404 f.), is so far from being obvious, that the contrary will rather impress itself upon every one who considers how decidedly the Pauline doctrine of predestination (Rom. ix.—xi.) finally makes the dualism with which it commences lose itself (xi. 30—36) in the complete unity of the final result (see above, p. 256 f.).

END OF PART I.

C. Green & Son, Printers, 178, Strand.

Lightning Source UK Ltd.
Milton Keynes UK
UKHW010755070121
376598UK00002B/593

9 783348 023245